A God Entranced Vision *of* All Things

$\mathcal{A}$ GOD ENTRANCED VISION *of* ALL THINGS

THE LEGACY OF JONATHAN EDWARDS

JOHN PIPER & JUSTIN TAYLOR

GENERAL EDITORS

CROSSWAY BOOKS

A DIVISION OF
GOOD NEWS PUBLISHERS
WHEATON, ILLINOIS

Library of Congress Cataloging-in-Publication Data
A God-entranced vision of all things : the legacy of Jonathan Edwards 300 years later / edited by John Piper and Justin Taylor.
  p. cm.
 Includes bibliographical references and index.
 ISBN 1-58134-563-1(pbb : alk. paper)
 1. Edwards, Jonathan, 1703-1758. I. Piper, John, 1946- . II. Taylor, Justin, 1976- .
BX7260.E3G63 2004
230'.58'092—dc22   2004004264

BP		13	12	11	10	09	08	07	06	05	04
15	14	13	12	11	10	9	8	7	6	5	4	3	2	1

To
Iain H. Murray

whose life and labors proclaim
a God-entranced vision of all things

CONTENTS

PART THREE
EXPOSITIONS OF EDWARDS'S MAJOR
THEOLOGICAL WORKS

CONTRIBUTORS

Sherard Burns. M.A.B.S., Reformed Theological Seminary, Orlando. Associate Pastor of Evangelism, Discipleship, and Assimilation, Bethlehem Baptist Church.

Mark Dever. Ph.D., Cambridge University. Senior Pastor, Capitol Hill Baptist Church, Washington, D.C.

Paul Helm. M.A., Oxford. J. I. Packer Chair in Theology and Philosophy, Regent College; Emeritus Professor, University of London.

Stephen J. Nichols. Ph.D., Westminster Theological Seminary, Philadelphia. Associate Professor, Lancaster Bible College and Graduate School.

J. I. Packer. D.Phil., Board of Governors' Professor of Theology, Regent College.

John Piper. D.theol., University of Munich. Preaching Pastor, Bethlehem Baptist Church.

Noël Piper. B.A., Wheaton College. Homemaker, writer, speaker.

Sam Storms. Ph.D., University of Texas at Dallas. President of Enjoying God Ministries, Kansas City.

Mark R. Talbot. Ph.D., University of Pennsylvania. Associate Professor of Philosophy, Wheaton College.

Justin Taylor. M.A.R. cand., Reformed Theological Seminary. Director of Theology, Executive Editor, Desiring God Ministries.

Donald S. Whitney. D.Min., Trinity Evangelical Divinity School; D.theol. cand., University of South Africa. Associate Professor of Spiritual Formation, Midwestern Baptist Theological Seminary.

Jonathan Edwards

Sarah Edwards

ACKNOWLEDGMENTS

We wish to express our gratitude to God for the gifts of several people who assisted with this project: Scott Anderson carried a heavy load in coordinating the original conference, without which this book would not exist; Vicki Anderson cheerfully assisted with numerous administrative duties that have made our jobs easier; Steve Nichols graciously answered a number of questions throughout this project; Ted Griffin did his usual helpful, thorough edits; and Carol Steinbach once again faithfully assembled the indexes with the assistance of Hannah Steller and Dan Brendsel. We would be remiss if we did not acknowledge our wives, Noël and Lea, and most importantly, our great God and Savior Jesus Christ.

INTRODUCTION

Justin Taylor

Twenty-five hundred people gathered in Minneapolis in October 2003 to celebrate the 300th birthday of Jonathan Edwards (1703-1758), considered by many to be "the greatest philosopher-theologian yet to grace the American scene."[1] The conference, hosted by Desiring God Ministries, was entitled "A God-Entranced Vision of All Things: The Unrivaled Legacy of Jonathan Edwards."

This book is a continuation and expansion of that tercentenary celebration, with the aim of introducing readers to Edwards, and more importantly, to his "God-entranced vision of all things." The phrase is adapted from Mark Noll's lament:

> Evangelicals have not thought about life from the ground up as Christians, because their entire culture has ceased to do so. Edwards' *piety* continued on in the revivalist tradition, his *theology* continued on in academic Calvinism, but there were no successors to his *God-entranced worldview* or his profoundly theological philosophy. The disappearance of Edwards' perspective in American Christian history has been a tragedy.[2]

The contributors to this volume pray that God will turn this tragic tide, and that the Bride of Christ will once again cherish and proclaim this Christ-exalting, God-entranced vision.

This vision is not properly Edwards's, but God's. God is the designer and definer of reality, and all of life must be lived to his glory. "Whether you eat or drink, or whatever you do, do all to the glory of God" (1 Cor. 10:31), working "heartily, as for the Lord and not for men" (Col. 3:23). We are commanded by Christ to "love the Lord [our] God with all [our] heart and with all [our] soul and with all [our] mind" (Matt. 22:37). If we

---

[1] Perry Miller, "General Editor's Note," *The Works of Jonathan Edwards*, vol. 1, *Freedom of the Will*, ed. Paul Ramsey (New Haven, Conn.: Yale University Press, 1957), viii.

[2] Mark Noll, "Jonathan Edwards, Moral Philosophy, and the Secularization of American Christian Thought," *Reformed Journal* 33 (February 1983): 26 (emphasis added).

do anything apart from faith in God, we have sinned (Rom. 14:23), and God is displeased (Heb. 11:6). "Chance" is a myth, "autonomy" is a lie, "neutrality" is impossible. Everything is created by God, everything is controlled by God, and everything's proper purpose is to be for God and his glory. All things are "from him and through him and to him. . . . To him be glory forever" (Rom. 11:36; cf. 1 Cor. 8:6). Or as Edwards put it: "the whole is of God, and in God, and to God, and God is the beginning, middle and end in this affair."[3] This is the God-given, God-centered, God-intoxicated, God-entranced vision of all things. Edwards did not invent this vision. But God gave him the grace to articulate this vision as well as or better than anyone ever has. To illustrate the flavor and contours of his vision, listen to Edwards's words as he preaches to his Northampton congregation on the beauty of God and our enjoyment of him:

> The enjoyment of God is the only happiness with which our souls can be satisfied. To go to heaven, fully to enjoy God, is infinitely better than the most pleasant accommodations here. Fathers and mothers, husbands, wives, or children, or the company of earthly friends, are but shadows; but God is the substance. These are but scattered beams, but God is the sun. These are but streams. But God is the ocean. Therefore it becomes us to spend this life only as a journey toward heaven, as it becomes us to make the seeking of our highest end and proper good, the whole work of our lives; to which we should subordinate all other concerns of life. Why should we labour for, or set our hearts on, any thing else, but that which is our proper end, and true happiness?[4]

EDWARDS'S NEGATIVE REPUTATION

While there has been an amazing resurgence of interest in and respect for Edwards in the academy,[5] he still suffers from an "identity problem" in the church. Most know little about him other than the fact that he delivered America's most famous sermon, "Sinners in the Hands of an Angry God," often reprinted in literature anthologies and American

---

[3] Jonathan Edwards, "The Dissertation Concerning the End for Which God Created the World," in *The Works of Jonathan Edwards*, vol. 8, *Ethical Writings*, ed. Paul Ramsey (New Haven, Conn.: Yale University Press, 1989), 531.

[4] Jonathan Edwards, "The Christian Pilgrim," in *The Works of Jonathan Edwards*, ed. Edward Hickman, 2 vols. (1834; reprint, Edinburgh: Banner of Truth, 1974), 2:244.

[5] See Sean Michael Lucas, "Jonathan Edwards Between Church and Academy: A Bibliographic Essay," in *The Legacy of Jonathan Edwards: American Religion and the Evangelical Tradition*, ed. D. G. Hart, Sean Michael Lucas, and Stephen J. Nichols (Grand Rapids, Mich.: Baker, 2003), 228-247.

History textbooks. Contemporary fire-and-brimstone preachers are often grating and graceless, and Edwards is imagined to be the same. But nothing could be further from the truth. What most of us don't know is that while "Edwards did know his hell . . . he knew his heaven better."[6] John Gerstner concludes his study on Edwards's view of heaven and hell in this way:

> If he spoke more of hell, it was only because he feared more people were going there, and he desired to set them on their way to heaven. . . . Even as he defended "the justice of God in the damnation of sinners" he triumphantly extolled the divine and everlasting mercy in the salvation of saints. Jonathan Edwards was in his truest element not as the faithful, fiery preacher of "sinners in the hands of an angry God"—though this he ever was and remained—but as the rhapsodic seer of the "beatific vision."[7]

It is true that Edwards's worldview often sounds strange to our modern ears. Some of what he writes is hard to understand; some of it is simply hard to accept. But as readers encounter Edwards, they would be well-advised to consider the counsel of biographer George Marsden:

> If there is an emphasis that appears difficult, or harsh, or overstated in Edwards, often the reader can better appreciate his perspective by asking the question: "How would this issue look if it really were the case that bliss or punishment for a literal *eternity* was at stake?"[8]

AN OVERVIEW OF THIS PRESENT VOLUME

Part One of this book examines Edwards's life and legacy. After arguing that God rests lightly upon the evangelical church today, John Piper shows why we need to recover the weight of the glory of God through Edwards's vision that "God is glorified not only by His glory's being seen, but by its being rejoiced in." He addresses the question of *how* this might happen and then lets Edwards answer several objections to this

---

[6] John H. Gerstner, *Jonathan Edwards on Heaven and Hell* (reprint, Morgan, Penn.: Soli Deo Gloria, 1998), 9.

[7] Ibid., 93. The most powerful ways to verify this judgment is to read Edwards's sermon, "Heaven Is a World of Love," in *The Works of Jonathan Edwards*, vol. 8, *Ethical Writings*, ed. Paul Ramsey (New Haven, Conn.: Yale University Press, 1989), 366-397. An excellent summary that captures both the content and the flavor of Edwards's view of heaven can be found in chapter 9 of Sam Storms's book, *One Thing: Developing a Passion for the Beauty of God* (Rosshire, England: Christian Focus, 2004).

[8] George M. Marsden, *Jonathan Edwards: A Life* (New Haven, Conn.: Yale University Press, 2003), 5.

worldview. Steve Nichols provides a chronological overview of Edwards's life, offering insight into the man, an introduction to his theology, and an exploration of his legacy in the academy and in the church. Noël Piper gives us a window into the godly, albeit imperfect Edwards home through a biography of Sarah, Jonathan's wife. Jonathan wrote to her on his deathbed that their marriage was an "uncommon union," and Mrs. Piper shows us that Sarah was Jonathan's "home and haven."

Part Two looks at the lessons, both positive and negative, that we might appropriate from Edwards for today. J. I. Packer unpacks Edwards's theology of revival as a reviving of religion for the glory of God, while also comparing the contribution of John Wesley (born in the same year as Edwards). Packer believes that Edwards's theology of revival is perhaps "the most important single contribution that Edwards has to make to evangelical thinking today,"[9] and in this essay he tells us why. Don Whitney explains what is meant by "spiritual disciplines," looks at how Edwards pursued his passion for God through them, and suggests lessons we can learn from his practice of these personal, biblical practices designed for the increase of godliness and Christlikeness. Mark Dever explains the circumstances surrounding the firing of Edwards from the pastorate in Northampton and explores the significant theological issues at stake, showing the implications for our doctrine of the church and the practice of church discipline. Finally, Sherard Burns has been assigned the difficult task of examining how Edwards could pursue a God-entranced vision of all things and yet own slaves. Burns explores the eighteenth-century context and also reminds us of the absolute sovereignty of God even over the pain and tragedy of America's "peculiar institution." He does all of this while weaving a careful path through the Scylla of callow condemnation on the one hand and the Charybdis of easy exoneration on the other.

For Part Three, we have asked three Edwards scholars to help us understand some of his most influential and demanding works: Paul Helm on *Original Sin*, Sam Storms on *Freedom of the Will*, and Mark Talbot on *Religious Affections*. These chapters re-present, as it were, Edwards's theses and arguments in an understandable way and show how his theology has contemporary application for our lives. Our hope

---

[9] J. I. Packer, *A Quest for Godliness: The Puritan Vision of the Christian Life* (Wheaton, Ill.: Crossway Books, 1990), 316.

is that these guides might encourage you to set about the task of working through these profound and challenging writings on your own.

Finally, we have included two appendices. The first is an Edwardsean sermon given by John Piper on 2 Corinthians 3:18—4:7. In the second, I attempt to answer some objections and recommend some resources regarding the challenge of reading Edwards today.

EDWARDS'S LEGACY: HE LEFT GOD WITH US

The risk in publishing a book about one man's vision of God is that the focus will be upon the man to the neglect of God himself. On the other hand, it is possible to *dishonor* God by not gladly receiving and appropriating the gifts he has given us. In fact, to neglect and to forget these forerunners in the faith is to be disobedient to God, who commands us through the author of Hebrews to "Remember your leaders, those who spoke to you the word of God. Consider the outcome of their way of life, and imitate their faith" (Heb. 13:7). Edwards spoke the word of God to us, and we are thus commanded to remember, to consider, and then to imitate him, insofar as he imitated the Lord (cf. 1 Thess. 1:6).

Perhaps the most fitting tribute we can give to Edwards comes from the words of Edwards himself. Here is how he counseled his flock to view faithful ministers of the gospel:

> Useful men are some of the greatest blessings of a people. To have many such is more for a people's happiness than almost anything, unless it be God's own gracious, spiritual presence amongst them; they are precious gifts of heaven. . . . Particularly, I would beseech and exhort those aged ones that yet remain, while they do live with us, to let us have much of their prayers, that when they leave the younger generations, they may leave God with them.[10]

Edwards was one of the greatest blessings the church has ever known. His life and writings have glorified God and increased our understanding of and happiness in God. He was a precious gift of heaven.

Upon hearing the news that Jonathan had died, his wife Sarah wrote in a letter to their daughter Lucy: "O what a legacy my husband, and

---

[10] Jonathan Edwards, "The Death of Faithful Ministers a Sign of God's Displeasure," in *The Salvation of Souls: Nine Previously Unpublished Sermons on the Call of Ministry and the Gospel by Jonathan Edwards*, ed. Richard A. Bailey and Gregory A. Wills (Wheaton, Ill.: Crossway Books, 2002), 34, 39.

your father, has left us! We are all given to God; and there I am, and love to be."[11] His legacy is that when he left this earth, he left God with his family—and with us.

Our prayer is that we all might recover and embrace this God-entranced vision of all things, growing in grace and knowledge, for the glory of God in Christ.

Soli Deo gloria.

---

[11] Sereno E. Dwight, "Memoirs of Jonathan Edwards," in *Works*, ed. Hickman, 1:clxxix.

PART ONE
THE LIFE AND LEGACY
OF EDWARDS

1

A GOD-ENTRANCED VISION OF ALL THINGS: WHY WE NEED JONATHAN EDWARDS 300 YEARS LATER

John Piper

One of the reasons that the world and the church need Jonathan Edwards 300 years after his birth is that his God-entranced vision of all things is so rare and yet so necessary. Mark Noll wrote about how rare it is:

> Edwards' piety continued on in the revivalist tradition, his theology continued on in academic Calvinism, but there were no successors to his God-entranced world view. . . . The disappearance of Edwards' perspective in American Christian history has been a tragedy.[1]

Evangelicalism today in America is basking in the sunlight of ominously hollow success. Evangelical industries of television and radio and publishing and music recordings, as well as hundreds of growing mega-churches and some public figures and political movements, give outward impressions of vitality and strength. But David Wells, Os Guinness, and others have warned of the hollowing out of evangelicalism from within.

The strong timber of the tree of evangelicalism has historically been the great doctrines of the Bible:

- God's glorious perfections
- man's fallen nature

---

[1] Mark Noll, "Jonathan Edwards, Moral Philosophy, and the Secularization of American Christian Thought," *Reformed Journal* 33 (February 1983): 26.

- the wonders of redemptive history
- the magnificent work of redemption in Christ
- the saving and sanctifying work of grace in the soul
- the great mission of the church in conflict with the world, the flesh, and the devil
- the greatness of our hope of everlasting joy at God's right hand

These unspeakably magnificent things once defined us and were the strong timber and root supporting the fragile leaves and fruit of our religious affections and moral actions. But this is not the case for many churches and denominations and ministries and movements in Evangelicalism today. And that is why the waving leaves of present evangelical success and the sweet fruit of prosperity are not as promising as we may think. There is a hollowness to this triumph, and the tree is weak even while the leafy branches are waving in the sun.

What is missing is the mind-shaping knowledge and the all-transforming enjoyment of the weight of the glory of God. The glory of God—holy, righteous, all-sovereign, all-wise, all-good—is missing. God rests lightly on the church in America. He is not felt as a weighty concern. Wells puts it starkly: "It is this God, majestic and holy in his being, this God whose love knows no bounds because his holiness knows no limits, who has disappeared from the modern evangelical world."[2] It is an overstatement. But not without warrant.

What Edwards saw in God and in the universe because of God, through the lens of Scripture, was breathtaking. To read him, after you catch your breath, is to breathe the uncommon air of the Himalayas of revelation. And the refreshment that you get from this high, clear, God-entranced air does not take out the valleys of suffering in this world, but fits you to spend your life there for the sake of love with invincible and worshipful joy.

In 1735 Edwards preached a sermon on Psalm 46:10, "Be still, and know that I am God." From the text he developed the following doctrine: "Hence, the bare consideration that God is God, may well be sufficient to still all objections and opposition against the divine sovereign dispensations."[3] When Jonathan Edwards became still and contem-

[2] David Wells, No Place for Truth: Or Whatever Happened to Evangelical Theology? (Grand Rapids, Mich.: Eerdmans, 1993), 300.
[3] Jonathan Edwards, "The Sole Consideration, That God Is God, Sufficient to Still All Objections to His Sovereignty," in The Works of Jonathan Edwards, ed. Edward Hickman, 2 vols. (1834; reprint, Edinburgh: Banner of Truth, 1974), 2:107.

plated the great truth that *God is God*, he saw a majestic Being whose sheer, absolute, uncaused, ever-being existence implied infinite power, infinite knowledge, and infinite holiness. And so he went on to argue like this:

> It is most evident by the Works of God, that his understanding and power are infinite. . . . Being thus infinite in understanding and power, he must also be perfectly holy; for unholiness always argues some defect, some blindness. Where there is no darkness or delusion, there can be no unholiness. . . . God being infinite in power and knowledge, he must be self-sufficient and all-sufficient; therefore it is impossible that he should be under any temptation to do any thing amiss; for he can have no end in doing it. . . . So God is essentially holy, and nothing is more impossible than that God should do amiss.[4]

When Jonathan Edwards became still and knew that God is God, the vision before his eyes was of an absolutely sovereign God, self-sufficient in himself and all-sufficient for his creatures, infinite in holiness, and therefore perfectly glorious—that is, infinitely beautiful in all his perfections. God's actions therefore are never motivated by the need to meet his deficiencies (since he has none), but are always motivated by the passion to display his glorious sufficiency (which is infinite). He does everything that he does—absolutely everything—for the sake of displaying his glory.

Our duty and privilege, therefore, is to conform to this divine purpose in creation and history and redemption—namely, to reflect the value of God's glory—to think and feel and do whatever we must to make much of God. Our reason for being, our calling, our joy is to render visible the glory of God. Edwards writes:

> All that is ever spoken of in the Scripture as an ultimate end of God's works is included in that one phrase, *the glory of God*. . . . The refulgence shines upon and into the creature, and is reflected back to the luminary. The beams of glory come from God, and are something of God and are refunded back again to their original. So that the whole is *of* God, and *in* God, and *to* God, and God is the beginning, middle and end in this affair.[5]

---

[4] Ibid., 107-108.

[5] Jonathan Edwards, "The Dissertation Concerning the End for Which God Created the World," in *The Works of Jonathan Edwards*, vol. 8, *Ethical Writings*, ed. Paul Ramsey (New Haven, Conn.: Yale University Press, 1989), 526, 531.

This is the essence of Edwards's God-entranced vision of all things! God is the beginning, the middle, and the end of *all things*. Nothing exists without his creating it. Nothing stays in being without his sustaining word. Everything has its reason for existing from him. Therefore nothing can be understood apart from him, and all understandings of all things that leave him out are superficial understandings, since they leave out the most important reality in the universe. We can scarcely begin to feel today how God-ignoring we have become, because it is the very air we breathe.

This is why I say that Edwards's God-entranced vision of all things is not only rare but also necessary. If we do not share this vision, we will not consciously join God in the purpose for which he created the universe. And if we do not join God in advancing his aim for the universe, then we waste our lives and oppose our Creator.

HOW TO RECOVER EDWARDS'S GOD-ENTRANCED VISION OF ALL THINGS

How then shall we recover this God-entranced vision of all things? Virtually every chapter in this book will contribute to that answer. So I will not try to be sweeping or comprehensive. I will focus on what for me has been the most powerful and most transforming biblical truth that I have learned from Edwards. I think that if the church would grasp and experience this truth, she would awaken to Edwards's God-entranced vision of all things.

No one in church history that I know, with the possible exception of St. Augustine, has shown more clearly and shockingly the infinite— I use the word carefully—importance of joy in the very essence of what it means for God to be God and what it means for us to be God-glorifying. Joy always seemed to me peripheral until I read Jonathan Edwards. He simply transformed my universe by putting joy at the center of what it means for God to be God and what it means for us to be God-glorifying. We will become a God-entranced people if we see joy the way Edwards saw joy.

JOY IS AT THE HEART OF WHAT IT MEANS FOR *GOD* TO BE GOD-GLORIFYING

Listen as he weaves together God's joy in being God and our joy in his being God:

> Because [God] infinitely values his own glory, consisting in the knowledge of himself, love to himself . . . *joy in himself*; he therefore valued the image, communication or participation of these, in the creature. And it is because he values himself, that he delights in the knowledge, and love, and joy of the creature; as being himself the object of this knowledge, love and complacence. . . . [Thus] God's respect to the creature's good, and his respect to himself, is not a divided respect; but both are united in one, as the happiness of the creature aimed at, is happiness in union with himself.[6]

In other words, for God to be the holy and righteous God that he is, he must delight infinitely in what is infinitely delightful. He must enjoy with unbounded joy what is most boundlessly enjoyable; he must take infinite pleasure in what is infinitely pleasant; he must love with infinite intensity what is infinitely lovely; he must be infinitely satisfied with what is infinitely satisfying. If he were not, he would be fraudulent. Claiming to be wise, he would be a fool, exchanging the glory of God for images. God's joy in God is part of what it means for God to be God.

Press a little further in with me. Edwards makes this plain as he sums up his spectacular vision of the inner life of the Trinity—that is, the inner life of what it is for God to be one God in three Persons:

> The Father is the deity subsisting in the prime, unoriginated and most absolute manner, or the deity in its direct existence. The Son is the deity [eternally] generated by God's understanding, or having an idea of Himself and subsisting in that idea. The Holy Ghost is the deity subsisting in act, or the divine essence flowing out and breathed forth in *God's infinite love to and delight in Himself*. And . . . the whole Divine essence does truly and distinctly subsist both in the Divine idea and Divine love, and that each of them are properly distinct persons.[7]

You cannot elevate joy higher in the universe than this. Nothing greater can be said about joy than to say that one of the Persons of the Godhead subsists in the act of God's delight in God—that ultimate and infinite joy is the Person of the Holy Spirit. When we speak of the place of joy in our lives and in the life of God, we are not playing games. We

---

[6] Ibid., 532-533 (emphasis added).
[7] Jonathan Edwards, "Essay on the Trinity," in *Treatise on Grace and Other Posthumously Published Writings*, ed. Paul Helm (Cambridge: James Clarke and Co., 1971), 118.

are not dealing with peripherals. We are dealing with infinitely important reality.

JOY IS AT THE HEART OF WHAT IT MEANS FOR *US* TO BE GOD-GLORIFYING

So joy is at the heart of what it means for God to be God. And now let us see how it is at the heart of what it means for us to be God-glorifying. This follows directly from the nature of the Trinity. God is Father *knowing* himself in his divine Son, and God is Father *delighting* in himself by his divine Spirit. Now Edwards makes the connection with how God's joy in being God is at the heart of how we glorify God. What you are about to read has been for me the most influential paragraph in all the writings of Edwards:

> God is glorified within Himself these two ways: 1. By appearing . . . to Himself in His own perfect idea [of Himself], or in His Son, who is the brightness of His glory. 2. By enjoying and delighting in Himself, by flowing forth in infinite . . . delight towards Himself, or in his Holy Spirit. . . . So God glorifies Himself toward the creatures also in two ways: 1. By appearing to . . . their understanding. 2. In communicating Himself to their hearts, and in their rejoicing and delighting in, and enjoying, the manifestations which He makes of Himself. . . . *God is glorified not only by His glory's being seen, but by its being rejoiced in.* When those that see it delight in it, God is more glorified than if they only see it. His glory is then received by the whole soul, both by the understanding and by the heart. God made the world that He might communicate, and the creature receive, His glory; and that it might [be] received both by the mind and heart. He that testifies his idea of God's glory [doesn't] glorify God so much as he that testifies also his approbation of it and his delight in it.[8]

---

[8] "Miscellanies," no. 448, in *The Works of Jonathan Edwards* (*WJE*), vol. 13, *The "Miscellanies*," ed. Thomas Schafer (New Haven, Conn.: Yale University Press, 1994), 495, emphasis added. See also "Miscellanies," no. 87 (251-252), no. 332 (410), and no. 679 (not in the New Haven volume). In another place where Edwards speaks of God's joy in being God and our joy in his being God, he makes explicit that this is why God's passion for our joy and his glory are not at odds.

> Because [God] infinitely values his own glory, consisting in the knowledge of himself, love to himself, [that is,] complacence and joy in himself; he therefore valued the image, communication or participation of these, in the creature. And it is because he values himself, that he delights in the knowledge, and love, and joy of the creature; as being himself the object of this knowledge, love and complacence. . . [Thus] God's respect to the creature's good, and his respect to himself, is not a divided respect; but both are united in one, as the happiness of the creature aimed at, is happiness in union with himself. "Dissertation Concerning the End for Which God Created the World" (532-533, emphasis added).

The implications of this paragraph for all of life are immeasurable. One of those implications is that the end and goal of creation hangs on *knowing* God with our minds and *enjoying* God with our hearts. The very purpose of the universe—reflecting and displaying the glory of God—hangs not only on true knowledge of God, but also on authentic joy in God. "God is glorified," Edwards says, "not only by His glory's being seen, but by its being rejoiced in."

Here is the great discovery that changes everything. God is glorified by our being satisfied in him. The chief end of man is not merely to glorify God *and* enjoy him forever, but to glorify God *by* enjoying him forever. The great divide that I thought existed between God's passion for his glory and my passion for joy turned out to be no divide at all, if my passion for joy is passion for joy *in God*. God's passion for the glory of God and my passion for joy in God are one.

What follows from this, I have found, shocks most Christians, namely, that we should be blood-earnest—deadly serious—about being happy in God. We should pursue our joy with such a passion and a vehemence that, if we must, we would cut off our hand or gouge out our eye to have it. God being glorified in us hangs on our being satisfied in him. Which makes our being satisfied in him infinitely important. It becomes the animating vocation of our lives. We tremble at the horror of not rejoicing in God. We quake at the fearful lukewarmness of our hearts. We waken to the truth that it is a treacherous sin not to pursue that satisfaction in God with all our hearts. There is one final word for finding delight in the creation more than in the Creator: *treason.*

Edwards put it like this: "I do not suppose it can be said of any, that their love to their own happiness . . . can be in too high a degree."[9] Of course, a passion for happiness can be misdirected to wrong objects, but it cannot be too strong.[10] Edwards argued for this in a sermon that he preached on Song of Solomon 5:1, which says, "Eat, friends, drink, and be drunk with love!" He drew out the following doctrine: "Persons need

---

[9] Jonathan Edwards, "Charity and Its Fruits," *WJE*, 8:255.

[10] It's the same thing C. S. Lewis said in *The Weight of Glory*:

> If we consider the unblushing promises of reward and the staggering nature of the rewards promised in the Gospels, it would seem that our Lord finds our desires not too strong, but too weak. We are half-hearted creatures, fooling about with drink and sex and ambition when infinite joy is offered us, like an ignorant child who wants to go on making mud pies in a slum because he cannot imagine what is meant by the offer of a holiday at the sea. We are far too easily pleased.

C. S. Lewis, *The Weight of Glory, and Other Addresses* (Grand Rapids, Mich.: Eerdmans, 1965), 2.

not and ought not to set any bounds to their spiritual and gracious appetites." Rather, he says, they ought

> to be endeavoring by all possible ways to inflame their desires and to obtain more spiritual pleasures. . . . Our hungerings and thirstings after God and Jesus Christ and after holiness can't be too great for the value of these things, for they are things of infinite value. . . . [Therefore] endeavor to promote spiritual appetites by laying yourself in the way of allurement. . . .[11] There is no such thing as excess in our taking of this spiritual food. There is no such virtue as temperance in spiritual feasting.[12]

This led Edwards to say of his own preaching and the great goals of his own ministry:

> I should think myself in the way of my duty to raise the affections of my hearers as high as possibly I can, provided that they are affected with nothing but truth, and with affections that are not disagreeable to the nature of what they are affected with.[13]

White-hot affections for God set on fire by clear, compelling, biblical truth was Edwards's goal in preaching and life, because it is the goal of God in the universe. This is the heart of Edwards's God-entranced vision of all things.

Perhaps the best way to unfold the implications of this vision is to let Edwards answer several objections that are raised.

Objections to Edwards

Objection #1: Doesn't this make me too central in salvation? Doesn't it put me at the bottom of my joy and make me the focus of the universe?

Edwards answers with a very penetrating distinction between the joy of the hypocrite and the joy of the true Christian. It is a devastating distinction for modern Christians because it exposes the error of defining God's love as "making much of us."

[11] Jonathan Edwards, "Sacrament Sermon on Canticles 5:1," sermon manuscript (1729), Beinecke Library, Yale University.

[12] Jonathan Edwards, "The Spiritual Blessings of the Gospel Represented by a Feast," in *The Works of Jonathan Edwards*, vol. 14, *Sermons and Discourses, 1723-1729*, ed. Kenneth Minkema (New Haven, Conn.: Yale University Press, 1997), 286.

[13] Jonathan Edwards, "Some Thoughts Concerning the Revival," in *The Works of Jonathan Edwards*, vol. 4, *The Great Awakening*, ed. C. C. Goen (New Haven, Conn.: Yale University Press, 1972), 387.

> This is . . . the difference between the joy of the hypocrite, and the joy
> of the true saint. The [hypocrite] rejoices in himself; self is the first
> foundation of his joy: the [true saint] rejoices in God. . . . True saints
> have their minds, in the first place, inexpressibly pleased and delighted
> with the sweet ideas of the glorious and amiable nature of the things
> of God. And this is the spring of all their delights, and the cream of
> all their pleasures. . . . But the dependence of the affections of hyp-
> ocrites is in a contrary order: *they first rejoice . . . that they are made
> so much of by God; and then on that ground, he seems in a sort, lovely
> to them.*[14]

The answer to the objection above is "no." Edwards's call for a God-
enthralled heart does not make the enthralled one central. It makes God
central. Indeed it exposes every joy as idolatrous that is not, ultimately,
joy in God. As St. Augustine prayed, "He loves thee too little who loves
anything together with Thee, which he loves not for thy sake."[15]

*Objection #2: Won't this emphasis on pleasure play into the central
corruption of our age, the unbounded pursuit of personal ease and comfort and pleasure? Won't this emphasis soften our resistance to sin?*

Many Christians think stoicism is a good antidote to sensuality. It
isn't. It is hopelessly weak and ineffective. And the reason it fails is that
the power of sin comes from its promise of pleasure and is meant to be
defeated by the superior promise of pleasure in God, not by the power
of the human will. Willpower religion, when it succeeds, gets glory for
the will. It produces legalists, not lovers. Edwards saw the powerlessness
of this approach and said:

> We come with double forces against the wicked, to persuade them to
> a godly life. . . . The common argument is the profitableness of religion,
> but alas, the wicked man is not in pursuit of profit; 'tis pleasure he
> seeks. Now, then, we will fight with them with their own weapons.[16]

In other words, Edwards says, the pursuit of pleasure in God is not only
not a compromise with the sensual world, but is the only power that can

---

[14] Jonathan Edwards, *The Works of Jonathan Edwards*, vol. 2, *Religious Affections*, ed. John Smith
(New Haven, Conn.: Yale University Press, 1959), 249-250 (emphasis added).

[15] Augustine, *Confessions*, X.24.

[16] Jonathan Edwards, "The Pleasantness of Religion," in *The Sermons of Jonathan Edwards: A Reader*,
ed. Wilson H. Kimnach, Kenneth P. Minkema, and Douglas A. Sweeney (New Haven, Conn: Yale
University Press, 1999), 23-24.

defeat the lusts of the age while producing lovers of God, not legalists who boast in their willpower. If you love holiness, if you weep over the moral collapse of our culture, I pray you will get to know Edwards's God-enthralled vision of all things.

Objection #3: Surely repentance is a painful thing and will be undermined by this stress on seeking our pleasure. Surely revival begins with repentance, but you seem to make the awakening of delight the beginning.

The answer to this objection is that no one can feel brokenhearted for not treasuring God until he tastes the pleasure of having God as a treasure. In order to bring people to the sorrow of repentance, you must first bring them to see God as their delight. Here it is in the very words of Edwards:

> Though [repentance] be a deep sorrow for sin that God requires as necessary to salvation, yet the very nature of it necessarily implies delight. Repentance of sin is a sorrow arising from the sight of God's excellency and mercy, but the apprehension of excellency or mercy must necessarily and unavoidably beget pleasure in the mind of the beholder. 'Tis impossible that anyone should see anything that appears to him excellent and not behold it with pleasure, and it's impossible to be affected with the mercy and love of God, and his willingness to be merciful to us and love us, and not be affected with pleasure at the thoughts of [it]; but this is the very affection that begets true repentance. How much soever of a paradox it may seem, it is true that repentance is a sweet sorrow, so that the more of this sorrow, the more pleasure.[17]

This is astonishing and true. And if you have lived long with Christ and are aware of your indwelling sin, you will have found it to be so. Yes, there is repentance. Yes, there are tears of remorse and brokenheartedness. But they flow from a new taste of the soul for the pleasures at God's right hand that up till now have been scorned.

Objection #4: Surely elevating the pursuit of joy to supreme importance will overturn the teaching of Jesus about self-denial. How can you affirm a passion for pleasure as the driving force of the Christian life and at the same time embrace self-denial?

Edwards turns this objection right on its head and argues that self-

---

[17] Ibid., 18-19.

denial not only does not contradict the quest for joy, but in fact destroys the root of sorrow. Here is the way he says it:

> Self-denial will also be reckoned amongst the troubles of the godly. . . . But whoever has tried self-denial can give in his testimony that they never experience greater pleasure and joys than after great acts of self-denial. Self-denial destroys the very root and foundation of sorrow, and is nothing else but the lancing of a grievous and painful sore that effects a cure and brings abundance of health as a recompense for the pain of the operation.[18]

In other words, the whole approach of the Bible, Edwards would say, is to persuade us that denying ourselves the "fleeting pleasures of sin" (Heb. 11:25) puts us on the path of "pleasures forevermore" at God's right hand (Ps. 16:11). There is no contradiction between the centrality of delight in God and the necessity of self-denial, since self-denial "destroys the root . . . of sorrow."[19]

Objection #5: Becoming a Christian adds more trouble to life and brings persecutions, reproaches, suffering, and even death. It is misleading, therefore, to say that the essence of being a Christian is joy. There are overwhelming sorrows.

This would be a compelling objection in a world like ours, so full of suffering and so hostile to Christianity, if it were not for the sovereignty and goodness of God. Edwards is unwavering in his biblical belief that God designs all the afflictions of the godly for the increase of their everlasting joy.

He puts it in a typically striking way: "Religion [Christianity] brings no new troubles upon man but what have more of pleasure than of trouble."[20] In other words, the only troubles that God permits in the lives of his children are those that will bring more pleasure than trouble with them—when all things are considered. He cites four passages of Scripture. "Blessed are you when others revile you and persecute you

---

18 Edwards, "The Pleasantness of Religion," 19.

19 Edwards explains the paradox of self-denial in another way: "There is no pleasure but what brings more of sorrow than of pleasure, but what the godly man either does or may enjoy" ("The Pleasantness of Religion," 18). In other words, there is no pleasure that godly people may not enjoy except those that bring more sorrow than pleasure. Or to put it in the astonishing way that makes it understandable: Christians may seek and should seek only those pleasures that are maximally pleasurable—that is, that have the least sorrows as consequences, including in eternity.

20 Edwards, "The Pleasantness of Religion," 18. He goes on to say, "Reproaches are ordered by God for this end, that they may destroy sin, which is the chief root of the troubles of the godly man, and the destruction of it a foundation for delight" (19).

and utter all kinds of evil against you falsely on my account. Rejoice and be glad, for your reward is great in heaven" (Matt. 5:11). "Count it all joy, my brothers, when you meet trials of various kinds, for you know that the testing of your faith produces steadfastness" (Jas. 1:2-3). "Then they left the presence of the council, rejoicing that they were counted worthy to suffer dishonor for the name" (Acts 5:41). "You joyfully accepted the plundering of your property, since you knew that you yourselves had a better possession and an abiding one" (Heb. 10:34).

In other words, yes, becoming a Christian adds more trouble to life and brings persecutions, reproaches, suffering, and even death. Yes, there are overwhelming sorrows. But the pursuit of infinite pleasure in God, and the confidence that Christ has purchased it for us, does not contradict these sufferings but carries them. By this joy and this hope we are able to suffer on the Calvary road of ministry and missions and love. "For the joy that was set before him" Jesus "endured the cross" (Heb. 12:2). He fixed his gaze on the completion of his joy. That gaze sustained the greatest act of love that ever was. The same gaze—the completion of our joy in God—will sustain us as well. The pursuit of that joy doesn't contradict suffering—it carries it. The completion of Christ's great, global mission will demand suffering. Therefore, if you love the nations, pursue this God-entranced vision of all things.

Objection #6: Where is the cross of Jesus Christ in all of this? Where is regeneration by the Holy Spirit? Where is justification by faith alone?

I will not answer these questions here, but rather in the sermon reprinted in the first appendix at the end of this book. Sometimes the more precious and important things you save for last.

Objection #7: Did not Edwards extol the virtue of "disinterested love" to God? How could love to God that is driven by the pursuit of pleasure in God be called "disinterested"?

It's true Edwards used the term "disinterested love" in reference to God.

I must leave it to everyone to judge for himself . . . concerning mankind, how little there is of this disinterested love to God, this pure divine affection, in the world.[21]

21 Jonathan Edwards, *The Works of Jonathan Edwards*, vol. 3, *Original Sin*, ed. Clyde A. Holbrook (New Haven, Conn.: Yale University Press, 1970), 144.

There is no other love so much above the selfish principle as Christian love is; no love that is so free and disinterested, and in the exercise of which God is so loved for himself and his own sake.[22]

But the key to understanding his meaning is found in that last quote. Disinterested love to God is loving God "for himself and his own sake." In other words, Edwards used the term "disinterested love" to designate love that delights in God for his own greatness and beauty, and to distinguish it from love that delights only in God's gifts. Disinterested love is not love without pleasure. It is love whose pleasure is in God himself.

In fact, Edwards would say there is no love to God that is not delight in God. And so if there is a disinterested love to God, there is disinterested delight in God. And in fact, that is exactly the way he thinks. For example, he says:

> As it is with the love of the saints, so it is with their joy, and spiritual delight and pleasure: the first foundation of it, is not any consideration or conception of their *interest in* divine things; but it primarily consists in the *sweet entertainment* their minds have in the view . . . of the divine and holy beauty of these things, as they are in themselves.[23]

The "interest" that he rules out does not include "sweet entertainment." "Interest" means the benefits received other than delight in God himself. And "disinterested" love is the "sweet entertainment" or the joy of knowing God himself.[24]

Objection #8: Doesn't the elevation of joy to such a supreme position in God and in glorifying God lead away from the humility and brokenness that ought to mark the Christian? Doesn't it have the flavor of triumphalism, the very thing that Edwards disapproved in the revival excesses of his day?

It could be taken that way. All truths can be distorted and misused.

---

[22] Jonathan Edwards, *Charity and Its Fruits* (Edinburgh: Banner of Truth, 1969), 174.

[23] Edwards, *Religious Affections*, 249, emphasis added.

[24] Norman Fiering is right in the following quote if you take "disinterested" in the absolute sense of no benefit whatever, not even the "sweet entertainment" of beholding God: "Disinterested love to God is impossible because the desire for happiness is intrinsic to all willing or loving whatsoever, and God is the necessary end of the search for happiness. Logically one cannot be disinterested about the source or basis of all interest." Norman Fiering, *Jonathan Edwards' Moral Thought in Its British Context* (Chapel Hill, N.C.: University of North Carolina Press, 1981), 161.

But if this happens, it will not be the fault of Jonathan Edwards. The God-enthralled vision of Jonathan Edwards does not make a person presumptuous—it makes him meek. Listen to these beautiful words about brokenhearted joy.

> All gracious affections that are a sweet odor to Christ, and that fill the soul of a Christian with a heavenly sweetness and fragrancy, are brokenhearted affections. A truly Christian love, either to God or men, is a humble brokenhearted love. The desires of the saints, however earnest, are humble desires: their hope is a humble hope; and their joy, even when it is unspeakable, and full of glory, is a humble brokenhearted joy, and leaves the Christian more poor in spirit, and more like a little child, and more disposed to a universal lowliness of behavior.[25]

The God-enthralled vision of Jonathan Edwards is rare and necessary, because its foundations are so massive and its fruit is so beautiful. May the Lord himself open our eyes to see it in these days together and be changed. And since we are great sinners and have a great Savior, Jesus Christ, may our watchword ever be, for the glory of God, "sorrowful, yet always rejoicing" (2 Cor. 6:10).

---

[25] Edwards, *Religious Affections*, 348-349.

2

JONATHAN EDWARDS:
HIS LIFE AND LEGACY

Stephen J. Nichols

Those prone to visit historical sites are likely to be disappointed when it comes to sites associated with the life of Jonathan Edwards. The home of his birth and early years in East Windsor, Connecticut, no longer stands. Neither does his home at Northampton, Massachusetts, nor his home at Stockbridge. At the former, a Roman Catholic church marks the spot; as for the latter, a sundial stands in its place. The church building where Edwards listened to his father preach in East Windsor has long been gone. The church at Northampton is actually the fifth building since Edwards last preached a sermon there; Stockbridge is on its fourth building. A rock along the side of the road marks the spot where the church at Enfield, Connecticut, once stood, the place where Edwards delivered the most famous American sermon of all time, "Sinners in the Hands of an Angry God."

The legacy of Edwards's life and thought, however, stands in stark contrast to the paucity of the remains of his homes and churches. In the nineteenth century, theologians and church leaders all vied for the claim to carry Edwards's mantle, asserting to be his true heir. In the twentieth and now the twenty-first century, scholars, clergy, and laity all continue to look to the New England divine for ideas and inspiration. In fact, Edwards may be even more well-known and discussed now than he was in his own lifetime. And greater still is the potential for the impact of his thought and life to direct future generations of the church toward a God-centered life.

This ongoing legacy has everything to do with the breadth of Edwards's writings and the depth of his encounter with God. While the material remains of Edwards's life may be scarce, the literary remains literally fill shelf after shelf. Among these writings are his great treatises, such as the classic theological text *Religious Affections* and the classic philosophical text *Freedom of the Will*.[1] Additionally, he left behind 1,400 sermons, the bulk of which have yet to be published. Add to this mix volumes of notes on a variety of subjects, the "Miscellanies," exegetical reflections that amount to biblical commentaries, scientific essays, and a host of letters. Edwards left enough material to keep scores of historians, philosophers, theologians, pastors, and laity quite busy. And busy they have been. No other colonial figure, not even Benjamin Franklin or George Washington, has generated the literature from dissertations to popular articles and treatments as Jonathan Edwards has. The number is fast approaching 4,000.[2]

The writings of Edwards comprise only part of the explanation for his legacy. The other part is the depth of his encounter with God. Edwards remarkably managed to hold together what we tend to split apart. He saw Christianity as engaging both head and heart, while much of popular evangelicalism suffers greatly from pendulum swings in this regard. He had an overwhelming vision of the beauty and excellency of Christ, the love and sweet communion of the Holy Spirit, and the glory and majesty of God, while simultaneously seeing wrath and judgment, punishment and justice, as also comprising the divine nature. He had a profound sense of grace and forgiveness, coupled with an acute sense of guilt and repentance. In short, Edwards knew the beauty of Christ because he knew palpably the ugliness of sin. In fact, it might just be the case that precisely because of his awareness of sin, he so exalted the sweetness of his Savior. And perhaps there is much for evangelicals of today and tomorrow to learn here.

Edwards learned these ideas in the trenches of his life, through the highs and lows of his ministry, through the times of rejoicing and mourning with his family, and in the twists and turns of his Christian pilgrimage. In the pages that follow, we will take a brief tour of this life, learning from his example and exploring his legacy for today.

---

[1] For summaries and expositions of these works, see the chapters in this volume by Mark Talbot and Sam Storms respectively.

[2] For a treatment of the recent literature on Edwards, see Sean Michael Lucas, "Jonathan Edwards Between Church and Academy: A Bibliographic Essay," in *The Legacy of Jonathan Edwards: American Religion and the Evangelical Tradition*, ed. D. G. Hart, Sean Michael Lucas, and Stephen J. Nichols (Grand Rapids, Mich.: Baker, 2003), 228-247.

LAST OF THE PURITANS

On a Sabbath day in January 1758, Jonathan Edwards preached his farewell sermon to a band of Mohican and Mohawk Indians and to a handful of English families along the plains of the Housatonic River, snaking through the Berkshire Mountains on the western frontier of Massachusetts. Edwards had come to Stockbridge from his pastorate in Northampton, a post he had held for twenty-three years. He was now leaving for Princeton, New Jersey, where he would be installed as president of Princeton University, holding office in good health for only six weeks. The manuscript for the sermon that day consists of some mere outline points and a few sketchy sentences, only shadows of the full parting words for his Indian flock. In typical sermon style, he ends with a series of applications, saving his final comments for those who "have made it [their] call to live agreeable to the gospel."[3]

Though hardly known, this sermon, and this line in particular, resonates deeply with that which is greatly known of his life. These comments serve not only as a fitting conclusion to his ministry at Stockbridge; they encompass the mission of his life. His first exposure to the gospel came in the parsonage of East Windsor, Connecticut, the home of Timothy Edwards and Esther Stoddard Edwards and their eleven children—Jonathan and his ten sisters. The Latin tutoring he received from his sisters, the love for reading his parents gave him that would only grow in the coming years, and his own omnivorous mind all fitted him to enter the recently established Yale University at twelve years of age. Graduating at the head of his class, he decided to stay at Yale in pursuit of a Master's degree.[4]

After completing his course work, but prior to writing his thesis, Edwards, still a teenager, accepted a call to pastor a Presbyterian church in New York City, in the vicinity of modern-day Broad and Wall Streets. He meticulously prepared his sermons, sometimes writing out a single sermon as many as five times before preaching it. He also spent many mornings horseback riding along the banks of the Hudson River. It was

---

[3] Jonathan Edwards, sermon manuscript on Hebrews 13:7-8 (1758), Beinecke Library, Yale University.

[4] For fuller biographical information, see Iain H. Murray, *Jonathan Edwards: A New Biography* (Edinburgh: Banner of Truth, 1987); Stephen J. Nichols, *Jonathan Edwards: A Guided Tour of His Life and Thought* (Phillipsburg, N.J.: P&R, 2001); and George M. Marsden, *Jonathan Edwards: A Life* (New Haven, Conn.: Yale University Press, 2003).

during these days that Edwards began writing his "Resolutions." Eventually reaching seventy in number, these rules and guidelines for his life became his mission statement. A sampling reveals his discipline and his desire to live wholeheartedly for God:

> 52. I frequently hear persons in old age say how they would live if they were to live their lives over again. Resolved, that I will live just so I can think I shall wish I had done, supposing I live to old age.

> 56. Resolved, never to give over, nor in the least to slacken my fight with my corruptions, however unsuccessful I may be.

> 70. Let there be something of benevolence in everything I speak.

The first resolution is even more instructive. Here Edwards commits his life to "do whatsoever I think to be most to God's glory and to my own good, profit, and pleasure." Here Edwards captures the vision of the first question and answer of the Westminster Shorter Catechism, which declares that the "chief end of man" is to both "glorify God and enjoy him forever." For Edwards, as for the Catechism, the two aims of God's glory and one's pleasure are in fact one and the same thing. What cannot be missed here is the centrality of this for Edwards's life. It is no less remarkable that Edwards learned and lived this as a nineteen-year-old.[5]

By the summer of 1723, however, his church in New York no longer needed him. The church he pastored had come into being through a split. Largely through the counsel and preaching of Edwards, the two groups reconciled, and the offshoot returned, a testimony to both Edwards's abilities and to his altruism, as helping them reconcile meant necessarily that he would be out of a job. He returned to New England, falling terribly ill and convalescing at home, during which time he finished his Master's thesis, an original composition in Latin in keeping with the custom of his day.[6]

Edwards now faced a crucial decision. He had obvious gifts for the ministry, while equally suited for the life of the scholar and an academic

---

[5] *Jonathan Edwards' Resolutions and Advice to Young Converts*, ed. Stephen J. Nichols (Phillipsburg, N.J.: P&R, 2001), 23-26, 17.

[6] For his thesis, "A Sinner Is Not Justified in the Sight of God Except Through the Righteousness of Christ Obtained by Faith," see *The Works of Jonathan Edwards*, vol. 14, *Sermons and Discourses, 1723-1729*, ed. Kenneth P. Minkema (New Haven, Conn.: Yale University Press, 1997), 60-66.

career. He decided to stay at Yale as a tutor, or member of the faculty. The rector of the college, Samuel Johnson, had recently left Yale due to his surprising conversion to Anglicanism—tantamount to heresy for the Congregationalists—leaving Yale rather unstable and without any leadership. During his brief tenure (1724-1726), the young Edwards largely held Yale together and brought it through these troublesome times. His academic career, however, came to an end when he received a call to serve as the assistant minister to the aging Solomon Stoddard, Edwards's maternal grandfather, at Northampton, Massachusetts. Northampton was located north of Edwards's home along the Connecticut River. It had grown to be a prosperous and large town, with an equally prominent pulpit. One would have to go to Boston to find a larger colonial church in New England.

Stoddard's reputation matched that of the town and church. Dubbed "Pope of the Connecticut River Valley," Stoddard's influence was felt far beyond the valley and even far beyond his death. During this brief time of mentoring, Edwards learned a great deal. He learned of the "seasons of harvest," or the times of revival in the church. He learned to be a passionate preacher, aiming sermons at moving the whole person toward a greater understanding of God and living for him. These two things he inherited from his grandfather. He, and the church at Northampton, also inherited some things not so pleasant. Chief among them was Stoddard's practice of admitting all to the Lord's Supper. This would come to be the center of the controversy between Edwards and his people, and Edwards's rejection of the practice would eventuate in his dismissal.[7] This was, however, many years over the horizon. Before the season of conflict came, he had many years of fruitful ministry at Northampton.

The Seasons of Ministry at Northampton

Although it is quite difficult to summarize an eventful twenty-three-year ministry, some highlights stand out. First, there is Edwards's preaching of his sermon "God Glorified in the Work of Redemption" to the ministers gathered for the Harvard commencement in Boston in 1731. Edwards was not of the ranks of Harvard alumni; he had gone to Yale.

---

[7] For a summary with contemporary application for today, see Mark Dever's chapter in this volume. For a full treatment of the "communion controversy" and of Edwards's writings on the issue, see *The Works of Jonathan Edwards*, vol. 12, *Ecclesiastical Writings*, ed. David D. Hall (New Haven, Conn.: Yale University Press, 1994).

He was also the successor to Stoddard. And he was young—many ministers waited their whole life to be called upon to deliver such a sermon. All of this is to say that the expectations on Edwards were great, and also to say that the odds were not in his favor. The outcome, however, could not have been better, not because of Edwards, but because of his message.

In the sermon, Edwards annihilated the pretense that human beings merit or warrant or even contribute anything to salvation. Instead, salvation is exclusively the work of God—the Triune God, that is. Edwards declares:

> We are dependent on Christ the son of God, as he is our wisdom, righteousness, sanctification, and redemption. We are dependent on the Father, who has given us Christ, and made him to be these things to us. We are dependent on the Holy Spirit, for it is of him that we are in Christ Jesus; it is the Spirit of God that gives faith in him. Whereby we receive him, and close [meet] with him.[8]

In this scheme of salvation, the creature is entirely dependent upon the Creator, and the redeemed give the glory to the Redeemer alone.

This view of salvation would be nothing new for Edwards's audience, which was well-versed in the Calvinistic tradition. Edwards, however, takes an intriguing next step. He makes the point that all of our good comes *from* God and comes to us *through* God. This encapsulates the blessings that are ours in salvation. But the chief blessing that we receive, our greatest good, comes to us *in* God. In other words, the greatest blessing that God gives us when he saves us is himself. Edwards puts it this way:

> God himself is the great good which [the redeemed] are brought to the possession of and enjoyment of by redemption. He is the highest good and the sum of all good which Christ purchased. God is the inheritance of the saints; he is the portion of their souls. God is their wealth and treasure, their food, their life, their dwelling place, their ornament and diadem, and their everlasting honor and glory.[9]

---

[8] *The Works of Jonathan Edwards*, vol. 17, *Sermons and Discourses, 1730-1733*, ed. Mark Valeri (New Haven, Conn.: Yale University Press, 1999), 201.
[9] Ibid., 208.

This preaching on the sovereignty of God in the work of redemption and on the sheer joy, delight, and pleasure of salvation was not contained in only one sermon of Edwards. It marked all of his preaching, eventually leading to new seasons of harvest and times of revival at Northampton. The first revival came in 1735-1737. During this time, not only Northampton but also churches along the Connecticut River experienced God at work in remarkable ways. Edwards described the experience in his own congregation:

> Our public assemblies were then beautiful, the congregation was then alive in God's service, everyone earnestly intent on the public worship, every hearer eager to drink in the words of the minister as they came from his mouth; the assembly in general were, from time to time in tears while the Word was preached; some weeping with sorrow and distress, others with joy and love, others with pity and concern for the souls of their neighbors.[10]

The converts grew in number, and soon the congregation outgrew its building. And here the revival fervor became smothered by the selfish interests, scheming, and posturing among the members. The wealthy citizens of the town vied for the most prominent pews in the new meeting-house under construction. Factions and backbiting ensued, growing to such a pitch that Edwards addressed it in the sermon "Peaceful and Faithful Amid Division and Strife" in May 1737. Here he speaks of "the old iniquity of this town," meaning Northampton, which he identifies as "Contention and a party spirit." He continues, "People have not known how to manage scarce any public business without siding and dividing themselves into parties." Though a bit of hyperbole, this was unfortunately characteristic of both civil and ecclesiastical life in Northampton.[11]

Edwards also notes the tragic consequence of the defaming of Christianity due to this contentious spirit, pointing out that "it has been very much taken notice of." This is especially the case since Northampton was so blessed of God through the few years prior to the time of revival. Edwards points out that while God "has most remark-

---

[10] Jonathan Edwards, "A Faithful Narrative of the Surprising Work of God," in *The Works of Jonathan Edwards,* vol. 4, *The Great Awakening,* ed. C. C. Goen (New Haven, Conn.: Yale University Press, 1972), 151.

[11] *The Works of Jonathan Edwards,* vol. 19, *Sermons and Discourses, 1734-1738,* ed. M. X. Lesser (New Haven, Conn.: Yale University Press, 2001), 670.

ably honored us by the great things he has done for us," many in Northampton are "industriously stirr[ing] up strife." This in miniature represents Edwards's ministry at Northampton. As in Dickens's novel, it, too, was the best of times and the worst of times. Yet, Edwards's preaching changed little during these oscillations of trial and triumph, and his ideas remained markedly consistent throughout. As this sermon concludes, he calls upon those who are faithful and who live peaceably, even in the throes of contention, to be peacemakers, to pursue "the best interest of God's people, [rather] than any private interest."[12]

Eventually the parishioners at Northampton once again began taking their faith seriously, and once again revival came. But this time it moved far beyond the bounds of the Connecticut River Valley, reaching throughout New England and beyond to encompass the colonies. The Great Awakening, from roughly 1740-1742, coincided with the trips of George Whitefield to the colonies and, as with the earlier revival, the preaching of Edwards.

The sermon receiving the most attention is the famous "Sinners in the Hands of an Angry God." Edwards preached this sermon the first time at Northampton with apparently little impact. A few months later, the occasion would arise for him to re-preach it, and this time the impact was legendary. Edwards was at Enfield, Connecticut, a healthy horse ride down the Connecticut River from Northampton. He wasn't there to preach, but to be preached to. The intended minister, however, was too ill to preach, and Edwards just happened to have the sermon manuscript in his saddlebag.

The sermon is replete with imagery of God's wrath for sinners. There is the famous spider dangling over a flame, hanging by a mere thread and vividly portraying our precarious position. A heavy lead weight sliding toward a bottomless gulf represents our inability to defer God's judgment, and a bent bow makes us acutely aware of the imminence of God's wrath. These are the images that have haunted readers ever since they first encountered the sermon in a high school American literature or history class. These images are what most people have when they hear of Edwards. Apologies for this dark side of Edwards are, however, not in order. For Edwards, the reality of hell's torments and God's wrath are the necessary corollaries to heaven's beauty and God's love.

---

[12] Ibid., 671-674, 663.

It is wrong, however, to caricature Edwards, as many do, as the consummate purveyor of hellfire and brimstone, incarnating the caricature of the Puritan as killjoy, the one who is always thinking and fearing that somewhere someone might just be having a good time.

This is certainly not the case in Edwards. One trips over the words *sweetness, beauty, happiness, joy, pleasure, excellency,* and *delight* throughout his writings. And even "Sinners in the Hands of an Angry God" is no exception. In addition to the imagery of God's wrath, there is also the imagery of God's mercy. Consider this example: "Now you have an extraordinary opportunity, a day wherein Christ has flung the door of mercy wide open and stands in calling, and crying with a loud voice to poor sinners."[13]

Many entered through that door of mercy that evening as they heard the sermon, and as the Awakening spread they were joined by countless others throughout the colonies. Because of Edwards's involvement in these early revivals, he stands at the headwaters of the revivals and of the revivalism that significantly serves to shape the American religious identity. He is often called upon either as inspiration for revivals or as justification for them and the phenomenon they might spawn. Some of the associations might very well cause Edwards to balk, if not object altogether. To all of the revival movements, however, Edwards has something quite meaningful to say.

Edwards wrote much on revivals and revivalism, with his mature thought expressed in *Treatise Concerning Religious Affections* (1746), which was first a sermon series. In this work he explores the nature of affections, what may not necessarily count as true signs of religious affections, and what counts as true signs. The twelfth and final sign of genuine religious affections is given as the life that bears fruit. This is quite instructive given the context. Edwards witnessed incredible enthusiasm for Christ at the height of the Awakening. But then the commitment faded, leaving Edwards rather confused. For him, this was no mere academic issue. He was a pastor, and he had a deep and abiding concern for the spiritual state of those under his care. Edwards learned through this experience that the Christian life is not a sprint, but a marathon.[14]

---

[13] *The Works of Jonathan Edwards,* vol. 22, *Sermons and Discourses, 1739-1742,* ed. Harry S. Stout and Nathan O. Hatch (New Haven, Conn.: Yale University Press, 2003), 416.

[14] See *The Works of Jonathan Edwards,* vol. 2, *Religious Affections,* ed. John E. Smith (New Haven, Conn.: Yale University Press, 1959), 383-461.

The revivalism approach to living the Christian life can tend to make it one that consists of fits and spurts. Edwards came to see that it was lived out, consistently, over the long haul. In the tradition of the Puritans, represented most strikingly in John Bunyan's *Pilgrim's Progress*, Edwards viewed the Christian life as a pilgrimage, a journey of progress toward heaven. This approach emphasizes a consistent living out of the Christian faith in all aspects of life, and even, or perhaps especially, in the ordinary experiences of daily living. The revivalism mentality tends toward highs and lows, with not much to say to ordinary experiences. Edwards can inspire us to yearn for the work of God in our lives and in our churches. But he also can help us see that sometimes that happens without bells and whistles.

Despite these seasons of fruitful ministry, his tenure at Northampton ended on a bitter note. He sensed a growing lethargy toward the things of God among his parishioners. He also sensed that his pastoral authority was waning. In some ways, what happened to Edwards at Northampton was merely a symptom of larger shifts in New England culture. In previous generations, the church, geographically located at the center of town, was to be the center of one's life. By Edwards's day, the church and the pastor were becoming increasingly marginal in the life of New Englanders. Edwards's vision of God and of the community of saints allowed for no such marginalization. Consequently, when he asserted his pastoral authority, calling for deep levels of commitment by his congregation, he ran counter to many in the church. The issue seized upon was his discontinuation of the practice started by Stoddard of admitting all, even the unregenerate, to Communion. Edwards was in the right; nevertheless, he was voted out of his church on June 22, 1750.[15]

Much has been written on the controversy and dismissal. Here we might simply focus on Edwards's response. Surely it must have been a crushing blow. Not so much because of the embarrassment to Edwards—although certainly it was an embarrassing episode—but more because of his disappointment in his aim for the congregation at Northampton. Long before the controversy, he preached a sermon series on Paul's famous poem on love in 1 Corinthians 13, which

---

[15] See Patricia J. Tracy, *Jonathan Edwards, Pastor: Religion and Society in Eighteenth-Century Northampton* (New York: Hill and Wang, 1980).

Edwards entitled "Charity and Its Fruits." The final installment in that series was the sermon, "Heaven Is a World of Love." Here he extols the sublime beauty and glory of the life to come. But this for Edwards was no mere ethereal vision. For all of his talk of heaven and the world to come, he had a good fix on life here and now in this world. Consequently, Edwards puts forth the thesis that "as heaven is a world of love, so the way to heaven is the way of love."[16]

What he longed for in his own life and in the lives of his congregation was that they would model this idea, living it out in their community. At times Edwards saw glimpses of it, and at times it even made more lasting manifestations. More often than not, however, his vision for his church went unrealized, as in the case of the late 1740s and in 1737 with the building of the new meetinghouse. We should not suppose Edwards to be naïve on this point. He knew of sin's spoiling effects that continue both individually and communally after one comes to Christ. That, of course, is the difference between the communion of saints here and that of the life to come. Yet, Edwards did not abandon the idea that the journey to heaven should strive to reflect the destination.

Perhaps we get the impression that Edwards lived a rather charmed life, untouched by the vicissitudes of defeat and loss, conflict and hardship. That simply is not the case. His conflict at Northampton raged for years, and when he left there for Stockbridge, he also found himself embroiled in controversy. Eventually at both places he was vindicated. A deacon at Northampton later admitted that the leadership of the church was in the wrong and that the dismissal was unjust. That was after the fact, however. It would have been quite easy for Edwards to have deep resentment throughout these trials, perhaps even to abandon his call to ministry altogether, but he did not. He did not lessen his grasp of the belief that if heaven is a world of love, then the way to heaven is the way of love—he strengthened it.

MISSIONARY AT STOCKBRIDGE

Once dismissed, Edwards received numerous offers, including pastorates overseas, at Boston, and even at Northampton by a group of loyal mem-

---

[16] *The Works of Jonathan Edwards*, vol. 8, *Ethical Writings*, ed. Paul Ramsey (New Haven, Conn.: Yale University Press, 1989), 396.

bers willing to start a new church. Edwards turned them all down, opting instead to head west. He went only forty miles, but the short distance could not mask the fact that he was literally moving to a new world. Stockbridge, Massachusetts, located on a beautiful plain along the Housatonic River and amidst the Berkshire Mountains, was the home of approximately 250 Mohicans, Mohawks, and Brothertons, as well as a dozen English families. It was a frontier mission post, only established a dozen years earlier. Prior Edwards scholarship viewed his time at Stockbridge as an exile and as a sabbatical during which he wrote his great treatises *Freedom of the Will*, *Original Sin*, and the posthumously published *Two Dissertations: Concerning the End for Which God Created the World* and *The Nature of True Virtue*. This is patently not the case. Edwards had a long-standing interest in Native Americans, as evidenced by his involvement on the board of trustees for Stockbridge and his editing and publishing of David Brainerd's journal. He also was very much involved in ministering to his flock of "Stockbridge Indians."[17]

One way this is seen is in his sermons. Edwards re-preached a number of sermons from earlier days once he got to Stockbridge. He also wrote many new ones. In all of them, he attempted to connect with his audience by making frequent allusions to nature—he often used such illustrations in his preaching, but here he increased the practice—and stating rather complicated matters in straightforward and clear prose. He preached a number of sermon series during this time, including treatments of the divine attributes, Christology and the deity and humanity of Christ, Revelation, the parables in Matthew 13, and, not surprisingly, the Lord's Supper. In the series on divine attributes, he included a sermon on God's mercy, which he likened to "a river that overflows all of its bounds."[18] In a sermon for the Mohawks, he declared, "We invite you to come and enjoy the light of the Word of God, which is ten thousand times better than [the] light of the sun."[19]

The great themes in his treatises and previous sermons also find expression in the pulpit at Stockbridge. In a sermon on Hebrews 11:16,

---

[17] For a fuller discussion, see Stephen J. Nichols, "Last of the Mohican Missionaries: Jonathan Edwards at Stockbridge," in *The Legacy of Jonathan Edwards*, 47-63.

[18] Jonathan Edwards, sermon manuscript on Exodus 34:6-7 (January 1753), Beinecke Library, Yale University.

[19] Jonathan Edwards, "To the Mohawks at the Treaty, August 16, 1751," in *The Sermons of Jonathan Edwards: A Reader*, ed. Wilson H. Kimnach, Kenneth P. Minkema, and Douglas A. Sweeney (New Haven, Conn.: Yale University Press, 1999), 109.

Edwards extols the virtues of heaven, the better country to come, in prose and imagery that rivals "Heaven Is a World of Love," though in outline format. Edwards explains that in heaven there is "no sin, no pride, no malice, [no] hating one another, no hurting one another, [no] killing one another . . . no death, no old age, no winter." Positively, heaven is a place of peace and love, where "hearts are full of love" and "full of joy and happiness."[20]

Edwards also exhorted the Stockbridge Indians to live holy lives, reminding them in a sermon on 1 Peter 1:15 "that Christians are under special obligation to be universally holy in their lives." By "universally holy" he meant that holiness should "extend itself to all God's commands, all employment and persons, all conditions, and all time."[21] He also realized, however, that such holiness is a duty of delight. As he taught in his sermon on 1 John 5:3, "True love to God makes the duties he requires of us easy and delightful," commending "the pleasure of communion with God." This idea, he explains in the application, moves us from approaching "religion as a hard task" to seeing it as "our delight and pleasure."[22]

It is clear from his sermons that the appraisal of Gerald McDermott is right: Edwards "seems to have developed genuine affection for his Indian congregation."[23] But even at Stockbridge, not all was smooth sailing. In addition to the Indians, Stockbridge was home to about a dozen English families. Chief among them was Colonel Ephraim Williams, of the ubiquitous Williams clan that appears throughout the Connecticut River Valley and that even gave Edwards difficulties at Northampton. Williams devoted his energies to acquiring land and wealth. He also oversaw the mission school, which was established at Stockbridge for the evangelization and education of Mohawks. Williams and his appointed schoolmaster Martin Kellogg, however, viewed the school as providing labor to work the land. This led to yet another drawn-out controversy as Edwards tried to wrest control of the school from Williams. Williams retaliated by boycotting the church and smearing Edwards's name, even accusing him of embezzlement. In time, Edwards was fully

---

[20] Jonathan Edwards, sermon manuscript on Hebrews 11:16 (January 1754), Beinecke Library, Yale University.

[21] Jonathan Edwards, sermon manuscript on 1 Peter 1:15 (n.d.), Beinecke Library, Yale University.

[22] Jonathan Edwards, sermon manuscript on 1 John 5:3 (n.d.), Beinecke Library, Yale University.

[23] Gerald McDermott, *Jonathan Edwards Confronts the Gods: Christian Theology, Enlightenment Religion, and Non-Christian Faiths* (Oxford: Oxford University Press, 2000), 203.

exonerated as Williams was shown to be embezzling funds and abusing his position. In the meantime, the disillusioned Mohawks left Stockbridge, leaving Edwards no choice but to close the school.

Here, as in Northampton, Edwards's ministry was one of highs and lows. He saw many converts and changed lives, while also experiencing the bitter root of controversy again. One example of his impact stands out in particular. Hendrick Aupaumut was most likely baptized by Edwards as an infant in 1757. Aupaumut was a hero in the Revolutionary War and a political leader of the Mohicans. He also was a spiritual leader, translating the Westminster Shorter Catechism into Mohican. Though the direct impact of Aupaumut is minimal at best, the indirect impact is great. Aupaumut wrote to Timothy Edwards, Jonathan's son who remained in Stockbridge after the family moved and presumably a friend of Aupaumut's, requesting copies of his father's books, wanting both *Freedom of the Will* and *Religious Affections*, testimony to Edwards's legacy among the Mohicans.[24]

THE UNCOMMON UNION: THE EDWARDS FAMILY

Edwards's time at Stockbridge was followed by a quite brief tenure as president of Princeton. He left Stockbridge in January, beginning his presidential duties later that month. Around the beginning of March, he took a smallpox inoculation, developed pneumonia, suffered intensely for about two weeks, and died on March 22, 1758. Perhaps the saddest element of this tragic episode is that at the time of his death Edwards was separated from his wife, Sarah. He had made the move to Princeton in the middle of winter. Given the difficulties of the travel, and also to allow Sarah to sell property and settle some financial affairs, it was decided that he would go ahead to Princeton and settle the home there and they would reunite in the spring. When they parted in January, it was the last time they were to see each other on earth. In now famous last words, his thoughts drifted toward Sarah as he said, dictating a letter to his daughter Lucy, "Give my kindest love to my dear wife, and tell her that the uncommon union, which has so long subsisted between us, has been such a nature as I trust is spiritual and so will continue for ever."[25]

---

[24] Hendrick Aupaumut to Timothy Edwards (1775), Stockbridge Historical Room, Stockbridge, Mass.
[25] See Heidi L. Nichols, "Those Exceptional Edwards Women," *Christian History* 22 (2003): 23-25. For more on Sarah and their relationship, see Noël Piper's essay in this volume.

Edwards had first met Sarah while he was a student at Yale in New Haven. Her father was a minister and a founding trustee of the college. From the first moment Jonathan met her, he was enraptured by her grace and elegance and charm, and also by her model spirituality. Through the years he surely kept up on the life of Sarah Pierpont, and he married her four years after he began his pastoral charge at Northampton. Like his own family at East Windsor, he and Sarah had eleven children of their own. He looked to Sarah to keep this bustling home together. Once, while Sarah was on a trip to Boston and Jonathan was left tending the family, he wrote a letter to his wife, informing her that the two oldest daughters were sick, adding, "We have been without you almost as long as we know how to be."[26]

Like other families of the colonial era, the Edwardses were no strangers to tragedy and difficulty. Though all of their children lived past infancy, not all of them survived their parents. Edwards preached the funeral sermon for his daughter Jerusha, who likely contracted tuberculosis while caring for the dying David Brainerd. Another daughter, Esther, lost her husband Aaron Burr, and there were the sad occurrences of the deaths of grandchildren. Further, Edwards, though it is hard for us as contemporary readers to think of this, lived on the frontier and faced the accompanying threat of Indian invasions. Distant relatives were taken captive, and at times both at Northampton and especially at Stockbridge tension ran high. One letter to Esther Edwards Burr from her father finds the family sheltered in a fort.

There were trying days, and there were days of celebration. Sometimes it was the challenges that provided for rich adventure in the Edwards home. When the family moved to Stockbridge, Jonathan Edwards, Jr., was just a boy. He played alongside the Mohicans and Mohawks, learning Mohican as he learned English. Later in his life he would become quite an advocate for Native Americans, even warranting the praise of George Washington. All visitors, and there were many, to the Edwards home commented on the grace of the hosts and the union of the family. Edwards, according to the custom for ministerial preparation in those days, also housed apprentices for the ministry in his home. This generation of ministers had a profound impact on New

---

[26] Jonathan Edwards to Sarah Pierpont Edwards (June 22, 1748), *The Works of Jonathan Edwards*, vol. 16, *Letters and Personal Writings*, ed. George S. Claghorn (New Haven, Conn.: Yale University Press, 1998), 247.

England. And before them, Edwards and his family lived out their faith in full view.

His hope for his family was the same as that for the congregations to which he ministered. Summed up best in a letter to his daughter Sarah when she was twelve years old and visiting relatives, Edwards writes, "I wish you much of the presence of Christ and communion with him, and that you might live so as to give him honor in [the] place where you are by an amiable behavior towards all."[27] When another daughter, Mary, was away in New Hampshire, Edwards took the occasion to remind her of God's care: "Though you are at so great distance from us, yet God is everywhere. You are much out of the reach of our care, but you are every moment in his hands. We have not the comfort of seeing you, but he sees you. His eye is always upon you."[28]

That his children learned this can be seen in some correspondence with his daughter, Esther Edwards Burr. Shortly after the death of her husband, her infant son, Aaron Burr, Jr., later to become America's third vice president, fell sick, being "brought to the Brink of the Grave." This was an intense time of suffering in Esther's life. No sooner had she finished writing to her mother about how God was comforting her at the loss of her husband, she took up the quill to write to her father of her "new tryals." In the letter, however, she reveals her deep resolve of faith in God, boldly claiming, "Altho all streams were cut off yet so long as my God lives I have enough—He enabled me to say altho' thou slay me yet will I trust in thee." She can declare, "O how good is God," she can say, "I saw the fullness there was in Christ," and she can testify that "a kind and gracious God h[as] been with me in six Troubles and in seven."[29] Her father had this to say in his response:

> Indeed, he is a faithful God; he will remember his covenant forever; and never will fail them that trust in him. But don't be surprised, or think some strange thing has happened to you, if after this light, clouds of darkness should return. Perpetual sunshine is not usual in this world, even to God's true saints. But I hope, if God should hide his face in

[27] Jonathan Edwards to Sarah Edwards (June 25, 1741), WJE, 16:96.
[28] Jonathan Edwards to Mary Edwards (July 26, 1749), WJE, 16:289.
[29] Esther Edwards Burr to Jonathan Edwards (November 2, 1757), The Journal of Esther Edwards Burr, 1754-1757, ed. Carol F. Karlsen and Laurie Crumpacker (New Haven, Conn.: Yale University Press, 1984), 295-296.

some respect, even this will be in faithfulness to you, to purify you, and fit you for further and better light.[30]

Perhaps Esther Edwards Burr's response to these times of trial in her life represents the true legacy of Edwards's ministry.

THE PURSUIT OF HAPPINESS: EDWARDS'S LEGACY

Many themes emerge from the life and thought of Edwards, and all of them provide for a rich legacy. Peter Thuesen once referred to Edwards as a "great mirror," intending to capture the notion that there is a breadth to Edwards's work that provides scholars and others from many different fields rich opportunities to see and reflect a variety of elements.[31] And that is certainly true as Edwards's literary remains abound. Amidst all of this material, some central themes and emphases shine through, calling for our attention as we contemplate Edwards's legacy for the church today.

His extensive and thorough understanding of the gospel, for one, compels attention. Edwards begins with a vision of the holiness and wrath of God, coupled with his infinite love and mercy as seen in the cross, then moves to portray vividly and powerfully humanity's desperate plight and utter need of a savior. He thoughtfully balances both a deep and abiding sense of our sin and lowliness alongside the exaltation of joy in Christ and delight in God. This approach serves well as an antidote to the often anemic and shallow presentations of the gospel today.

Secondly, we could learn from the example of his well-trained eye to see the beauty of God in nature and to see God at work both in the Word and in the world. This led Edwards to view his engagement of the world in an entirely new way. He could learn of God in the Bible, to be sure, but as he watched the flying spider, for instance, he could see something of the pleasure of God, and as he rode through the picturesque Connecticut River Valley he marveled at God's creativity and goodness. As George Marsden, commenting on this comprehensive vision of Edwards, observes, "The key to Edwards' thought is that everything is related because everything is

---

[30] Jonathan Edwards to Esther Edwards Burr (November 20, 1757), *WJE*, 16:730.

[31] Peter J. Thuesen, "Jonathan Edwards as Great Mirror," *Scottish Journal of Theology* 50 (1997): 39-60.

related to God."[32] Seeing the world this way brings new perspective to the Christian at work, enjoying nature, participating in the arts, and engaging culture.

Finally, Edwards, unlike any other, gracefully portrays life as relishing in the gifts and world of the Triune God, heralding that ultimately we find true fulfillment in relishing God himself. This last point is worth exploring in depth.

Somewhat endemic to American identity is the pursuit of happiness. Enshrined by Thomas Jefferson, these words and what they mean are often the talk of American historians, and in many ways are often the goal of American citizens. Happiness and its pursuit was of no less interest to Edwards. He differed quite a bit from his contemporaries, however. Most notable in this regard is Benjamin Franklin, one of the key shapers of the meaning of those words. In Franklin's hands, the pursuit of happiness largely came to mean self-fulfillment accomplished through self-reliance. Of course, Franklin advocated public virtue and the common good as well. But his aphorisms in the quite popular *Poor Richard's Almanac* and his own *Autobiography* point to a certain self-centeredness in Franklin's pursuit. "Early to bed, early to rise, makes one healthy, wealthy, and wise," illustrates the point.

Edwards could not disagree more. Rather than seeing self-centeredness as the goal achieved through self-reliance, Edwards advocated God-centeredness achieved through dependence on him. There is, however, a great irony here. The irony is summed up in Christ's words: "Whoever finds his life will lose it, and whoever loses his life for my sake will find it" (Matt. 10:39). To state the irony directly, self-centeredness through self-reliance leads to self-defeat, in the truest and fullest sense possible. When, however, God is at the center, the self is most realized, most fulfilled, and most happy.

It is worth noting that Edwards emphasized, as well, God-dependence over self-dependence. Again it was Franklin who said, "God helps those who help themselves." Through such statements, self-reliance has become a distinctly American ideal, and American evangelicalism is not necessarily immune from its effects. Conversely, Edwards sees us as helpless, standing before God entirely empty-handed. His emphasis on the sovereignty of God caused him to exalt God in the

---

[32] Marsden, *Jonathan Edwards*, 460.

work of redemption and in sanctification, to come to him and to live for him only through dependence upon him. This crucial aspect of Edwards's legacy is worth remembering.

Edwards has a different definition of happiness and a different means by which it is achieved than Franklin and most pursuers of the American dream. He also knows that these differences lead to different objects that fill out that definition and mark the pursuit. In his sermon "Heaven Is a World of Love," he notes that the pleasures of heaven are not just for heaven; they are to be enjoyed now. Consequently, he admonishes that our desires "must be taken off the pleasure of this world."[33] This is not deprivation. Edwards simply does not want our desires to be so small as to cause us to miss the true happiness and pleasure of what God has for us both now and in the world to come.

Edwards longed for his parishioners at Northampton and Stockbridge and for his family and for himself to be "happified" in and through Christ, a word that only he could coin, and a word that he truly spent his life in pursuit of. Sometimes that happiness came in times of triumph. Sometimes it came to him on the anvil of suffering, conflict, and hardship. But in all aspects of this remarkable life we see the legacy of God glorified and enjoyed forever, which is still instructive 300 years later and hopefully for years to come.

---

[33] Edwards, "Heaven Is a World of Love," *WJE*, 8:394.

3

SARAH EDWARDS:
JONATHAN'S HOME AND HAVEN

Noël Piper

We are interested in Jonathan Edwards because of his influence on our way of understanding the world and seeing God. Of course, that makes us curious about his wife, Sarah. But I'd be wasting our time if I were satisfied just to dig around for interesting tidbits. So I pray that this biography and our time in it will be biblical and will be for our edification and encouragement.

Biography *is* important, and the book of Hebrews is a good place to remind ourselves of that. Perhaps 13:7-8, in particular, can help us read with clearer purpose the story of a saint, of one who leads us in our faith.

> Remember *your leaders, those who spoke to you the word of God. Consider the outcome of their way of life, and* imitate *their faith. Jesus Christ is the same yesterday and today and forever.*

Remember. Consider. Imitate. We should never think that we can't be a saint like Sarah Edwards. I expect that Sarah Edwards would be the first to tell us that she isn't great. She would tell us she has a great God—the same God we have. "Jesus Christ is the same yesterday and today and forever." Let us look for him as we consider Sarah's story.

THE BACKDROP

For the sake of context, let's remember that Jonathan and Sarah's whole lives were lived in the colonies of the New World—*colonies*, not one country. Thirteen small British colonies hugged the Atlantic coast. And a vast western wilderness stretched who knew how far into the unknown.

New *England* and the other colonies were Britain's fragile fingertip grasp on the edge of the continent. The colonists were British citizens surrounded by territories of other nations. Florida and the Southwest were Spain's. The Louisiana Territory was France's. The French, in particular, were eager to ally themselves with local Indians against the British. Today the Edwards story should elicit the sight of garrisons on hilltops, the sounds of shots in the distance, the discomfort of soldiers billeting in their homes, the shock and terror of news about massacres in nearby settlements. This was the backdrop, to a greater or lesser degree, throughout much of their lives.

THE COURTSHIP OF JONATHAN EDWARDS AND SARAH PIERREPONT

In 1723, at age nineteen, Jonathan had already graduated from Yale and had been a pastor in New York for a year. When his time in that church ended, he accepted a job at Yale and returned to New Haven where Sarah Pierrepont lived. It's possible that Jonathan had been aware of her for three or four years, since his student days at Yale. In those student days, when he was about sixteen, he probably would have seen her when he attended New Haven's First Church where her father had been pastor until his death in 1714.[1]

Now, on his return in 1723, Jonathan was twenty and Sarah was thirteen. It was not unusual for girls to be married by about sixteen.

As this school term's work began for him, it seems he may have been somewhat distracted from his usual studiousness. A familiar story finds him daydreaming over his Greek grammar book, which he probably intended to be studying to prepare to teach. Instead we find now on the front page of that grammar book a record of his real thoughts.

> They say there is a young lady in [New Haven] who is loved of that Great Being, who made and rules the world, and that there are certain seasons in which this Great Being, in some way or other invisible, comes to her and fills her mind with exceeding sweet delight; and that she hardly cares for anything, except to meditate on Him. . . . [Y]ou could not persuade her to do any thing wrong or sinful, if you would give her all the world, lest she should offend this Great Being. She is of

---

[1] Iain H. Murray, *Jonathan Edwards: A New Biography* (Edinburgh: Banner of Truth, 1987), 91.

a wonderful sweetness, calmness, and universal benevolence of mind; especially after this Great God has manifested himself to her mind. She will sometimes go about from place to place, singing sweetly; and seems to be always full of joy and pleasure. . . . She loves to be alone, walking in the fields and groves, and seems to have some one invisible always conversing with her.[2]

All the biographers mention the contrast between the two of them. Sarah was from one of the most distinguished families in Connecticut. Her education had been the best a woman of that era typically received. She was accomplished in the social skills of polite society. She enjoyed music and perhaps knew how to play the lute. (In the year of their marriage, one of the shopping reminders for Jonathan when he traveled was to pick up lute strings.[3] That may have been for a wedding musician, or it may have been for Sarah herself.) People who knew her mentioned her beauty and her way of putting people at ease. Samuel Hopkins, who knew her later, stressed her "peculiar loveliness of expression, the combined result of goodness and intelligence."[4]

Jonathan, on the other hand, was introverted, shy, and uneasy with small talk. He had entered college at thirteen, and graduated valedictorian. He ate sparingly in an age of groaning dining tables, and he was not a drinker. He was tall and gangly and awkwardly different. He was *not* full of social graces. He wrote in his journal: "A virtue which I need in a higher degree is gentleness. If I had more of an air of gentleness, I should be much mended."[5] (In that time, *gentleness* meant "appropriate social grace," as we use the word today in *gentle*man.)

One thing they had in common was a love for music. He pictured music as the most nearly perfect way for people to communicate with each other.

---

[2] Quoted in ibid., 92.

[3] George M. Marsden, *Jonathan Edwards: A Life* (New Haven, Conn.: Yale University Press, 2003), 110.

[4] Quoted in Elisabeth D. Dodds, *Marriage to a Difficult Man: The Uncommon Union of Jonathan and Sarah Edwards* (Laurel, Miss.: Audubon Press, 2003), 15. In the writing of this short biography of Sarah Edwards, I am indebted especially to Dodds's book. I have known this work so long, it is possible that I sometimes have incorporated its thought without appropriate footnote references. I realize there are weaknesses in Dodds's presentation (see my Foreword to the 2003 edition of *Marriage to a Difficult Man*). So I do recommend that interested readers go to Marsden's *Jonathan Edwards: A Life* and Murray's *Jonathan Edwards: A New Biography* for more careful chronology, theological interpretation, and understanding of the man who so shaped Sarah's life and was so affected by Sarah.

[5] Quoted in Dodds, *Marriage to a Difficult Man*, 17.

The best, most beautiful, and most perfect way that we have of expressing a sweet concord of mind to each other, is by music. When I would
form in my mind an idea of a society in the highest degree happy, I
think of them as expressing their love, their joy, and the inward concord and harmony and spiritual beauty of their souls by sweetly singing
to each other.[6]

That imagery was just the first thought-step into a leap from human
realities to heavenly realities, where he saw sweet human intimacy as
only a simple ditty compared to the symphony of harmonies of intimacy
with God.

As Sarah grew older, and Jonathan grew somewhat mellower, they
began to spend more time together. They enjoyed walking and talking
together, and he apparently found in her a mind that matched her
beauty. In fact, she introduced him to a book she owned by Peter van
Mastricht, a book that later was influential in his thinking about the
Covenant.[7] They became engaged in the spring of 1725.

Jonathan was a man whose nature was to bear uncertainties in
thought and theology as if they were physical stress. The years of wait-
ing until Sarah was old enough to marry must have added even greater
pressure. Here are some words he used to describe himself, from a couple of weeks of his journal in 1725, a year and a half before they would
marry:

December 29	Dull and lifeless
January 9	Decayed
January 10	Recovering[8]

Perhaps it was his emotions for Sarah that sometimes caused him
to fear sinning with his mind. In an effort to remain pure, he resolved,
"When I am violently beset with temptation or cannot rid myself of evil
thoughts, to do some sum in arithmetic or geometry or some other study,
which necessarily *engages all my thoughts* and unavoidably keeps them
from wandering."[9]

6 Quoted in Marsden, *Jonathan Edwards*, 106.
7 Dodds, *Marriage to a Difficult Man*, 21. (Dodds spelled the name as Peter Maastricht.)
8 Quoted in ibid., 19.
9 Quoted in ibid.

The Beginnings of Their Married Life

Jonathan Edwards and Sarah Pierrepont were finally married on July 28, 1727. She was seventeen. He was twenty-four. He wore a new powdered wig and a new set of white clerical bands given him by his sister Mary. Sarah wore a boldly-patterned green satin brocade.[10]

We get only glimmers and glimpses into the heart of their love and passion. One time, for instance, Jonathan used the love of a man and a woman as an illustration of our limited grasp of another person's love toward God. "When we have the idea of another's love to a thing, if it be the love of a man to a woman . . . we have not generally any further idea at all of his love, we only have an idea of his *actions* that are the *effects* of love. . . . We have a faint, vanishing notion of their *affections*."[11]

Jonathan had become the pastor in Northampton, following in the footsteps of his grandfather, Solomon Stoddard. He began there in February 1757, just five months before their wedding in New Haven.

Sarah could not slip unnoticed into Northampton. Based on the customs of the time, Elisabeth Dodds imagines Sarah's arrival in the Northampton church:

> Any beautiful newcomer in a small town was a curio, but when she was also the wife of the new minister, she caused intense interest. The rigid seating charts of churches at that time marked a minister's family as effectively as if a flag flew over the pew. . . . So every eye in town was on Sarah as she swished in wearing her wedding dress.
>
> Custom commanded that a bride on her first Sunday in church wear her wedding dress and turn slowly so everyone could have a good look at it. Brides also had the privilege of choosing the text for the first Sunday after their wedding. There is no record of the text Sarah chose, but her favorite verse was "Who shall separate us from the love of Christ?" (Rom 8:35), and it is possible that she chose to hear that one expounded.
>
> She took her place in the seat that was to symbolize her role—a high bench facing the congregation, where everyone could notice the least flicker of expression. Sarah had been prepared for this exposed position every Sunday of her childhood on the leafy common of New

---

[10] Ibid., 22.
[11] Ibid.

Haven, but it was different to be, herself, the Minister's Wife. Other women could yawn or furtively twitch a numbed foot in the cold of a January morning in an unheated building. Never she.[12]

Marsden says, "By fall 1727 [about three months after the wedding] Jonathan had dramatically recovered his spiritual bearings, specifically his ability to find the spiritual intensity he had lost for three years."[13]

What made the difference? Perhaps he was better fitted for a church situation than for the academic setting at Yale. In addition, it seems likely to me that the recovery was closely related to their marriage. For at least three years prior to this, in addition to his rigorous academic pursuits, he had also been restraining himself sexually and yearning for the day when he and Sarah would be one. When their life together began, he was like a new man. He had found his earthly home and haven.

And as Sarah stepped into this role of wife, she freed him to pursue the philosophical, scientific, and theological wrestlings that made him the man we honor.

Edwards was a man to whom people reacted. He was different. He was intense. His moral force was a threat to people who settled for routine. After he'd thought through the biblical truth and implications of a theological or church issue, he didn't back down from what he'd discovered.

For instance, he came to realize that only believers should take Communion in the church. The Northampton church was not happy when he went against the easier standards of his grandfather who had allowed Communion even for unbelievers if they weren't participating in obvious sin.[14] This kind of controversy meant that Sarah, in the background, was also twisted and bumped by the opposition that he faced.

He was a thinker who held ideas in his mind, mulling them over, taking them apart and putting them together with other ideas, and testing them against other parts of God's truth. Such a man reaches the heights when those separate ideas come together into a larger truth. But he also is the kind of man who can slide into deep pits on the way to a truth.[15]

A man like that is not easy to live with. But Sarah found ways to

---

[12] Ibid., 25.
[13] Marsden, *Jonathan Edwards*, 111.
[14] For more on this, see Mark Dever's chapter in this volume.
[15] Dodds, *Marriage to a Difficult Man*, 57.

make a happy home for him. She made him sure of her steady love, and then she created an environment and routine where he was free to think. She learned that when he was caught up in a thought, he didn't want to be interrupted for dinner. She learned that his moods were intense. He wrote in his journal: "I have had very affecting views of my own sinfulness and vileness; very frequently to such a degree as to hold me in a kind of loud weeping . . . so that I have often been forced to shut myself up."[16]

The town saw a composed man. Sarah knew what storms there were inside him. She knew the at-home Jonathan.

Samuel Hopkins wrote:

> While she uniformly paid a becoming deference to her husband and treated him with entire respect, she spared no pains in conforming to his inclination and rendering everything in the family agreeable and pleasant; accounting it her greatest glory and there wherein she *could best serve God and her generation* [and ours, we might add], *to be the means in this way of promoting his usefulness and happiness.*[17]

So life in the Edwards house was shaped in large degree by Jonathan's calling. One of his journal entries said, "I think Christ has recommended rising early in the morning by his rising from the grave very early."[18] So it was Jonathan's habit to awake early. The family's routine through the years was to wake early with him, to hear a chapter from the Bible by candlelight, and to pray for God's blessing on the day ahead.

It was his habit to do physical labor sometime each day for exercise—for instance, chopping wood, mending fences, or working in the garden. But Sarah had *most* of the responsibility for overseeing the care of the property.

Often he was in his study for thirteen hours a day. This included lots of preparation for Sundays and for Bible teaching. But it also included the times when Sarah came in to visit and talk or when parishioners stopped by for prayer or counsel.

In the evening the two of them might ride into the woods for exer-

---

[16] Quoted in ibid., 31.
[17] Quoted in ibid., 29-30 (emphasis added).
[18] Quoted in ibid., 28.

cise and fresh air and to talk. And in the evening they would pray together again.

The Growing Family

Beginning on August 25, 1728, children came into the family—eleven in all—at about two-year intervals: Sarah, Jerusha, Esther, Mary, Lucy, Timothy, Susannah, Eunice, Jonathan, Elizabeth, and Pierpont.[19] This was the beginning of Sarah's next great role, that of mother.

In 1900 A. E. Winship made a study contrasting two families. One had hundreds of descendants who were a drain on society. The other, descendants of Jonathan and Sarah Edwards, were outstanding for their contributions to society. He wrote of the Edwards clan:

> Whatever the family has done, it has done ably and nobly. . . . And much of the capacity and talent, intelligence and character of the more than 1400 of the Edwards family is due to Mrs. Edwards.

By 1900 when Winship made his study, this marriage had produced:

- thirteen college presidents
- sixty-five professors
- 100 lawyers and a dean of a law school
- thirty judges
- sixty-six physicians and a dean of a medical school
- eighty holders of public office, including:
  - three U.S. senators
  - mayors of three large cities
  - governors of three states
  - a vice president of the U.S.
  - a controller of the U.S. Treasury

Members of the family wrote 135 books. . . . edited 18 journals and periodicals. They entered the ministry in platoons and sent one hundred missionaries overseas, as well as stocking many mission boards with lay trustees.[20]

---

[19] Pierpont's name was spelled different than Sarah's maiden name. Standardized spelling hadn't become common yet.

[20] Dodds, *Marriage to a Difficult Man,* 31-32.

Winship goes on to list kinds of institutions, industries, and businesses that have been owned or directed by Edwards's descendants. "There is scarcely a Great American industry that has not had one of this family among its chief promoters." We might well ask with Elisabeth Dodds, "Has any other mother contributed more vitally to the leadership of a nation?"[21]

Six of the Edwards children were born on Sundays. At that time some ministers wouldn't baptize babies born on Sundays, because they believed babies were born on the day of the week on which they had been conceived, and that wasn't deemed an appropriate Sabbath activity.

All of the Edwards children lived at least into adolescence. That was amazing in an era when death was always very close, and at times there was resentment among other families.

THE HOUSEHOLD

In our centrally-heated houses, it's difficult to imagine the tasks that were Sarah's to do or delegate: breaking ice to haul water, bringing in firewood and tending the fire, cooking and packing lunches for visiting travelers, making the family's clothing (from sheep-shearing to spinning and weaving to sewing), growing and preserving produce, making brooms, doing laundry, tending babies and nursing illnesses, making candles, feeding poultry and produce, overseeing butchering, teaching the boys whatever they didn't learn at school, and seeing that the girls learned homemaking creativity. That's only a fraction of that for which she was responsible.

How could she have known the gift she was giving *us* as she freed Jonathan to fulfill his calling?

Once when Sarah was out of town and Jonathan was in charge, he wrote almost desperately, "We have been without you almost as long as we know how to be."[22]

Much of what we know about the inner workings of the Edwards family comes from Samuel Hopkins, who lived with them for a while. He wrote:

---

[21] Ibid., 32.
[22] Quoted in Marsden, *Jonathan Edwards*, 323.

She had an excellent way of governing her children; she knew how to make them regard and obey her cheerfully, without loud angry words, much less heavy blows. . . . If any correction was necessary, she did not administer it in a passion; and when she had occasion to reprove and rebuke she would do it in few words, without warmth [that is, vehemence] and noise. . . .

Her system of discipline was begun at a very early age and it was her rule to resist the first, as well as every subsequent exhibition of temper or disobedience in the child . . . wisely reflecting that until a child will obey his parents he can never be brought to obey God.[23]

Their children were eleven different people, proving that Sarah's discipline did not squash their personalities—perhaps because an important aspect of their disciplined life was that, as Samuel Hopkins wrote, "for [her children] she constantly and earnestly prayed and bore them on her heart before God . . . and that even before they were born."[24]

Dodds says:

Sarah's way with their children did more for Edwards than shield him from hullabaloo while he studied. The family gave him incarnate foundation for his ethic. . . . The last Sunday [Edwards] stood in the Northampton pulpit as pastor of the church he put in this word for his people: "Every family ought to be . . . a little church, consecrated to Christ and wholly influenced and governed by His rules. And family education and order are some of the chief means of grace. If these fail, all other means are like to prove ineffectual."[25]

As vital as Sarah's role was, we mustn't picture her raising the children alone. Jonathan and Sarah's affection for each other and the regular family devotional routine were strong blocks in the children's foundation. And Jonathan played an integral part in their lives. When they were old enough, he would often take one or another along when he traveled. At home, Sarah knew Jonathan would give one hour every day to the children. Hopkins describes his "entering freely into the feelings and concerns of his children and relaxing into cheerful and animate conversation accompanied frequently with sprightly remarks

---

[23] Quoted in Dodds, *Marriage to a Difficult Man*, 35-36.
[24] Quoted in ibid., 37.
[25] Ibid., 44-45.

and sallies of wit and humor . . . then he went back to his study for more work before dinner."[26] This was a different man than the parish usually saw.

It is possible to piece together a lot about the Edwards household because they were paper savers. Paper was expensive and had to be ordered from Boston. So Jonathan saved old bills, shopping lists, and first drafts of letters to stitch together into small books, using the blank side for sermon writing. Since his sermons were saved, this record of everyday, sometimes almost modern details was saved as well. For instance, many of the shopping lists included a reminder to buy chocolate.[27]

It was understood by travelers in that colonial time that if a town had no inn or if the inn was unsavory, the parson's house was a welcoming overnight place. So from the beginning in Northampton, Sarah exercised her gifts of hospitality. Their home was well-known, busy, and praised.

THE WIDER SPHERE OF INFLUENCE

Sarah was not only mother and wife and hostess—she also felt spiritual responsibility for those who entered her house. A long line of young apprentice pastors showed up on their doorstep over the years, hoping to live with them and soak up experience from Jonathan. That's why Samuel Hopkins was living with them and had the occasion to observe their family. He arrived at the Edwards home in December 1741. Here's his account of the welcome he received.

> When I arrived there, Mr. Edwards was not at home, but I was received with great kindness by Mrs. Edwards and the family and had encouragement that I might live there during the winter. . . . I was very gloomy and was most of the time retired in my chamber. After some days, Mrs. Edwards came . . . and said as I was now become a member of the family for a season, she felt herself interested in my welfare and as she observed that I appeared gloomy and dejected, she hoped I would not think she intruded [by] her desiring to know and asking me what was the occasion of it. . . . I told her . . . I was in a Christless, graceless state . . . upon which we entered into a free conversation and

[26] Quoted in ibid., 40.
[27] Ibid., 38; Ola Elizabeth Winslow, *Jonathan Edwards, 1703-1758: A Biography* (New York: Macmillan, 1940), 136.

... she told me that she had [prayed] respecting me since I had been in the family; that she trusted I should receive light and comfort and doubted not that God intended yet to do great things by me.[28]

Sarah had seven children at the time—ages thirteen down to one and a half—and yet she also took this young man under her wing and encouraged him. He remembered it all his life.

The impact of Sarah Edwards's assurance in God's working did not stop in that personal conversation. Hopkins went on to become a pastor in Newport, Rhode Island, a town dependent on the slave economy. He raised a strong voice against it, even though many were offended. But one young man was impressed. William Ellery Channing had been adrift till then, looking for purpose in his life. He had long talks with Hopkins, went back to Boston, became a pastor who influenced Emerson and Thoreau, and had a large part in the abolitionist movement.[29]

We all have quiet conversations that might be forgotten. Sarah's with Samuel would have been forgotten except for Hopkins's journal. Their talk was part of a chain that led onward at least as far as Emerson and Thoreau, and *that* certainly wasn't the end of it—we just don't have the records of what happened next, and next, and next. We usually *don't* know how God winds the threads of our lives on and on and on.

Hopkins obviously admired Sarah Edwards. He wrote that "she made it her rule to speak well of all, so far as she could with truth and justice to herself and others. . . ." This sounds a lot like Jonathan's early flyleaf musings about Sarah—confirmation that he hadn't been blinded by love.

When Hopkins watched the relationship between Jonathan and Sarah he saw that:

> In the midst of these complicated labors . . . [Edwards] found at home one who was in every sense a help mate for him, one who made their common dwelling the abode of order and neatness, of peace and comfort, of harmony and love, to all its inmates, and of kindness and hospitality to the friend, the visitant, and the stranger.[30]

---

[28] Quoted in Dodds, *Marriage to a Difficult Man*, 50.
[29] This chain of influence is described by Dodds in *Marriage to a Difficult Man*, 50-51.
[30] Ibid., 64.

Another person who observed the Edwards family was George Whitefield, when he visited America during the Awakening. He came to Northampton for a weekend in October 1740 and preached four times. Also, on Saturday morning he spoke to the Edwards children in their home. Whitefield wrote that when he preached on Sunday morning, Jonathan wept during almost the whole service. The Edwards family had a great effect on Whitefield as well:

> Felt wonderful satisfaction in being at the house of Mr. Edwards. He is a Son himself, and hath also a Daughter of Abraham for his wife. A sweeter couple I have not yet seen. Their children were dressed not in silks and satins, but plain, as becomes the children of those who, in all things ought to be examples of Christian simplicity. She is a woman adorned with a meek and quiet spirit, talked feelingly and solidly of the Things of God, and seemed to be such a help meet for her husband, that she caused me to renew those prayers, which, for many months, I have put up to God, that he would be pleased to send me a daughter of Abraham to be my wife.[31]

The next year Whitefield married a widow whom John Wesley described as a "woman of candour and humanity."[32]

THE SPIRITUAL TURNING POINT

The second phase of the Awakening crested in the spring and summer of 1741, the same time Jonathan was asking the church for a set salary due to the financial demands of his large family. This caused the parish to watch very closely the lifestyle of the Edwards family, to be on the lookout for extravagance. A salary committee of the church ruled that Sarah had to keep an itemized statement of all expenditures.

In January 1742 we come to an event in Sarah's life that was a turning point for her. Our efforts to understand this period remind us of the difficult task a biographer has in trying to record fairly a person's life, and how hard it can be to evaluate what you read in biography or history.

An obvious problem arises when a biographer's worldview makes him blind to important aspects of his subject's life. Iain Murray sees this problem when he takes note of prominent Edwards biographers and

---

[31] Winslow, *Jonathan Edwards, 1703-1758*, 188.
[32] Dodds, *Marriage to a Difficult Man*, 74-75.

observes that Ola Winslow (1940) rejected Edwards's theology and that later, in Perry Miller (1949), "anti-supernatural animus comes to its fullest expression."[33]

It's amazing to think that someone could write a highly-acclaimed biography of Edwards that lauds his philosophy but rejects his view of God and anything supernatural. And then, from our perspective as readers, what if that lopsided view were *all* we knew about Edwards? That's the challenge for a biography reader—trying to find and recognize a well-balanced approach.

In January 1742 Sarah underwent a crisis that is approached very differently by different biographers, leaving us with the challenge of trying to understand what really happened.

Winslow, who rejected Edwards's theology, used the account of Sarah's experience to minimize the impact of Jonathan's acceptance of outward, active manifestations of the Holy Spirit. Winslow wrote, "The fact that his wife was given to these more extreme manifestations no doubt inclined him to a more hospitable attitude toward them. . . ."[34] The implication seems to be that under normal circumstances he would have been less accepting of such "enthusiasm," but his perception was skewed by having to account for Sarah's experience.

Miller, who rejected the idea of anything supernatural, could only conclude that Sarah's story provided Jonathan with a proof-case to use against those who thought "enthusiasm" was from Satan. Miller's implication seems to be that although we modern people know such manifestations couldn't really be supernatural, Edwards was old-fashioned and mistakenly thought something supernatural was going on. So, Miller might say, it was convenient for Edwards to have an experience at hand to try to use as proof against doubters.[35]

Dodds describes Sarah as "limply needful, grotesque—jabbering, hallucinating, idiotically fainting."[36] She calls it a breaking point and attributes it to Sarah's previous stoicism, her coping with her difficult husband and many children, the financial stresses, Jonathan's criticism of her handling of a certain person, and her jealousy over the success of

[33] Murray, *Jonathan Edwards*, xxix.
[34] Winslow, *Jonathan Edwards, 1703-1758*, 205.
[35] Miller's attitude colors his recounting of this event: Perry Miller, *Jonathan Edwards* (New York: W. Sloane Associates, 1949), 203-206 .
[36] Dodds, *Marriage to a Difficult Man*, 81. Dodds describes Sarah's experience in chapter 8.

a visiting pastor while Jonathan was away from home. Dodds says we can't know if it was a religious transport or a nervous breakdown.[37]

Over against all these interpretations stands Sarah's own account of this time. She speaks unambiguously of the experience as a spiritual encounter.

What really happened? We would be wise to hear some of Sarah's own words, as transcribed by Jonathan. He published her account in "Some Thoughts Concerning the Present Revival of Religion."[38] For privacy's sake, he didn't reveal her name or gender.

> The soul dwelt on high, was lost in God, and seemed almost to leave the body. The mind dwelt in a pure delight that fed and satisfied it; enjoying pleasure without the least sting, or any interruption. . . .
>
> [There were] extraordinary views of divine things, and religious affections, being frequently attended with very great effects on the body. Nature often sinking under the weight of divine discoveries, and the strength of the body was taken away. The person was deprived of all ability to stand or speak. Sometimes the hands were clinched, and the flesh cold, but the senses remaining. Animal nature was often in a great emotion and agitation, and the soul so overcome with admiration, and a kind of omnipotent joy, as to cause the person, unavoidably to leap with all the might, with joy and mighty exultation. . . .[39]
>
> The thoughts of the perfect humility with which the saints in heaven worship God, and fall down before his throne, have often overcome the body, and set it into a great agitation.[40]

There is more. And rather than finding yourself subject to *my* choice of what to emphasize, you can read it for yourself in "Some Thoughts Concerning the Present Revival of Religion in New England."[41]

We mustn't imagine that she was shut away by herself during all this time. Jonathan was away from home all except the first two days. So she was responsible for the home—caring for the seven children and the

---

[37] Ibid., 90.

[38] The section that tells Sarah's story is published as Appendix E in *Marriage to a Difficult Man* (2003 edition), 209-216.

[39] Jonathan Edwards, "Some Thoughts Concerning the Present Revival in New England," in *The Works of Jonathan Edwards*, ed. Edward Hickman, 2 vols. (1834; reprint, Edinburgh: Banner of Truth, 1974), 1:376.

[40] Ibid., 377.

[41] Ibid., 376-378. Also published as Appendix A in Dodds, *Marriage to a Difficult Man*, 187.

guests and attending special gatherings at church. Probably no one grasped at the time how completely God was shaking and shaping her when she was alone.

This was only a month after Samuel Hopkins had moved into their home, so his impressions of the family were being formed in the midst of Sarah's most life-changing days.

Was Sarah's experience psychological or spiritual? Did it spring from the frustrations and pressures of her life? I suppose that none of us ever has *totally* pure motives or actions or causes in our spiritual activities, but there is no doubt that both Jonathan and Sarah recognized her experiences as being *from* God and *for* her spiritual delight and benefit. They have proved themselves to be people whose judgment in spiritual matters we can usually trust. So I don't feel inclined to explain away her understanding of her experiences. Nor would I want to minimize Jonathan's confirmation, implicit in his making the account public.

Stresses over finances, distress at having upset her husband, jealousy about another's ministry—all those things were real in Sarah's life. But we have seen from our own experience that God reveals himself through what is happening to us and around us. God used such things to show Sarah she needed him, to uncover her own weakness. And then, when the almost-physical sensations of God's presence came upon her, he was all the more precious and sweet to her, because of what he had forgiven and overcome for her.

Also I think back to Jonathan's early description of her, written in his Greek book. Granted, he was an infatuated lover. But he didn't make up his description out of nothing. He was writing about a certain kind of person, and we can see the shape of her, even if it is through Jonathan's rose-colored glasses.

> . . . there are certain seasons in which this Great Being, in some way or other invisible, comes to her and fills her mind with exceeding sweet delight; and that she hardly cares for anything, except to meditate on Him.[42]

That is very close to how she described this adult experience. And remember that as a thirteen-year-old, she loved "to be alone, walking in the fields and groves, and seems to have some one invisible always conversing with her."[43]

Thirteen-year-olds who are energized by being alone usually grow up to be adults who are energized by being alone. Where is that solitude for a woman with a newborn every other year, with a steady stream of travelers and apprentices living in her house, and with a town who notices every twitch of her life?

Here are some other reasons I believe she experienced God, and not just psychological distress or breakdown.

First, I don't know anyone who has, for no apparent reason, suddenly snapped out of psychological breakdown and been just fine after that. (Dodds seems to try to evade this argument by suggesting that when Jonathan had her sit down and tell him everything that had happened, he was acting as an unwitting forerunner of psychotherapy.[44])

Second, Jesus said, "You will recognize them by their fruits" (Matt. 7:16). Sarah's life was different after these weeks—different in the ways you would expect after God had specially visited someone. Jonathan said she exhibited

> a great meekness, gentleness, and benevolence of spirit and behaviour; and a great alteration in those things that formerly used to be the person's failings; seeming to be much overcome and swallowed up by the late great increase of grace, to the observation of those who are most conversant and most intimately acquainted.[45]

He also reassured his reader that she had not become too heavenly-minded to be any earthly good.

> Oh how good, said the person once, is it to work for God in the daytime, and at night to lie down under his smiles! High experiences and religious affections in this person have not been attended with any disposition at all to neglect the necessary business of a secular calling . . . but worldly business has been attended with great alacrity, as part of the service of God: the person declaring that, it being done thus, it was found to be as good as prayer.[46]

---

[43] Ibid.
[44] Edwards, "Thoughts on the Revival," 378.
[45] Ibid.
[46] Dodds, *Marriage to a Difficult Man*, 216.

Her changed life bore the fingerprint of God, not of psychological imbalance. It is clear that Jonathan agreed with her belief that she had encountered God:

> If such things are enthusiasm, and the fruits of a distempered brain, let my brain be evermore possessed of that happy distemper! If this be distraction, I pray God that the world of mankind may be all seized with this benign, meek, beneficent, beatifical, glorious distraction![47]

THE WILDERNESS

After more than twenty years, Jonathan was ousted from his church in Northampton. I'm not going to dwell on that, because it's a fairly well-known part of his life. But it is worth a moment of our time to empathize with the emotional and financial stress it would have been for Sarah. Her husband had been rejected. But until he had another position, they had to remain in Northampton. So for one year Sarah lived in a hostile setting and managed their large household with no salary coming in.

In Stockbridge there was a community of Indians and a few whites. They were urgently searching for a pastor at the same time that Jonathan was seeking God's next step for his life. In 1750 the Edwardses moved to Stockbridge, out on the western side of Massachusetts, on the pioneer edge of the British fingerhold on the continent.

In 1871 *Harpers New Monthly Magazine* ran an article featuring Stockbridge. This was more than one hundred years after Edwards's death, and yet he had come to bear international esteem surpassed (perhaps!) only by George Washington. Many paragraphs described his noteworthy role in the history of the town of Stockbridge. And though decades had passed, they hadn't forgotten the Northampton controversy that led to Jonathan's call to Stockbridge.

> There succeeded to that vacant office in the wild woods one whose name is not only highly honored throughout this land, but better known and more honored abroad, perhaps, than that of any of our countrymen except Washington. As a preacher, a philosopher, and a person of devoted piety he is unsurpassed.... But ... after a most successful ministry of more than 20 years, a controversy had arisen

---

[47] Edwards, "Thoughts on the Revival," 378.

between him and his people, and they had thrust him out from them rudely and almost in disgrace. The subsequent adoption of his views, not only at Northampton but throughout the churches of New England, has abundantly vindicated his position in that lamentable controversy. . . .

He was not too great in his own estimation to accept the place now offered him [in the small outpost of Stockbridge]. . . .

Edwards was almost a thinking machine. . . .

That a man thus thoughtful should yet be indifferent to many things of practical importance would not be strange. Accordingly we are told that the care of his domestic and secular affairs was devolved almost entirely upon his wife, who happily, while of kindred spirit with him in many respects, and fitted to be his companion, was also capable of assuming the cares which were thus laid upon her. It is said that Edwards did not know his own cows, nor even how many belonged to him. About all the connection he had with them seems to have been involved in the act of driving them to and from pasture occasionally, which he was willing to do for the sake of needful exercise. A story is told in this connection, which illustrates his obliviousness of small matters. As he was going for the cows once, a boy opened the gate for him with a respectful bow. Edwards acknowledged the kindness and asked the boy whose son he was. "Noah Clark's boy," was the reply. . . . On his return, the same boy . . . opened the gate for him again. Edwards [asked again who he was]. . . . "The same man's boy I was a quarter of an hour ago, Sir."[48]

THE LAST CHAPTER

This was a family who had hardly tasted death, yet they were very aware of its constant nearness. How easily might a woman die in childbirth. How easily might a child die of fever. How easily might one be struck by a shot or an arrow of war. How easily might a fireplace ignite a house fire, with all asleep and lost.

When Jonathan wrote to his children, he often reminded them—not morbidly, but almost as a matter of fact—how close death might be. For Jonathan, the fact of death led automatically to the need for eternal life. He wrote to their ten-year-old Jonathan, Jr., about the death of a playmate. "This is a loud call of God to you to prepare for death. . . . Never

---

[48] "A New England Village," *Harper's New Monthly Magazine*, November 1871, http://www.rootsweb.com/~maberksh/harpers/ (accessed 12-31-03).

give yourself any rest unless you have good evidence that you are converted and become a new creature."[49]

A family tragedy was the opening page of the final chapter of their lives.

Their daughter Esther was the wife of Aaron Burr, the president of
the College of New Jersey, which would later be called Princeton. On
September 24, 1757, this son-in-law of Jonathan and Sarah died suddenly, leaving Esther and two small children. This would be the first of
five family deaths in a year.

Aaron Burr's death left the presidency open at the College of New
Jersey, and Edwards was invited to become president of the college.
Jonathan had been extremely productive in his thinking and writing during the six Stockbridge years; so it was not easy to leave. But in January
1758 he set off for Princeton, expecting his family to join him in the spring.

George Marsden pictures the moment:

> He left Sarah and his children in Stockbridge, as 17-year-old Susannah
> later reported, "as affectionately as if he should not come again."
> When he was outside the house, he turned and declared, "I commit you
> to God."[50]

He had hardly moved into the President's House at Princeton when
he received news that his father had died. As Marsden says, "A great
force in his life was finally gone, though the power of the personality had
faded some years earlier."[51]

In this final chapter of Jonathan's and Sarah's lives, there are key
moments that encapsulate and confirm God's work through Sarah
Edwards in the main roles she had been given by him.

Sarah's Role as a Mother, with the Desire to Raise Godly Children

When Aaron Burr died, we catch a glimpse of how well the mother had
prepared the daughter for unexpected tragedy. Esther wrote to her
mother, Sarah, two weeks after he died:

> God has seemed sensibly near, in such a supporting and comfortable
> manner that I think I have never experienced the like. . . . I doubt not

---

[49] Marsden, *Jonathan Edwards*, 412.
[50] Ibid., 491.
[51] Ibid.

but I have your and my honoured father's prayers, daily, for me, but give me leave to entreat you to request earnestly of the Lord that I may never . . . faint under this his severe stroke. . . . O I am afraid I shall conduct myself so as to bring dishonour on . . . the religion which I profess.[52]

At the darkest moment of her life, she fervently desired not to dishonor God.

Sarah's Role as the Wife of Jonathan

Soon after Jonathan arrived in Princeton, Jonathan was inoculated for smallpox. This was still an experimental procedure. He contracted the disease, and on March 22, 1758, he died, while Sarah was still back in Stockbridge, packing for the family's move to Princeton. Fewer than three months had passed since he had said good-bye at their doorstep. During the last minutes of his life, his thoughts and words were for his beloved wife. He whispered to one of his daughters:

It seems to me to be the will of God, that I must shortly leave you; therefore give my kindest love to my dear wife, and tell her, that the uncommon union, which has so long subsisted between us, has been of such a nature, as I trust is spiritual, and therefore will continue for ever: and I hope she will be supported under so great a trial, and submit cheerfully to the will of God.[53]

A week and a half later Sarah wrote to Esther (it had been only six months since Esther's husband had died):

My very dear child, What shall I say? A holy and good God has covered us with a dark cloud. O that we may kiss the rod, and lay our hands upon our mouths! The Lord has done it. He has made me adore his goodness, that we had him so long. But my God lives; and he has my heart. O what a legacy my husband, and your father, has left us! We are all given to God; and there I am, and love to be.

Your affectionate mother,
Sarah Edwards[54]

---

52 Dodds, *Marriage to a Difficult Man*, 160.
53 Sereno E. Dwight, "Memoirs of Jonathan Edwards," in *Works*, 1:clxxviii.
54 Ibid., 1:clxxix.

Esther never read her mother's letter. On April 7, less than two weeks after her father's death, Esther died of a fever, leaving behind little Sally and Aaron, Jr. Sarah traveled to Princeton to stay with her grandchildren for a while and then take them back to Stockbridge with her.

Her Role as a Child of God

In October Sarah was traveling toward Stockbridge with Esther's children. While stopping in the home of friends, she was overcome with dysentery, and her life on earth ended. It was October 2, 1758. She was forty-nine. The people with her reported that "she apprehended her death was near, when she expressed her entire resignation to God and her desire that he might be glorified in all things; and that she might be enabled to glorify him to the last; and continued in such a temper, calm and resigned, till she died."[55]

Hers was the fifth Edwards death in a year, and the fourth Edwards family grave in the Princeton Cemetery during that year.

WHO WAS SARAH EDWARDS?

She was the supporter and protector and home-builder for Jonathan Edwards, whose philosophy and passion for God is still vital 300 years after his birth.

She was the godly mother and example to eleven children who became the parents of outstanding citizens of this country, and—immensely more important to her—many are also citizens of heaven.

She was the hostess and comforter and encourager of Samuel Hopkins, and who knows how many others, who went on to minister to others, who went on to minister to others, who went on . . .

She was an example to George Whitefield, and who knows how many others, of a godly wife.

At the heart of all she was, she was a child of God, who from early years experienced sweet, spiritual communion with him, and who over the years grew in grace, and who at least once was very dramatically visited by God in a way that changed her life.[56]

---

[55] Dodds, *Marriage to a Difficult Man*, 169.
[56] Besides the references cited throughout the footnotes in this chapter, the following resources may also be of interest to the reader: Sharon James, *In Trouble and in Joy: Four Women Who Lived for God*

A Timeline of Sarah Edwards[57]

October 5, 1703	Jonathan born, East Windsor, CT
January 9, 1710	Sarah born, New Haven, CT
1723	Jonathan writes "Apostrophe to Sarah Pierpont" in his Greek book
October 26, 1726	Jonathan begins preaching in Northampton, under leadership of Solomon Stoddard
February 15, 1727	Jonathan is ordained, Northampton
July 28, 1727	Jonathan and Sarah marry, New Haven
August 25, 1728	Sarah born
February 11, 1729	Solomon Stoddard dies; Jonathan becomes pastor
December 1729	Jonathan's sister, Jerusha, dies
April 26, 1730	Daughter Jerusha born
February 13, 1732	Esther born
1734	Great Awakening begins in Northampton
April 7, 1734	Mary born
February 10, 1736	Jonathan's grandmother, Esther Mather Stoddard, dies
August 21, 1736	Jonathan's sister Lucy dies of "throat distemper"
August 31, 1736	Daughter Lucy born
July 25, 1738	Timothy born
March 1740	Measles epidemic; several of the Edwards children ill
1740	Sarah's portrait painted
June 20, 1740	Susannah (Sukey) born
October 17-19, 1740	Whitefield in Northampton
Spring 1741	Jonathan asks for set salary
July 1741	Jonathan preaches "Sinners in the Hands of an Angry God" in Enfield
December 1741	Samuel Hopkins arrives
January 19—February 4, 1742	Sarah's extraordinary spiritual experience
May 9, 1743	Eunice born
1744	Request for higher salary
May 26, 1745	Son Jonathan born
May 6, 1747	Elizabeth born
May 28, 1747	David Brainerd arrives
October 9, 1747	Brainerd dies

(Auburn, Mass.: Evangelical Press USA, 2003); Carol F. Karlsen and Laurie Crumpacker, eds., *The Journal of Esther Edwards Burr, 1754-1757* (New Haven, Conn.: Yale University Press, 1986); Doreen Moore, *Good Christians, Good Husbands? Leaving a Legacy in Marriage & Ministry* (Rosshire, England: Christian Focus, 2004), chapter on Jonathan Edwards; Heidi L. Nichols, "Those Exceptional Edwards Women," *Christian History* 22 (2003): 23-25 (available on the Internet at http://www.christianitytoday.com/ch/2003/001/9.23.html).

[57] This chronology is gleaned from my own reading, with clarification of details by Kenneth Minkema, "A Jonathan Edwards Chronology," http://www.yale.edu/wje/html/chronology.html (accessed 1-29-04).

February 14, 1748	Jerusha dies
April 8, 1750	Pierrepont born
June 11, 1750	Daughter Sarah and Elihu Parsons marry
June 22, 1750	Jonathan dismissed from NH church
July 2, 1750	Jonathan preaches farewell sermon
November 8, 1750	Mary and Timothy Dwight marry
August 8, 1751	Installation at Stockbridge
October 18, 1751	Family moves to Stockbridge
1752	Sarah ill, almost dies
May 14, 1752	Grandchild born, Mary's Timothy
May 29, 1752	Grandchild born, Sarah's Esther
June 29, 1752	Esther and Aaron Burr marry
April, 1753	Timothy leaves home to live with Burrs and study at Princeton
December, 1753	Grandchild born, Sarah's Elihu
1754	Grandchild born, Esther's Sarah
1754-1763	French and Indian War
February 6, 1756	Grandchild born, Esther's Aaron
1756	Grandchild born, Mary's Erastus
September 24, 1757	Aaron Burr dies, leaving presidency of Princeton open
January 27, 1758	Jonathan's father dies
February 16, 1758	Jonathan becomes president of Princeton
February 23, 1758	Jonathan is inoculated against smallpox
March 22, 1758	Jonathan dies
April 7, 1758	Esther dies
October 2, 1758	Sarah dies

PART TWO
LESSONS FROM EDWARDS'S LIFE AND THOUGHT

4

The Glory of God and the Reviving of Religion: A Study in the Mind of Jonathan Edwards

J. I. Packer

It is a privilege and a pleasure to bring a presentation—perhaps I ought to say, a present—to help celebrate Jonathan Edwards's 300th birthday. Such celebration is welcome; it reflects wisdom. Though yesterday's great Christians must not be idolized, they should be remembered, and their legacy kept in appreciative view; for God gave them their strength and insight in order to enrich not just their own generation but all who would come after. So then, I now invite attention to some aspects of Edwards's thought that I, for one, have especially valued and that seem to me to have much to say to others of us at this time.

Let me be more specific about what I owe to Edwards. First, for almost sixty years I have been hungry for the wisdom of the Puritans, and Edwards has fed my appetite, for, to echo Perry Miller, Puritanism is what Edwards was.[1] Again, for almost sixty years, ever since I read Charles Finney's very able and forceful *Lectures on Revivals of Religion*,[2] revival has been a heart-interest of mine, and it was Edwards's classic writings on the Northampton visitation of 1734 and the Great Awakening of 1740-42 that brought the theme into biblical focus for me (before that, not surprisingly to anyone who knows Finney, it was somewhat skewed in my mind). Furthermore, I repeatedly urge in varied com-

---

[1] "Many definitions of Puritanism have been offered by historians. . . . I suspect that the most useful would be simply that Puritanism is what Edwards is." Perry Miller, *Jonathan Edwards* (New York: William Sloane Associates, 1949), 194.

[2] First published, 1835; many editions since.

pany that evangelicalism is Christianity without additions, subtractions, or dilutions—Christianity, that is, in its purest and most authentic form. And to make the point I picture historic Christianity as a broad river whose main stream flows along a central channel while eddies, stagnant pools, backwaters, and expanses of mud abound along its banks. Then I cite the teaching of such men as Augustine, Luther, Calvin, Owen, and Warfield, and Edwards with them, as so many buoys marking out the central channel for all who are concerned to be found in it. Thus, under God I owe a lot to Edwards and am glad to have this opportunity of acknowledging my debt.

My aim now is to show in detail how Edwards's view of God shaped his thinking about revival. But first it will be good to make sure that we have a clear view of this remarkable man, saint, pastor, polymath, theologian, metaphysician, apologist, and educator as he was; and we may do that most vividly, I think, by setting alongside him the other evangelical leader whose 300th birthday we celebrated in 2003—John Wesley.[3] A glance at some of the similarities and differences between these two men will help us to see them both more clearly than otherwise we might do.

EDWARDS AND WESLEY

So how do they compare? They were different human types, to start with: Edwards was tall, gaunt, grave, taciturn with strangers, and always somewhat withdrawn, while Wesley was short, slight (regularly weighing 128 pounds, so he tells us), cheerful and outgoing to everyone, and a chatty conversationalist in all company. Neither seems to have had much of a sense of humor, but Wesley was a great storyteller, while Edwards was not. Their backgrounds were different. Wesley was a native Englishman, a sometime Oxford don, tirelessly traversing his homeland as a visiting fireman for God. Edwards was a settled New England colonial, serving smallish pastorates, who was caught constantly in the family rivalries and small-town politics of frontierland. Both were Bible-believing Protestants, scholarly children of the early Enlightenment, reading and thinking men with well-trained minds, wide in their interests and widely read, and masters of a fluent precision of language for preaching, teaching, and debat-

---

[3] On Wesley, I commend two recent brief books: Iain H. Murray, *Wesley and Men Who Followed* (Edinburgh: Banner of Truth, 2003) and Stephen Tomkins, *John Wesley: A Biography* (Oxford, UK: Lion/Grand Rapids, Mich.: Eerdmans, 2003).

ing. But Wesley was an activist, while Edwards was an analyst, and Wesley's practical theology of religion—new birth, justification, and holiness, all by faith—though serviceable enough for his purposes,[4] is not in the same league as Edwards's exact explorations and demonstrations of the plans, works, and ways of the Triune God, according to the Scriptures and the developed Reformed faith.

Again, both were clergy, born into clergy families, who embraced the family theology; which made Wesley an eighteenth-century Anglican post-Calvinist (all his life Wesley had an anti-Calvinist obsession[5]), while Edwards remained a seventeenth-century Calvinistic Puritan at heart. So when Wesley came to publish Edwards's *Religious Affections* in 1773, he reduced "one of the most complete systems of what has been strikingly called 'spiritual diagnostics'" (the words are B. B. Warfield's[6]) to half length, declaring that in its original form it had in it "much wholesome food . . . mixed with much deadly poison." Iain Murray, who records this, notes that in Wesley's view, "Christian experience is so basically simple that it is needless to attempt distinctions between the real and the false in those who claim to be rejoicing in Christ. If a person who has assurance of salvation later loses it, and abandons the Christian practice which he once followed, he is plainly a case of a person losing his salvation. So Wesley thought. Edwards would have been almost nonplussed by such an approach. . . ."[7] No comment necessary, I think.

The pastoral ministries of the two men, though both centering for substance on the preaching of regeneration and sanctification in Christ, were very different in form and style. Wesley traveled constantly throughout Britain, carving out for himself the role of chief pastor— para-bishop, you might say—of the countrywide Methodist societies. By the end of Wesley's eighty-seven-year life the British societies had over

---

[4] Wesley developed a theology of religion, personal and corporate, rather than a systematic account of God. Though widely read and sharp-minded, he equivocated somewhat on the work of God in both justification and sanctification, causing great consternation thereby (see Murray, *Wesley and Men Who Followed*, 76-79, chaps. 9-10). Murray is correct: "His beliefs in their totality made up a loose synthesis, an amalgam, rather than a coherent system" (76). Wesley might better be described as a highest-grade catechist than as a theologian in the full sense.

[5] Tutored to some extent by his mother, an ex-Puritan, ex-Calvinist, Wesley was always convinced that a consistent believer in divine sovereignty could not offer Christ to all, nor stave off Antinomianism, and he was impervious to argument on both points.

[6] B. B. Warfield, *Studies in Theology* (*Works*, vol. 9) (New York: Oxford University Press, 1932; repr. Grand Rapids, Mich.: Baker, 1981), 524.

[7] Iain H. Murray, *Jonathan Edwards: A New Biography* (Edinburgh: Banner of Truth, 1987), 259-260.

70,000 members (and the American societies, led by Thomas Coke and Francis Asbury, had 50,000 more). In a little over fifty years Wesley had preached over 40,000 times, festooning familiar outlines with an easy extempore flow of stories, illustrations, and applications adapted to each congregation, averaging two sermons most days. "I know," he wrote, "were I myself to preach one whole year in one place, I should preach both myself and most of my congregation to sleep."[8]

That was the challenge facing homebody Edwards, who for twenty-four years was sole pastor of a town of some 1,200 adults and then for six years shepherded a village settlement of perhaps 100 Anglo-Saxons and 200 native Indians, and who always aimed to spend thirteen hours each weekday in his study. The 1,200 manuscript sermons that survive (one for most Sundays of his ministry) show him tackling most seriously the task of keeping everyone, including himself, spiritually awake.[9] In Edwards's sermons riveting expository skill combines with a wide thematic range, a wealth of evangelical thought, a pervasive awareness of eternal issues, and a compelling logical flow to make them arresting, searching, devastating, and Christ-centeredly doxological to the last degree. His preaching style, though quiet, was commanding and by all accounts was almost hypnotic in its power to fix his hearers' minds on divine things. Charles Simeon was later to say that his own sermons were planned to humble the sinner, to exalt the Savior, and to promote holiness; Edwards could have used exactly those words about his.

Two more contrasts before our profile ends. Both Edwards and Wesley were accused of being proud and stubborn. With Wesley the activist, it was because of his habit of always assuming leadership, intellectual and organizational, and never recognizing superiors or peers in any circumstance whatever. (Was this Paul-like care for the churches? Or Diotrephes-like love of preeminence? Faithful stewardship of the gospel or natural hubristic arrogance? Or a blend of both? All these views are taken, and the jury is still out.) With Edwards the analyst, however, there is no room for doubt: What gave offense was his unflinching loyalty to

---

[8] John Telford, ed., *Letters of John Wesley* (London: Epworth, 1931), 3:195; cited from Murray, *Wesley and Men Who Followed*, 85.

[9] This had a literal aspect. In a sermon weightily titled "When the Spirit of God Has Been Remarkably Poured out on a People, a Thorough Reformation of Those Things That Before Were Amiss Amongst Them Ought to Be the Effect of It," Edwards speaks against sleeping in church and urges that "persons would avoid laying down their bodies in their seats in the midst of public worship." *The Blessing of God: Previously Unpublished Sermons of Jonathan Edwards*, ed. Michael D. McMullen (Nashville: Broadman & Holman, 2003), 270.

what he took to be biblical truth, as his open-eyed courting of dismissal from Northampton by pressing the principle that the Lord's Supper is for believers only clearly showed.[10]

Then, too, both men had wives: But whereas Jonathan's thirty-one-year "uncommon union" with Sarah was a love match and a true partnership throughout,[11] John Wesley's thirty-year bond with Molly was a disaster from start to finish—a marriage of convenience that quickly became the precise opposite, a woeful tale of hurt, hostility, and separation. "I married because I needed a home in order to recover my health," Wesley wrote grimly at one stage, "and I did recover it. But I did not seek happiness thereby, and I did not find it."[12] Oh dear. Let us tiptoe on.

Four major things should be remembered as we round off our set of contrasts. First, whatever their frailties and conceptual differences, both of these men preached substantially the same gospel of ruin through sin, redemption through Christ, and regeneration through the Holy Spirit, laying special stress on the reality of ruined human nature because they both believed that only out of self-despair would anyone ever turn wholeheartedly to God (which is why each of them took time out to rebut John Taylor's denial of original sin, both of their books appearing in 1757).[13] Second, they explicitly embraced holiness both as their personal goal and as their ministry target, and both came to see and set forth holiness with increasing clarity as consisting essentially of love to God and man. Wesley's commitment here went back to his reading of Thomas à Kempis, Jeremy Taylor, and William Law in 1725, thus antedating Aldersgate Street by thirteen years, and later he often declared that God had raised up Methodism precisely "to spread scriptural holiness throughout the land." Edwards wrote of himself as having from early on

---

[10] For the details of which, see the chapter by Mark Dever in this volume.

[11] On his deathbed in Princeton, Edwards said to Lucy, his youngest daughter: "Give my kindest love to my dear wife, and tell her that the uncommon union, which has so long subsisted between us, has been of such a nature, as I trust is spiritual, and therefore will continue for ever." Murray, *Jonathan Edwards*, 441. See Elisabeth D. Dodds, *Marriage to a Difficult Man: The "Uncommon Union" of Jonathan and Sarah Edwards* (Philadelphia: Westminster Press, 1971; repr.: Laurel, Miss.: Audobon Press, 2003).

[12] Murray, *Wesley and Men Who Followed*, 45.

[13] Full titles: John Taylor, *The Scripture-Doctrine of Original Sin Proposed to Free and Candid Examination*, 1738. John Wesley, *The Doctrine of Original Sin, According to Scripture, Reason, and Experience*, in *The Works of John Wesley* (3rd ed., 1872, repr. Grand Rapids, Mich.: Baker, 1986), 9:191-464. Jonathan Edwards, "The Great Christian Doctrine of Original Sin Defended," in *The Works of Jonathan Edwards*, ed. Edward Hickman, 2 vols. (1834; reprint, Edinburgh: Banner of Truth, 1974), 1:143-233.

in his adult Christian life pursued "an increase of grace and holiness, and a holy life, with much more earnestness than ever I sought grace before I had it,"[14] and the seventy Resolutions that he drew up for himself as early as 1722-23 would seem abundantly to bear this out.[15]

Third, in their pastoral ministries both saw the value of "societies" (that is, small-group fellowships, as we would call them) for fanning the flames of spiritual life, though Wesley's developed infrastructure of "bands" and "classes" and the "select society" within each Methodist community, a setup learned largely from the Moravians, went far beyond the prayer groups and instructional get-togethers that Edwards put in place in Northampton. Fourth—and this is reflected in all that we have looked at so far, even Wesley's unhappy marriage, which came to grief through his unwillingness to reduce his ministry just because he had a wife—they were both spiritually alive in Christ in a quite breathtaking way; they were both wonderfully single-minded, and magnificently firm and courageous in the face of criticism and opposition; and overall, according to their own lights, they both were utterly selfless in the service of their God and Savior, just as they were both truly wise in dealing with the upheavals of revival.

Our portrait of Edwards is now sufficiently drawn; so we move Wesley out of the picture and go forward ourselves to look next at the makeup of Edwards's theology.

The Mind of Jonathan Edwards

Let us begin at the beginning, with an *orientation* to Edwards's overall outlook.

Edwards has been described as God-*centered*, God-*focused*, God-*intoxicated*, and God-*entranced*, and so indeed he was. There is no overstatement here. Every day, from morning till night, he sought to live in conscious communion with God, whether walking, riding, studying on his own, or relaxing in the bosom of his large and, it seems, happy and often extended family. He was not a mystic in the sense of seeking God-drenched states of soul that leave rationality behind; on the contrary, it was precisely through deep and clear thoughts that God warmed and

---

[14] Murray, *Jonathan Edwards*, 51. "He had pursued holiness, he subsequently reflected: 'with far greater diligence and earnestness than ever I pursued anything in my life'" (101).

[15] The Resolutions are set out in *Works*, ed. Hickman, 1:xx-xxii.

thrilled his heart. Rationally biblical and biblically rational understanding of everything was his constant quest, and John Gerstner was right to title his three-volume exposition *The Rational Biblical Theology of Jonathan Edwards*.[16] Edwards's basic wavelength—theological, moral, devotional, and doxological—was Puritan, as has been said, and the theology of the mid- and late seventeenth century was his anchorage. "As to my subscribing to the substance of the Westminster Confession," he wrote in 1750, when the possibility of his moving to minister in Scotland was mooted, "there would be no difficulty."[17] Convictionally and confessionally, he was a tenacious adherent of the Puritan theology that had shaped New England, and coming at a time when the fires of that heritage were burning low, he gave it a new lease of intellectual and communal life.

A man is known both by his own friends and his own books, and also by the books he recommends to others. "Take Mastricht [Peter Van Mastricht, *Theologia Theoretico-Practica*, 1699] for divinity in general, doctrine, practice, and controversy," Edwards wrote to young Joseph Bellamy in 1747, ". . . much better than Turretin [Francis Turretin, *Institutio Theologiae Elencticae*, 1688][18] or any other book in the world, except the Bible, in my opinion."[19] Van Mastricht was Voetius's successor in the theology chair at Utrecht University. Voetius, a pillar of Holland's Second Reformation, had pioneered a solid blend of developed Calvinism with English Puritan wisdom on the Christian life, and Van Mastricht maintained this, laying out his treatment of each topic in four sections: explanatory (i.e., exegetical), doctrinal (i.e., systematic), argumentative (i.e., controversial), and practical (i.e., applicatory). His work is thus a user-friendly textbook of Reformed-Puritan-Pietist stripe for anyone who can read Latin and wants to know the full range and strength of the Puritan brand of Christianity.

---

[16] John Gerstner, *The Rational Biblical Theology of Jonathan Edwards*, 3 vols. (Powhatan, Va.: Berean/Orlando, Fla.: Ligonier, 1991-93).

[17] Murray, *Jonathan Edwards*, 346.

[18] Turretin's work is now available in English: trans. George M. Giger, ed. James T. Dennison, 3 vols., Phillipsburg, N.J.: Presbyterian & Reformed, 1992-97.

[19] Murray, *Jonathan Edwards*, 282. One section of Van Mastricht's work is available in English: *A Treatise on Regeneration*, ed. Brandon Withrow (Morgan, Penn.: Soli Deo Gloria, 2002). "We need to recognize, as Van Mastricht recognized, that the theological task is not complete unless we have distinguished four basic elements in Christian theology: exegesis, positive doctrine, historical analysis and defense, and practice" (Richard Muller, "Giving Direction to Theology: The Scholastic Dimension," *Journal of the Evangelical Theological Society* 28 [1985]: 191). Van Mastricht divides up his treatment of each topic accordingly; his four divisions are rendered in Withrow's volume Explanatory, Doctrinal, Argumentative, and Practical.

From our overall orientation to Edwards's theological system we now advance to a specific *description* of it. It is a fully integrated whole that we can sketch out as follows.

Shaping everything is the view of the Triune God's plan of grace that the Westminster Standards set forth: a plan that turns upon two hinges—namely, the covenant of redemption that expresses God's appointment of his Son to save sinners, and the covenant of grace that expresses the divine commitment to all whom the Father saves through the mediation of the Son and the life-giving gift of the Holy Spirit. Within this frame are set the Son's course of past humiliation, present exaltation, and future vindication; the individual salvation of each elect and regenerate person; and the ongoing life and service of the church.

Sin-blinded humans are unacquainted with, and unclear and uncertain about, the abiding realities of which the Bible testifies and to which its inspired words point. But the "divine and supernatural light" of illumination by the Holy Spirit brings a knowledge of these things that is as immediate, sure, and indubitable as is the seeing of physical objects with our bodily eyes. From this illumination comes belief of biblical truth, and out of that grows the Christian life—the life, that is, of assured trust in Christ as one's all-sufficient Savior, of increasing insight into the actual guilt and inward corruption from which Christ brings deliverance, of disciplined labor for holiness and virtue, and of sustained joy in knowing, worshiping, and appreciating God. Without this illumination, all forms of religious observance are hollow and empty, whether one realizes this or not. To see unilluminated formalism become real religion must therefore be a pastor's constant goal.

God shows himself by word and deed in the processes and events of human history, which is thus in the most literal sense "his story." The Bible's interpretation of the histories, communal and personal, that it records is the model for interpreting our own history, from the same redemption-centered point of view, in terms of which alone will the history of any Christian person ever make real sense. As George Marsden states Edwards's position:

> History, according to Edwards, was in essence the communication of God's redemptive love in Christ. The history of redemption was the very purpose of creation. Nothing in human history had significance on its own. . . . Christ's saving love was the center of all history and

defined its meaning. Human events took on significance only as they related to God's redemptive action in bringing increasing numbers of human beings into the light of that love or as they illustrated human blindness in joining Satan's warfare against all that was good.[20]

Following up this modern-sounding insight, Edwards hoped one day (so he told the Princeton trustees shortly before his death) to write "a body of divinity [i.e., a systematic theology] in an entire new method, being thrown into the form of an history."[21] It would not, one supposes, abandon the decretal foundation on which Reformed systematic theology had regularly been set since Theodore Beza and William Perkins, but would trace out from Scripture the progressive fulfillment of God's decretal plan. Edwards did not live to fulfill his hope, but the posthumous publication of his 1739 sermons titled *A History of the Work of Redemption* gives us some faint idea of what the proposed work would have been like,[22] and his evident grasp of the appropriate architectonic and hermeneutical implications of the fact that history is the Bible's backbone, God's self-revelation being essentially historical in form and substance, put him at this point ahead of all his contemporaries. Had he lived as long as Wesley did and written his proposed treatise, showing the significance of history within a Bible-believing frame long before liberal scholars started using history to support their own skepticism, the course of Protestant theology during the past two centuries might have been very different. But we cannot pursue that thought here.

Edwards saw clearly that Scripture reveals God to be a society with a unity—a triune society, eternally bonded in mutual love—and he ventured to think of our salvation as, so to speak, a welcome into the transcendent family circle. God's plan, he once wrote, is that "[Christ] and his Father and they [Christians] should be as it were one family; that his people should be in a sort admitted into the society of the three persons in the Godhead."[23] Within this conception Edwards's probing mind offers a variety of ideas about the sense and way in which the Son is the

---

[20] George M. Marsden, *Jonathan Edwards: A Life* (New Haven, Conn.: Yale University Press, 2003), 488-489.

[21] Ibid., 482.

[22] Ibid., 483-486.

[23] "Miscellanies" no. 571, in *Works of Jonathan Edwards,* vol. 18, *The "Miscellanies," 501-832,* ed. Ava Chamberlain (New Haven, Conn.: Yale University Press, 2000), 110.

image of the Father and the Spirit is the divine love personalized. Whether in these he went beyond Scripture is moot, but he certainly did not intend to do that. At the end of the day, so he writes, "I am far from pretending to explaining [sic] the Trinity so as to render it no longer a mystery [i.e., a divine fact beyond our understanding]. I think it to be the highest and deepest of all mysteries still, notwithstanding anything I have said or conceived about it. I don't intend to explain the Trinity."[24] As John Owen made so clear in his battles with Socinianism,[25] confessional Trinitarianism is and must be presupposed in all articulations of Reformed covenant theology or else that theology collapses. Edwards knew this, and his grasp of the reality and centrality of the mystery of the transcendent eternal Trinity was firm.

Finally, just as Edwards presented all that has been stated thus far as clearly taught in specific Scriptures, so he brought it all to bear on the never-ending task of interpreting the Bible as a whole and every part of it, and fixing the standpoint and perspective of our receiving what God has to say to us in and through it. In other words, he worked in terms of the hermeneutical principle that all Reformed exegetes since Calvin had followed—namely, the analogy of faith or of Scripture (both phrases were used). This is the principle of the internal consistency of biblical teaching, as being first to last the product of a single divine mind. So he unfolded the Bible within its own theological frame, duly detecting and displaying its biggest and most pervasive themes—the sovereignty of God in creation, providence, and grace; the love of God to sinners, supremely expressed in the mediatorial ministry of the Lord Jesus Christ; and the power of God renewing hearts, generating faith and repentance, and transforming believers' character and conduct.

And in doing this he constantly led his hearers to the pervasive biblical injunctions to look back and around and ahead, discerning as clearly as possible what God has done, is doing, and will do, praising and adoring, trusting and obeying, and hoping and enduring accordingly. As beyond a certain distance a view of scenery may get lost in mist,

---

[24] Jonathan Edwards, "An Essay on the Trinity," in *Treatise on Grace and Other Posthumously Published Writings*, ed. Paul Helm (Cambridge, UK: James Clarke/Greenwood, S.C.: Attic Press, 1971), 121-122.

[25] See John Owen, *Vindiciae Evangelicae, Works XII*, ed. W. Goold (London: Banner of Truth, 1966) and his running battle with Socinian exegetes in his *Exposition of the Epistle to the Hebrews* (7 vols., Edinburgh: Banner of Truth, 1991). See also Carl R. Trueman, *The Claims of Truth: The Trinitarian Theology of John Owen* (Carlisle, UK: Paternoster, 1998).

so beyond a certain point our sight of God's works and our knowledge of his purposes, seen as it were through biblical field glasses that bring them up with maximum clarity, will nonetheless dissolve into mystery: The God who has told us so much about himself is still not a God about whom we do, or can, ever know everything. So here is a limit, a line to approach and walk but not to overstep. Edwards walks this line with classic skill.

Such, then, is the framework of Edwards's theology. It had to be laid out first in order to put us in a position to understand what he says about the two linked themes of our title—the glory of God and the reviving of religion. Now, however, we can move straight to them, and shall do so.

THE GLORY OF GOD

Edwards inherited a dispute among the learned: Was God's goal in creation his own glory, as Reformed theology maintained, or man's happiness, as Arminians and Deists thought? In his *Dissertation on the End for Which God Created the World*, posthumously published, Edwards resolved this question with startling brilliance. As his son, Jonathan Edwards, Jr., put it:

> It was said that, as God is a benevolent being . . . he could not but form creatures for the purpose of making them happy. Many passages of Scripture were quoted in support of this opinion. On the other hand, numerous and very explicit declarations of Scripture were produced to prove that God made all things for his own glory. Mr. Edwards was the first, who clearly showed, that both these were the ultimate end of the creation . . . and that they are really one and the same thing.[26]

Edwards clinched his case on this by surveying the biblical use of the word "glory" (Hebrew, *kabod*; Greek, LXX and NT, *doxa*). Having stated correctly that etymologically *kabod* implies "weight, greatness, abundance" and in use often conveys the thought of "God in fullness," Edwards traces the term thus:

> Sometimes it is used to signify what is *internal*, *inherent*, or in the possession of a person [i.e., glory that *belongs* to someone]: and sometimes for *emanation*, *exhibition*, or *communication* of this internal glory [i.e.,

---

[26] Sereno E. Dwight, "Memoirs," in *Works*, ed. Hickman, 1:cxcii.

glory that *appears* to someone]: and sometimes for the *knowledge*, or *sense* of these [communications], in those to whom the exhibition or communication is made [i.e., glory that is *seen*, or *discerned*, by someone]; or an *expression* of this knowledge, sense, or effect [i.e., glory that is *given* to someone, by praise and thanks in joy and love].[27]

And the conclusion he offers—on the basis of both biblical texts that speak of glory and of glorifying in these four distinct though connected ways and also analytical argument surrounding this exegesis—is that God's internal and intrinsic glory consists of his knowledge (omniscience with wisdom) plus his holiness (spontaneous virtuous love, linked with hatred of sin) plus his joy (supreme endless happiness); and that his glory (wise, holy, happy love) flows out from him, like water from a fountain, in loving spontaneity (grace), first in creation and then in redemption, both of which are so set forth to us so as to prompt praise; and that in our responsive, Spirit-led glorifying of God, God glorifies and satisfies himself, achieving that which was his purpose from the start.

The chief end of man, as the famous first answer of the Westminster Shorter Catechism memorably puts it, is to glorify God and enjoy him forever. God so made us that in praising, thanking, loving, and serving him, we find our own supreme happiness and enjoyment of God in a way that otherwise we would not and could not do. We reach our highest enjoyment of God in and by glorifying him, and we glorify him supremely in and by enjoying him. In fact, we enjoy him most when we glorify him most, and vice versa. And God's single-yet-complex end, now in redemption as it was in creation, is his own happiness and joy in and through ours. His great goal here and now is to glorify himself through glorifying, and being glorified by, rational human beings who out of their fallenness come to saving faith in Jesus Christ. Thus the *emanation* (outflow) of divine glory in the form of creative and redemptive action results in a *remanation* (returning flow) of glory to God in the form of celebratory devotion. And so God's goal for himself (Father, Son, and Spirit, the "they" who are "he" within the Triune unity), the goal that includes his goal for all Christian humankind, is achieved by means of a singly unitary process, which itself is ongoing and unending.

The unimaginable endlessness of this reciprocal sequencing that is

---

[27] Jonathan Edwards, "The End for Which God Created the World," in *Works*, ed. Hickman, 1:116.

in truth the end for which God created the world can only be indicated formulaically and analogically (to use a couple of non-Edwardsean terms). This is done for us in a normative way in Revelation 21, and C. S. Lewis most tellingly did it at the close of his final Narnia story, *The Last Battle*, where the children have been brought through a rail crash into the real Narnia that is to be their home forever. The key sentences are these:

> Then Aslan [the Christ-like lion] turned to them and said:
> "You do not yet look so happy as I mean you to be . . . all of you are (as you used to call it in the Shadowlands) dead. The term is over; the holidays have begun. The dream is ended: this is the morning."
> . . . We can most truly say that they all lived happily ever after. But for them it was only the beginning of the real story. All their life in this world and all their adventures in Narnia had only been the cover and the title page: now at last they were beginning Chapter One of the Great Story which no one on earth has read: which goes on for ever: in which every chapter is better than the one before.[28]

This picks up exactly, in mythical-parabolic terms, the point that Edwards, in his more prosaic way, was concerned to make. Amy Plantinga Pauw capsules it as follows:

> Because "heaven is a progressive state," the heavenly joy of the saints, and even of the triune God, will forever continue to increase. . . . Saints can look forward to an unending expansion of their knowledge and love of God, as their capacities are stretched by what they receive . . . there is no intrinsic limit to their joy in heaven. . . . As the saints continue to increase in knowledge and love of God, God receives more and more glory. This heavenly reciprocity will never cease, because the glory God deserves is infinite, and the capacity of the saints to perceive God's glory and praise him for it is ever increasing.[29]

Here, finally, is how Edwards himself, in his rather more severe and abstract manner, sums the matter up. ("The creature" in what follows is the believer.)

---

[28] C. S. Lewis, *The Last Battle* (Harmondsworth, UK: Penguin, 1964), 165.
[29] Amy Plantinga Pauw, *"The Supreme Harmony of All": The Trinitarian Theology of Jonathan Edwards* (Grand Rapids, Mich.: Eerdmans, 2002), 180-181.

And though the emanation of God's fulness, intended in the creation, is to the creature as its *object*; and though the creature is the *subject* of the fulness communicated, which is the creature's good; yet it does not necessarily follow that, even in doing so, God did not make *himself* his end. It comes to the same thing. God's respect to the creature's good, and his respect to himself, is not a divided respect; but both are united in one, as the happiness of the creature aimed at is happiness in union with himself. . . . The more happiness the greater union. . . . And as the happiness will be increasing to eternity, the union will become more and more strict [i.e., closely bound] and perfect; nearer and more like to that between God the Father and the Son; who are so united, that their interest is perfectly one. . . .

Let the most perfect union with God be represented by something at an infinite height above us; and the eternally increasing union of the saints with God, by something that is ascending constantly towards that infinite height . . . and that is to continue thus to move to all eternity.[30]

The two-way street of this unceasing process, says Edwards, embodies and expresses the true end for which God created the world: namely, the endless advancement of his glory, in union with us, through the endless advancement of ours, in union with him. Those who have in any measure tasted the refreshment and joy of heart that flow from faith in, friendship with, and worship of the holy Three (or shall I say the holy One, or One-in-Three) will latch on to Edwards's thinking here as a complete answer to any who fancy that the Christian heaven would be static and dull, and will themselves look forward to the awaiting glory with ever-growing eagerness.

THE REVIVING OF RELIGION

What Edwards has analyzed out concerning the glory of God and of the godly is no more, just as it is no less, than a dotting of the i's and a crossing of the t's in what earlier Puritan and Reformed teachers had already said. It is, however, an important ingredient in our present line of thought because of the clarity with which it focuses Edwards's God-centered concept of religion. Living as we do in a human-centered culture shaped by the Enlightenment, and surrounded as we are by

---

[30] Edwards, "The End for Which God Created the World," 120.

human-centered forms of religion in as well as outside the churches, following Edwards at this point calls us to an effort of rethinking, reimagining, re-centering our attention, reeducating our desires, and refocusing our affections that is almost beyond our strength. Evangelical and liberal theology are, to be sure, always and necessarily at logger-heads, because cognitive revelation, on which evangelicalism builds, and cognitive relativism, which is basic to liberalism, are totally antithetical.

But for two centuries now evangelical and liberal pietists have been joining hands to give personal religion, previously defined as knowledge and service of God, a subjective twist that effectively redefines it as the experience of reaching after, and trying to maintain, some knowledge and service of God amid the ups and downs and strains and pains of daily life. The reference-point has moved; the study of religion—professedly Christian religion, that is—has become a study of human feelings, attitudes, and struggles rather than of God's gifts and calling and works and ways with humans, which was Edwards's agenda. Edwards has, indeed, an unquenchable interest in Christian and pseudo-Christian religious experience, which he describes and dissects with great clinical skill; but his interest is theocentric rather than anthropocentric, intellectual rather than sentimental, theological rather than anthropo-logical, and doxological rather than psychological. Set his *Treatise on the Religious Affections* alongside William James's justly famous Gifford lectures, *The Varieties of Religious Experience*, and you see at once that a watershed has been passed. Evangelical theologian and spiritual diag-nostician Edwards asks, what is of God in all this; pragmatist philoso-pher and amateur psychologist James simply asks what happens. And today's pietistic evangelicals and liberals both tend only to ask what is inside us that makes us feel as we do at this moment, and what has God for us here and now to make us feel better. What a downhill slide there has been!

What Edwards, standing in the Reformational mainstream, meant by religion is very clear. It is the life of regeneration, repentance, and assured faith and hope in Christ, based on knowing oneself to be a jus-tified and adopted child of God whom the Triune Lord has loved from eternity, whom the Son has redeemed by dying on the cross, and whom the Holy Spirit, the divine change agent, now indwells. It is the life of loving both the written Word of the Lord and the living Lord of the Word. It is a life of rigorous self-watch and self-discipline, for the deforming, distracting, desensitizing, demonic power of sin in one's spiritual system must be detected and resisted. It is a life of reckoning with our temperamental limitations, whatever mixture of sanguine, choleric, melancholic, and phlegmatic we find we are, and seeking to transcend those shortcomings. It is a life of prayer—praise and petition; complaint and confession; meditation and celebration. And with that it is a quest for full Christlikeness of character and action, inasmuch as Christ "exhibited to the world such an illustrious pattern of humility, divine love, discreet zeal, self-denial, obedience, patience, resignation, fortitude, meekness, forgiveness, compassion, benevolence, and universal holiness, as neither men nor angels ever saw before."[31] Finally, religion honors God by goodwill and integrity in all relationships and by enterprise in seizing such opportunities for "good works" of benevolence and help as present themselves.

What then is the reviving of religion? Again the idea is very clear. It is God pouring out his Spirit, and thereby ratcheting up the power and speed of the Spirit's work in human hearts to further the many facets of supernatural spiritual life that have just been referred to. When Edwards uses the word "revival," it is as a synonym for "reviving," and usually he adds "of religion" to make his meaning explicit. For him, the reviving of religion is rooted in the intensified realization of divine realities through God's work of making the sense of his own reality, and of the realities of sin and salvation, so vivid as to be overwhelming and inescapable. This creates in the heart a correspondingly intense urgency to get, and stay, right with God, and an equally intense joy of assurance and exaltation in worship when one's acceptance with God is out of doubt. That joy grows into the larger enjoyment of God in his beauty and goodness that was spoken of earlier and that operates as the driving force of God-glorifying life. Whatever else occurs springs from this source.

Under the impact of such joyful excitement, persons with inner scars and weaknesses due to previous bad experiences, bad relationships, and bad habits may fall into exaggerated emotionalism, hysterical eccentricities, and what was called "enthusiasm" (we would call it fanaticism)—namely, belief in direct divine revelations to oneself. But these phenomena are no sure signs of God at work, and when God is at work

---

[31] Jonathan Edwards, "The Life and Diary of the Rev. David Brainerd," *Works*, ed. Hickman, 2:313.

there is still nothing spiritually significant about them, though pride may prompt the persons concerned to think otherwise. What Edwards, in the title of a 1741 publication, called *The Distinguishing Marks of a Work of the Spirit of God*[32] are (1) honor to Christ, (2) opposition to sin, (3) submission to Scripture, (4) awakening to truth, (5) love to God and man. These are the true, and only true, fruits and tokens of revival.

Edwards was in the thick of the reviving work of God, first in Northampton in 1734 and then in New England's Great Awakening, 1740-42, and his revival writings have classic status.[33] Should we, then, call him a revivalist—as even B. B. Warfield did, introducing him in 1912 as "saint and metaphysician, revivalist and theologian,"[34] and so making it look as if revival involvement was the most important part of his public life? Surely the label is inappropriate. Since Charles Finney in the 1830s, *revivalist* has been used to mean a specialist in what Finney called "protracted meetings" (modern equivalents are "revivals," "crusades," and "renewal missions")—that is, special series of preachments designed to invigorate Christians and convert unbelievers.[35] But that is not what Edwards was at all. He was a preaching pastor, the long-term servant of a regular congregation, and as such he was a meticulous textual expositor who in a broad sense was preaching the gospel in what he hoped was an awakening way all the time, as indeed his surviving sermons clearly reveal. Such special sermons as he produced during and after the revivals were, so far as we know, diagnostic and didactic rather than evangelistic.[36] "Sinners in the Hands of an Angry God," which so drastically impacted the church at Enfield and has so fixed the image of Edwards in North American culture, was for him a fairly standard treatment of hell-torment, a recurring theme in his own pulpit; it was in fact a sermon he had already preached at Northampton without anyone apparently turn-

---

[32] An enlarged version of Edwards's commencement address to a turbulent Yale community in 1741: *Works,* ed. Hickman, 2:257-277. See Marsden, *Jonathan Edwards,* 233-238.

[33] These writings are: *A Narrative of Surprising Conversions,* 1735; *Distinguishing Marks of a Work of the Spirit of God,* 1741; *Thoughts Concerning the Present Revival of Religion in New England,* 1742; *A Treatise Concerning Religious Affections,* 1746; *The Life of David Brainerd,* 1749.

[34] Warfield, *Studies in Theology,* in *Works,* 9:515: opening sentence of article, "Edwards and New England Theology," in *Encyclopaedia of Religion and Ethics,* ed. James Hastings (New York: Charles Scribner's Sons, 1912), p. 221.

[35] See on this Iain H. Murray, *Revival and Revivalism: The Making and Marring of American Evangelicalism, 1750-1858* (Edinburgh: Banner of Truth, 1994).

[36] *Charity and Its Fruits* was a sermon series in 1738; *A History of the Work of Redemption* was a sermon series in 1739; *Religious Affections* was a sermon series in 1742-43. *Distinguishing Marks of a Work of the Spirit of God* (see notes 32, 33 above) also belongs here.

ing a hair. So when scholars, even great men like Warfield, call Edwards a revivalist, I wince and wish they had not done it.

The Great Awakening was controversial in its own day, and the reviving of religion is still something of a disputed question among evangelicals.[37] To clear the ground for our further advance, it will be helpful at this point to offer Edwardsean comment on some current opinions.

CURRENT OPINIONS ON REVIVAL

"There is no doctrine of revival in the Bible." If the meaning here is that no Bible writer discusses the reviving of religion in the formal, intentional way in which Paul treats justification in his letter to the Romans and John projects the divine saviorhood of Jesus Christ in his Gospel and epistles, we may agree without argument. But the Edwardsean comment is that doctrine, the explanatory declaration of God's doings and man's duty, is to be drawn from the biblical history of God's words and acts set together, and that there are in the Bible many words from God, especially in the prophets, and many recorded prayers from the godly setting forth the need and hope of spiritual reviving, alongside many narratives of religion actually revived, and out of these materials a doctrine of God's way of reviving his work in this world may properly be distilled. (Edwards, a postmillennialist, expected successive waves of revival eventually to convert the world.)

"Revival is concerned with saving souls." If the meaning is that many are converted when revivings of religion occur, again we may agree. It happened so among respectable colonists in Northampton, and throughout New England during the Great Awakening, and among native Indians at Crossweeksung and the Forks of Delaware under the ministry of David Brainerd, whose life and papers Edwards published as a paragon example of personal godliness and missionary fruitfulness.[38] But the Edwardsean comment must be that since religion is centrally concerned with holiness and the glorifying and enjoying of God as a way of life, the reviving of religion must center here too, and the conversions that command so much Christian attention at revival times must be seen as the entry into what really matters to God rather than as

---

[37] See Iain H. Murray, *Pentecost Today?* (Edinburgh: Banner of Truth, 1998); J. I. Packer, *Collected Shorter Writings*, vol. 2, *Serving the People of God* (Carlisle, UK: Paternoster, 1998), 57-155.

[38] Jonathan Edwards, "The Life and Diary of the Rev. David Brainerd," in *Works*, ed. Hickman, 2:313-458. See Marsden, *Jonathan Edwards*, 329-334; Murray, *Jonathan Edwards*, 300-309.

the heart of the divine concern. Certainly, true conversion, the correlate of divine illumination of the mind and regeneration of the heart, is a great thing. Edwards rates it greater than the creation of the world and even than the resurrection of Jesus, since in new birth the rule of sin in the heart has to be overcome; but to limit one's concern in revival to conversions alone would actually be a Spirit-quenching mistake.

"Revival is the action of God, but we can and must pray it down." If this simply means that Christians should pray for the reviving of religion because the Bible tells them to and revival is something that in any case they long for, there would be no problem here. Edwards himself argues all of that in the mini-treatise he wrote to commend some Scottish ministers' proposal of an international concert of prayer each Saturday evening, each Sunday morning, and the first Tuesday each quarter for seven years, interceding for the conversion of the world. Its title page ran *An Humble Attempt to Promote Explicit Agreement and Visible Unity of God's People Through the World, in Extraordinary Prayer, for the Revival of Religion, and the Advent of Christ's Kingdom on Earth, Pursuant to Scripture Promises and Prophecies Concerning the Last Time.*[39] To get the Christian world (that is, for Edwards, the Protestant communities everywhere) praying for revival was for Edwards hugely important, as the grandiose terms of his title seem to indicate. Nor is there a problem if the thought is simply that very earnest prayer is appropriate when very great blessing is being sought, for, as Edwards knew, that indeed is so. But the Edwardsean comment must be that we cannot directly induce a reviving visitation from God by the quantity or quality of our praying, and it would be arrogant presumption for us to think we could. God always answers faithful prayers in a positive way, but not always precisely when, where, and how we were hoping. God reserves the right to give better answers in better ways than we have thought to ask for. But the one in charge is always he, never we, and Edwards strikes this note at the end of his *Humble Attempt* by reminding his readers of the biblical link between

> Praying and Not Fainting. . . . It is very apparent from the word of God, that he is wont often to try the faith and patience of his people, when crying to him for some great and important mercy, by withholding the

---

[39] Jonathan Edwards, "Humble Attempt," *Works*, ed. Hickman, 2:278-312.

mercy sought, for a season; and not only so, but at first to cause an increase of dark appearances. And yet he, without fail, at last succeeds those who continue instant in prayer, with all perseverance, and "will not let him go except he blesses. . . ."[40]

This, Edwards urges, is a truth of which the saints must never lose sight.

"Revival is the answer to all the church's problems." To some of them, such as the problem of spiritual apathy and deadness and bickering in the congregation, yes; but a reviving visitation from God brings its own problems, problems of spiritual life overflowing in disorder and counterfeited in fanaticism, and problems of alienation, opposition, and division between those who welcome the visitation and those who do not. No one knew this better than Edwards, whose revival writings are from one standpoint a series of attempts to deal with this unhappy state of affairs.

ELEMENTS IN REVIVAL

What exactly happens in a reviving visitation from God, gradual or sudden, brief or prolonged, large- or small-scale, as the case may be? From Scripture, and particularly from the Acts of the Apostles, which is a narrative from the archetypal revival era, we can put together a general answer to that question, all the specifics of which can be illustrated, one way or another, from Edwards's revival writings. To be sure, no two episodes of revival are identical, if only because the various individuals and communities to which, and the various cultural backgrounds against which, the reviving of religion takes place have their own unique features, and in every narrative of revival these should be noted. But the same generic pattern appears everywhere. Revival is God touching minds and hearts in an arresting, devastating, exalting way, to draw them to himself through working from the inside out rather than from the outside in. It is God accelerating, intensifying, and extending the work of grace that goes on in every Christian's life, but is sometimes overshadowed and somewhat smothered by the impact of other forces. It is the near presence of God giving new power to the gospel of sin and grace. It is the Holy Spirit sensitizing souls to divine realities and so generating deep-level responses to God in the form of faith and repentance,

---

[40] Ibid., 312.

praise and prayer, love and joy, works of benevolence and service and initiatives of outreach and sharing. The pattern can be analyzed as follows:

1. *God comes down.* There is no clearer way to characterize the sharpened sense of God's close presence in his transcendent power, holiness, and grace than this phrase from Isaiah 64:1. God is felt to be inescapable as he searches our hearts, measures our lives, makes us know what he thinks of us, moves us to call on him for help, shows us his mercy, and fills us with joy because of it. Preoccupation with God and religion, both for sorrow and for joy, continues as long as the visitation lasts.

2. *God's Word pierces.* Late in the seventeenth century, John Howe bewailed from the pulpit the fact that Puritan preachers were no longer able to "get within" their hearers as they had been able to do a generation earlier.[41] Puritanism had once abounded in preachers whose gift was to "rip up" consciences, as the Puritans regularly put it, but that was no longer so. What that meant was not that veteran Puritans like Howe no longer knew how to make the searching applications that had once marked their movement, but that the Commonwealth period and the decades leading up to it had been an era of revival, which the post-Restoration period was not. In revival times, Bible teaching about God and sin, death and eternal life, spiritual lostness and divine salvation is always felt to come with the authority of God. When Paul reminded the Thessalonians that they had accepted his gospel "not as the word of men but as what it really is, the word of God, which is at work in you believers" (1 Thess. 2:13), and when he asked them to pray that in his ongoing ministry "the word of the Lord may speed ahead and be honored, as happened among you" (2 Thess. 3:1), this is what he was referring to. ("Run and be glorified" is the literal rendering of the Greek verbs used here, and "be glorified" conveys the thought of being venerated as coming from God and displaying his glory in its declaration of what he has done.) Under revival conditions the ministry of the Word of God—

---

[41] "It is plain . . . that there is a great retraction of the Spirit of God even from us [ministers]. We know not . . . how to get within you: our words die in our mouths . . . We speak not as persons . . . that expect to make you serious, heavenly, mindful of God, and to walk more like Christians. The methods of alluring and convincing souls, even that some of us have known, are lost from among us in a great part . . . when such an effusion of the Spirit shall be as is here [in the text, Ezek. 39:29] signified, they shall know how to speak to better purpose, with more compassion and sense [i.e., feeling], with more seriousness, with more compassion and allurement, than we now find we can." John Howe, preaching in 1678; cited from Iain H. Murray, *The Puritan Hope* (London: Banner of Truth, 1971), 245.

rather, the divine Word ministered, whether through preaching, reading, gossip, or however—strikes the conscience with piercing and convincing authority.

3. *Man's sin is seen.* The divinely inspired Old Testament prophets set forth the sins of God's people with all the lurid ugliness that their oriental imaginations could command, but people were unmoved; as we say today, they simply did not see it. When, however, the Spirit was poured out at Pentecost and Peter spoke to the crowd of their sin in crucifying the now risen and enthroned Christ, they were "cut to the heart" (the Greek verb is ordinarily used of sawing) and asked aloud what they should do to get rid of their guilt (Acts 2:37). At times of revival, deep conviction of personal sin, particularly of the dishonor that unlove and unbelief do to Christ, fastens upon heart and conscience as the Spirit applies the truth, thus fulfilling Jesus' own words recorded in John 16:8-11.

4. *Christ's cross is valued.* "We preach Christ crucified . . . the power of God and the wisdom of God" (1 Cor. 1:23-24). "Far be it from me to boast except in the cross of our Lord Jesus Christ" (Gal. 6:14). So wrote Paul, himself both a convert and a preacher under revival conditions. Discernment of the cross as an atoning sacrifice, and faith in the crucified Lord, and exultation in the forgiveness of sins are further elements in the reviving of religion, whenever and wherever it occurs. Christianity that is alive in the heart is always cross-centered.

5. *Change goes deep.* Repentance, flowing from faith, is a change of mind expressed in a changed way of life. Thinking differently, we behave differently. The essence of the change is to stop living to oneself in self-will and sin and to start living to God in obedience and holiness. At revival times the inward pressure thus to change and leave the past behind becomes very strong and may prompt dramatic and violent gestures of renunciation, like the burning of a fortune's worth of occultist literature that Luke describes in Acts 19:18-19. The best exegesis of the violence that takes the kingdom of God by force understands it as the drastic changes that true repentance requires and that true converts actually make (Matt. 11:12; cf. Luke 16:16).

6. *Love breaks out.* "The town seemed to be full of the presence of God: it never was so full of *love* . . . as it was then."[42] Knowledge of being the object of God's saving love generates grateful love to him and joy-

---

[42] Jonathan Edwards, "A Faithful Narrative," in *Works*, ed. Hickman, 1:348.

ful love to all others. The seemingly extravagant mutual love and care that the New Testament writers celebrate as fact in the first churches (Acts 2:44-45, 4:32; 2 Cor. 8:1-4; Col. 1:8; 1 Thess. 4:9; etc.) is part of the evidence of revival conditions at that time.

7. *Joy fills hearts.* Peter, writing to Jewish Christians all over Asia Minor (1 Pet. 1:1), many of whom he could not have known personally, nonetheless declares of them all: "Though you do not now see [Christ], you believe in him and rejoice with joy that is inexpressible and filled with glory" (1:8; the Greek says literally, "with glorified joy"). Thinking of today's church, we wonder how Peter could have felt entitled to generalize in this way, but the answer stares us in the face: Under first-century revival conditions, inexpressible joy in Christ was virtually a standard and universal experience among Christian believers. When God is reviving his work, intense joy, alongside generous love, becomes the norm.

8. *Each church becomes itself*—becomes, that is, the people of the divine presence in an experiential, as distinct from a merely notional, sense. God is felt to be there, present to bless, in the midst of those who are his. In 1 Corinthians 14:24-25 Paul says that if in church all speech from all parties takes the form of intelligible declaration of gospel grace (which is what "prophesy" means here), then an unbeliever, wandering in, "is convicted by all, he is called to account by all, the secrets of his heart are disclosed, and so, falling on his face, he will worship God and declare that God is really among you." Paul's point, that prophecy does more good than tongues in church, would gain no force from his saying this unless something of this kind had already happened in the Corinthian church, so that it made sense to expect it to happen again. Under revival conditions the sense of God's presence among his people is vivid, and such things do in fact happen.

9. *The lost are found.* The blessing overflows; the saints reach out; unconverted people seek and find Christ. Earlier the point was made that revival is about more than conversions, but that does not mean it is not about conversions at all. Revivals of religion are ordinarily times of evangelistic fruitfulness, as was the case in Jerusalem after Pentecost and in Northampton in 1734-35. The cautious Edwards writes:

> I am far from pretending to be able to determine how many have lately been the subjects of . . . mercy; but if I may be allowed to declare any

thing that appears to me probable in a thing of this nature, I hope that more than 300 souls were savingly brought home to Christ, in this town, in the space of half a year.[43]

Later he thought he had overestimated. But the point—that there is always an evangelistic overflow when God revives religion, as was the case in Jerusalem long ago (Acts 2:41, 47; 4:4; 5:14; 6:7)—remains.

10. *Satan keeps pace*. The devil is not a creator but a destroyer. He is always busy trying to wreck the work of God. He is a cunning and resourceful adversary who at revival times, over and above his regular trapping routines, uses the false fire of fanaticism, the false zeal of errant teachers, and the false strategies of orthodox overdoers and divisive firebrands majoring in minors to discredit and demolish what God has been building up. Under revival conditions, as at other times, Christians need to take and use the complete armor of God, as described by Paul in Ephesians 6:10-20, in order to stand against him.

These, then, are the processes of revival, clinically stated. In medical studies, physiology explores the healthy working of all body parts, while pathology, applying physiological knowledge, investigates physical malfunctions and asks what can be done to put them right. Edwards was a spiritual pathologist of great clinical brilliance and thus was a shrewd guide in all aspects of communion with God, most outstandingly in the context of religious excitement as God revives religion and Satan keeps pace. Surveying his work in this field, as his own writings witness to and explicate it, we see in him three special strengths for this task.

First strength: a true understanding of religion. Edwards knows that *sin* is an anti-God allergy found in every human soul, the taproot of all active disobedience, all bad habits and inability to break them, all egocentric and self-serving motivations, all desires (lusts) in which the I-want syndrome called original sin finds expression, and all the unbelief of and unresponsiveness to the Word of God that mark our lives. He knew that regeneration is the supernatural renewing of the heart in the motivational image of the Lord Jesus, so that the urge to love and honor and serve and please and exalt and glorify God the Father now dominates and becomes the mainspring of faith, of repentance, of righteousness, of real worship, prayer, joy, and neighbor-love, and of all good

---

[43] Ibid., 350.

works (good inwardly, in motivation, as well as outwardly, in performance). And he knew that holiness means, negatively, renouncing and avoiding moral and spiritual evil and, in positive terms, actively loving God and man. This knowledge equips him to identify and instill truly pure religion at all times.

Second strength: a true understanding of the nature of revival, what God does when he revives religion. The ten-point analysis set out above mirrors Edwards's view here. This knowledge equipped him to distinguish between the authentic and the phony, that which was of the Spirit of God and that which was carnal and satanic, and to write about the difference in a way that remains standard for all time.

Third strength: a true understanding of God's wisdom and sovereignty in reviving religion according to the church's need and his people's prayers. Knowing that those who pray for revivings of religion are inevitably, whether they realize it or not, asking for trouble, and foreseeing what trouble will come, God yet keeps times and seasons in his own power as his own secret and does what he does in answer to those prayers according to his own discretion. Therefore we must learn to combine eagerness in prayer and boldness in diagnosing deadness and challenging sin with submission to providence and to sustain all three for as long as we have to, confident that if our stance triggers new troubles for us and our petitions are not granted in our own lifetime, an answer will be given in some form someday. Edwards's teaching on patient persistence in prayer for revival blessing that will change the world reflects abidingly valid insight at this point.

So, of all theological writers on the reviving of religion, I hail Jonathan Edwards as not only the first but also the best. Now back to his own big picture.

We should now note that such revivings of religion as we have analyzed, and as Edwards had experienced, had a key place in his understanding of God's plan for world history. What is nowadays called postmillennialism seemed to him clear in Scripture—Old Testament prophecy, including Daniel, and the book of the Revelation, interpreted in historicist terms, being the main sources. He thought the final era of history, when knowledge of God would fill the earth as the waters cover the sea, had begun. The book of Acts tells how, at the start of the new-covenant dispensation, an outpouring of the Holy Spirit produced an impetus that took the gospel from Jerusalem to Rome. Edwards seems to have thought this paradigmatic, for he taught that through such out-pourings the gospel would circle the world, and the mass of humans would be converted. This would be the full realization of the kingdom of Christ, who was central in all God's purposes. The role of the church in Edwards's day and in future days, therefore, was to match the church's role in Acts—that is, to become through its ministers the instrumental means of spreading the gospel. Ecclesiology is more the frame than the focus of Edwards's thought about God's plan. Understandably, Reformers and Puritans were constantly laboring to get and keep churches in scriptural shape, whatever else claimed their attention. Edwards, however, could take the Reformed church order of New England for granted, and so, equally understandably, his point of reference when looking ahead was less the perfecting of the church than the triumph of the kingdom of Christ, of which the church was the executive agent. Edwards was not weak in his ecclesiology, as witnessed by his willingness to lose his job, as he did, for insisting on classic New England discipline at the Lord's Table. Characteristically, though, his thought about the church was an aspect of his thought about the kingdom.

Today the older churches worldwide are under threat, so it is natural for biblically informed minds within them to strategize for the renewing and reviving of churches (congregations, that is) as units and in their life together. For Edwards, however, the focus of thought was always the reviving of religion in and through the churches for the conversion of the world. What difference this makes is a matter worth discussing, but we cannot do that here.

WRAP-UP

The initial goal of this essay was to elucidate Edwards's understanding of revival, distinguishing it from more general ideas of renewal as the reanimating of the church's corporate life. For it is in my view important to see that what is meant when we hear of congregational renewal, biblical renewal, liturgical renewal, ecumenical renewal, lay renewal, and so on is something less than Edwards's conception of a reviving of religion—that is, a deepening and energizing of personal communion with God according to the Scriptures. Edwards, however, like Calvin, was a very organic as well as a very powerful, Bible-centered, God-focused thinker, and it soon became clear that the project required some account to be given of how Edwards understood the fellowship with God that constitutes religion and the God with whom Christians commune; and so the essay grew into its present shape. Out of the material surveyed, the following questions for us now seem to arise:

First, do we acknowledge Edwards's God—that is, the biblical profile and lineaments of the Creator as Edwards presents them from the Scriptures? Sadly, for many in the churches today the word *God* has no clear meaning. Talking-points about God among the church's intellectuals include the anti-trinitarian monism into which Process Theology has finally mutated, the non-hierarchical social Trinity of some post-liberals, and the ultra-Arminian open theism of some evangelicals. But neither God's holiness, nor his glory, nor the punitive pain involved in being finally condemned by one's Creator receive much serious attention. Yet if Edwards is right, when God revives religion, these truths, faithfully taught, make an enormous impact; and about their prominence in the Bible there can be no question. So we do well to ask ourselves whether we have come to terms with them as of now.

Second, do we understand religion as Edwards did? Specifically, do we understand Christian existence as the joy of enjoying God in Christ, framed by the struggles of a life of repentance, self-denial, and suffering in its various forms? Much is heard today of spirituality as self-discovery and self-fulfillment in God and of a relationship with God that brings happiness, contentment, satisfaction, and inward peace. But of bearing the cross, battling wrong desires, resisting temptation, mortifying sin, and making those decisions that Jesus pictured as cutting off a limb and plucking out an eye, little or nothing gets said. Yet this is the living out of repentance, and without realistic emphasis on this more demanding side of the Christian life, a great deal of self-deceived shallowness and a great many false professions of faith from persons ignorant of the cost of discipleship are bound to appear. Now it is precisely the life of repentance, of cross-bearing, of holiness under pressure and joy within pain—the life, in other words, of following Jesus on his own stated terms—that God revives, for this is the reality of religion. Again, we do well to ask ourselves whether this is something we have come to terms with as of now.

Third, would we recognize a reviving of religion if we were part of one? I ask myself that question. For more than half a century the need of such reviving in the places where I have lived, worshiped, and worked has weighed me down. I have read of past revivals. I have learned, through a latter-day revival convert from Wales, that there is a *tinc* in the air, a kind of moral and spiritual electricity, when God's close presence is enforcing his Word. I have sat under the electrifying ministry of the late Martyn Lloyd-Jones, who as it were brought God into the pulpit with him and let him loose on the listeners. Lloyd-Jones's ministry blessed many, but he never believed he was seeing the revival he sought. I have witnessed remarkable evangelical advances, not only academic but also pastoral, with churches growing spectacularly through the gospel on both sides of the Atlantic and believers maturing in the life of repentance as well as in the life of joy. Have I seen revival? I think not—but would I know? From a distance, the difference between the ordinary and extraordinary working of God's Spirit looks like black and white, a difference of kind; to Edwards, however, at close range, it appeared a matter of degree, as his *Narrative* and his Brainerd volume (to look no further) make clear. Some evangelicals need to be asked, Are you not expecting too little from God in the way of moral transformation? But others need to be asked, Are you not expecting too much from God in the way of situational drama? Do we always know when we are in a revival situation?

To bring Wesley back for a moment before we say good-bye: Had I been mentored through the successive levels of one of his brilliantly structured Methodist Societies, from trial band (a small group of four to ten, exploring whether I truly wanted God in my life) to class membership in the United Society and to a band of believers, and on in due course to the Select Society, a fellowship of bands seeking to live a life of holy love, would it have been clear to me at any stage that I was part of a nationwide work of God's reviving religion?[44] I do not know. Here is an uncertainty with which, I think, we must all learn to live. Touches of reviving, I suspect, surround us, and we are not always aware of them.

What is certain, however, is this: God calls us, and wisdom directs us, to seek for ourselves the full reality of religion as Edwards describes it, and to pray for the further reviving of religion, by God's grace and for God's glory, that all our communities have need of at this time.

---

[44] For a fuller description of the structure of Wesley's countrywide United Societies, see Robert G. Tuttle, Jr., *John Wesley: His Life and Theology* (Grand Rapids, Mich.: Zondervan, 1978), 276-282, 318-319, and Tim Stafford and Tom Albin, "Finding God in Small Groups," *Christianity Today* 47 (August 2003): 42-44. "The whole Wesley revival is really a revival of pastoral care and spiritual guidance" (43).

5

PURSUING A PASSION
FOR GOD THROUGH
SPIRITUAL DISCIPLINES:
LEARNING FROM
JONATHAN EDWARDS

Donald S. Whitney

Jonathan Edwards is a spiritual hero to many Christians, and rightly so. Probably the main reason you're reading this is because he's a spiritual hero of yours. The Bible commands us to have the right kind of spiritual heroes. In Hebrews 13:7 we're told, "Remember those who led you, who spoke the word of God to you; and considering the result of their conduct, imitate their faith."[1]

We acknowledge, of course, that even the holiest human heroes are inconsistent ones. All our heroes are imperfect and sinful. As the next verse in this passage reminds us, only the perfect and sinless Hero, only "Jesus Christ is the same yesterday and today and forever" (v. 8). Nevertheless, the right kind of heroes, because they were devoted followers of Christ and people of his Word, will guide and protect us far more than they will mislead us.

Jonathan Edwards is just such a spiritual hero. Like those whom the first recipients of the letter to the Hebrews were to follow, Edwards is one "who spoke the word of God" to us through his life and works. As such, he is a hero whose life we should "remember," "consider," and "imitate" after the fashion of Hebrews 13:7. The purpose of this chapter is to help us remember, consider, and imitate Edwards's example of pursuing a passion for God through spiritual disciplines.

---

[1] All Scripture references in this chapter are from the NASB.

WHAT ARE THESE SPIRITUAL DISCIPLINES THROUGH WHICH EDWARDS PURSUED HIS PASSION FOR GOD?

The spiritual disciplines are the practical ways whereby we obey the command of 1 Timothy 4:7: "discipline yourself for the purpose of godliness." The goal of every spiritual discipline is—as this verse teaches—godliness. Godliness is another way of describing holiness, sanctification, and Christlikeness. To put it in other terms, the purpose of the spiritual disciplines is intimacy with Christ and conformity (both internal and external) to Christ.

To further clarify what spiritual disciplines are, think of them as:

Practices. A spiritual discipline is something you do, not something you are. Disciplines should not be confused with graces, character qualities, or the fruit of the Spirit. Prayer, for example, is a spiritual discipline, while joy, strictly speaking, is not. As practices, the spiritual disciplines are first about doing, then about being. The spiritual disciplines are right doing that leads to right being. That is, the purpose of doing the practices known as spiritual disciplines is the state of being described in 1 Timothy 4:7 as "godliness." Thus the discipline of prayer, rightly practiced, should result in godly joy. So while they should not be separated from each other, it is important to distinguish the *practices* known as the spiritual disciplines from the *fruit* that should result from them.

Biblical practices. We may not properly call just anything we do a spiritual discipline. Regardless of the benefit we may derive from a given activity, it is best to reserve the biblical term "discipline" for practices taught by precept or example in the Bible. Otherwise, anything and everything will eventually be called a spiritual discipline. Someone could claim that washing dishes—which, admittedly, ought to be done in the presence of and to the glory of God (1 Cor. 10:31)—is as spiritually beneficial to themselves as prayer is to others. But if we allow this, what basis for disagreement over what is and what isn't a spiritual discipline will exist except personal experience and preference?

Sufficient for godliness. Despite the spiritual help—real and perceived—that we may gain by practices not found in Scripture, the spiritual disciplines taught or modeled in the Bible are sufficient "for the purpose of godliness." Only the spiritual disciplines found in Scripture are "inspired by God and profitable for teaching, for reproof, for correction, for training in righteousness; so that the man of God may be adequate, equipped for every good work" (2 Tim. 3:16-17). And "every good work" for which Scripture makes us "adequate" and "equipped" would certainly include "the purpose of godliness."

Means to godliness, not ends. A person is not automatically godly just because he or she practices the spiritual disciplines. This was the error of the Pharisees, for although they prayed, memorized Scripture, fasted, and practiced other disciplines, Jesus pointed to them as the epitome of *un*godliness. Godliness is the result of God's Spirit changing us into Christlikeness *through* the means of the disciplines. Apart from faith and the right motives when practicing them, the disciplines can be dead works. The purpose for practicing the spiritual disciplines is not to see how many chapters of the Bible we can read or how long we can pray, nor is it found in anything else that can be counted or measured. We're not necessarily more godly because we engage in these biblical practices. Instead, these biblical practices should be the *means* that result in true godliness—that is, intimacy with and conformity to Christ.

Personal and interpersonal. Some spiritual disciplines are practiced alone; some are practiced with others. For instance, the Bible instructs us to pray in private, but it also teaches us to pray with the church. Some disciplines, like silence and solitude, are almost exclusively practiced in isolation from people. Yet some, like fellowship and communion, cannot be experienced alone. Our individual personalities incline each of us toward the disciplines of privacy or the disciplines of society. However, both personal and interpersonal disciplines are necessary for a balanced Christlikeness, for Jesus practiced both the disciplines of withdrawal and the disciplines of engagement.

As Edwards was not only a minister himself but grew up in a minister's home, his involvement with the interpersonal (congregational) disciplines is taken for granted. Instead of those corporate practices, this chapter is concerned with the role that the personal spiritual disciplines played in Edwards's life.

These timeless and universal disciplines are not mere biblical responsibilities; rather they are the God-given means of experiencing God. Because of the presence of the Holy Spirit within, Christians can experience God everywhere and in all circumstances. But there are certain means God has revealed in Scripture—the spiritual disciplines—that he has ordained especially for the purpose of seeking and savoring him. And it was through these God-given means that Jonathan Edwards pursued his passion for God.

God indeed was a passion and delight for Edwards from the first daybreak of God's grace upon his soul in the spring of 1721. Years afterward he wrote about that divine daybreak, a spiritual sunrise that occurred when he was in his late teens:

> The first instance that I remember of that sort of inward, sweet delight in God and divine things, that I have lived much in since, was on reading those words, 1 Tim. 1:17, "Now unto the King, eternal, immortal, invisible, the only wise God, be honor and glory forever and ever, Amen." As I read the words, there came into my soul, and was as it were diffused through it, a sense of the glory of the Divine Being; a new sense, quite different from any thing I ever experienced before. Never any words of Scripture seemed to me as these words did. I thought with myself, how excellent a Being that was, and how happy I should be, if I might enjoy that God, and be rapt up to him in heaven; and be as it were swallowed up in him forever! I kept saying, and as it were singing, over these words of Scripture to myself; and went to pray to God that I might enjoy him; and prayed in a manner quite different from what I used to do, with a new sort of affection.[2]

Notice that it was through the means of Scripture reading, prayer, singing, and worship—biblical spiritual disciplines—that Edwards experienced his enjoyment of God. From the biographies, and especially the pages of his own pen, we learn more of the specific details of . . .

How Jonathan Edwards Pursued a Passion for God Through the Spiritual Disciplines

Bible Intake

All forms of encountering Scripture are gathered under the heading of "Bible Intake." This includes hearing, reading, studying, and memorizing God's Word. Although there is evidence that Edwards engaged in each of these, I want to focus in particular on how Edwards models what is arguably the best way of experiencing the sweetness of Scripture—medita-

---

[2] Sereno E. Dwight, "Memoirs of Jonathan Edwards," in *The Works of Jonathan Edwards*, ed. Edward Hickman, 2 vols. (1834; reprint, Edinburgh: Banner of Truth, 1974), 1:xiii.

tion. While there is no one ideal method of meditating on the Bible, essentially it involves thinking in a prolonged and focused way about something found in the text while hearing, reading, studying, or memorizing it.

Meditation on Scripture was Edwards's practice from his first days as a disciple of Jesus. Later, describing the time soon after his conversion, he wrote, "I seemed often to see so much light exhibited by every sentence, and such a refreshing food communicated, that I could not get along in reading; often dwelling long on one sentence to see the wonders contained in it, and yet almost every sentence seemed to be full of wonders."[3]

Edwards seemed particularly fond of meditating on Scripture while walking in solitude or while on horseback, whether riding for relaxation or on a journey. What is most important, of course, is the result of this practice. In his *Personal Narrative*, Edwards wrote of the impact of meditation on Scripture on his soul:

> Sometimes, only mentioning a single word caused my heart to burn within me; or only seeing the name of Christ, or the name of some attribute of God. . . . The sweetest joys and delights I have experienced, have not been those that have arisen from a hope of my own good estate, but in a direct view of the glorious things of the gospel.
>
> Once, as I rode out into the woods for my health, in 1737, having alighted from my horse in a retired place, as my manner commonly has been, to walk for divine contemplation and prayer, I had a view that for me was extraordinary, of the glory of the Son of God, as Mediator between God and man, and his wonderful, great, full, pure and sweet grace and love, and meek and gentle condescension. This grace that appeared so calm and sweet, appeared also great above the heavens. The person of Christ appeared ineffably excellent with an excellency great enough to swallow up all thought and conception—which continued, as near as I can judge, about an hour; which kept me the greater part of the time in a flood of tears and weeping aloud. I felt an ardency of soul to be, what I know not otherwise how to express, emptied and annihilated; to lie in the dust, and to be full of Christ alone; to love Him with a holy and pure love; to trust in Him; to live upon Him; to serve and follow Him; and to be perfectly sanctified and made pure, with a divine and heavenly purity. I have, several other times, had views very much of the same nature, and which have had the same effects.[4]

---

[3] Ibid., xiv.
[4] Ibid., xlvi-xlvii.

Like Edwards, we *feel* most deeply about things when we *think* most deeply about them. Why is it that we can read a passage of Scripture at home, and it may affect us very little, but then our pastor can preach on that same passage and we are deeply stirred? It's because when we read it at home, our eyes pass over the words in a few seconds, we close the Bible, and the words immediately leak out of our minds. But when we sit under a preacher who focuses our attention on that same passage for several minutes—pointing out details of the text, comparing it with other passages, illustrating and applying it—our emotions are kindled, and we begin to feel more deeply about what God says in that section of Scripture.

The tendency of most Christians in our hurried, overburdened times is to close the Bible as soon as we've read it and turn to the next thing on our to-do list. If pressed, we'd usually have to admit—immediately after closing the Bible—that we don't remember a thing we've read. Reading alone will seldom give us the encounter with God, the spiritual nourishment, that our souls need.

Reading is the exposure to Scripture—and that's the starting place— but meditation is the absorption of Scripture. And it is the absorption of Scripture that causes the water of the Word of God to percolate deeply into the parched soil of the soul and refresh it.

Prayer

Edwards was so devoted to prayer that it is hard to find a daily routine for him that wasn't permeated with it. He prayed alone when he arose, then had family prayer before breakfast. Prayer was a part of each meal, and he prayed again with the family in the evening. He prayed over his studies, and he prayed as he walked in the evenings. Prayer was both a discipline and a part of his leisure.

Biographer George Marsden draws a similar portrait of Edwards's life of prayer:

He began the day with private prayers followed by family prayers, by candlelight in the winter. Each meal was accompanied by household devotions, and at the end of each day Sarah joined him in his study for prayers. Jonathan kept secret the rest of his daily devotional routine, following Jesus' command to pray in secret. Throughout the day, his goal was to remain constantly with a sense of living in the presence of

God, as difficult as that might be. Often he added secret days of fasting and additional prayers.[5]

Prayer, then, for Edwards was both planned and informal, scheduled and spontaneous, on a daily basis. From the time when his teenage soul first began to experience what he called "that sort of inward, sweet delight in God and divine things," it was as though Edwards could not think long of God without speaking or singing to him. "Prayer seemed natural to me," he wrote of the change in his life, "as the breath by which the inward burnings of my heart had vent."[6]

Prayer was so essential to Edwards's Christianity that the idea of a Christian who did not pray was preposterous. Some of the most sobering words he ever spoke were directed toward those who claimed to be followers of Jesus but who never prayed in private. In his sermon on "Hypocrites Deficient in the Duty of Prayer," Edwards solemnly declared:

> I would exhort those who have entertained a hope of their being true converts—and who since their supposed conversion have left off the duty of secret prayer, and ordinarily allow themselves in the omission of it—to throw away their hope. If you have left off calling upon God, it is time for you to leave off hoping and flattering yourselves with an imagination that you are children of God.[7]

It was inconceivable that anyone could know the God he knew and not be compelled by the sweetness, love, and satisfaction found in God to pray. It seemed contrary to Edwards's understanding of Scripture that anyone could be indwelled by the Spirit who causes God's children to "cry out, 'Abba! Father!'" (Rom. 8:15; cf. Gal. 4:6) and yet not cry out to the Father in regular private prayer. Edwards testifies that when a person has a passion for God, he prays.

Private Worship

Here I want to concentrate on Edwards's habit of singing in his private worship of God. Just as most Christians could not imagine pub-

---

[5] George M. Marsden, *Jonathan Edwards: A Life* (New Haven, Conn.: Yale University Press, 2003), 133.

[6] Dwight, "Memoirs," xiii.

[7] Jonathan Edwards, "Hypocrites Deficient in the Duty of Prayer," in *Works*, ed. Hickman, 2:74.

lic worship without singing, apparently Edwards could not conceive of private worship without it. But he did not sing praises to God when alone merely because he felt obligated to do so. Rather, Edwards spoke of his private, spontaneous songs to God as that which "seemed natural" and flowed from the sweetness of his contemplations of God.

He writes of this in his *Personal Narrative* as he describes the early years of his Christian life:

> I often used to sit and view the moon for a long time; and in the day, spent much time in viewing the clouds and sky, to behold the sweet glory of God in these things; in the mean time, singing forth, with a low voice, my contemplations of the Creator and Redeemer. And scarce any thing, among all the works of nature, was so sweet to me as thunder and lightning; formerly nothing had been so terrible to me. Before, I used to be uncommonly terrified with thunder, and to be struck with terror when I saw a thunderstorm rising; but now, on the contrary, it rejoiced me. I felt God, if I may so to speak, at the first appearance of a thunderstorm; and used to take the opportunity, at such times, to fix myself in order to view the clouds and see the lightnings play, and hear the majestic and awful voice of God's thunder, which oftentimes was exceedingly entertaining, leading me to sweet contemplations of my great and glorious God. While thus engaged, it always seemed natural to me to sing or chant forth my meditations; or, to speak my thoughts in soliloquies with a singing voice.[8]

As he matured in his relationship with God, Edwards continued singing in his frequent times of private worship. In his *Personal Narrative* he continues to describe his experience "year after year; often walking alone in the woods, and solitary places, for meditation, soliloquy, and prayer, and converse with God; and it was always my manner, at such times, to sing forth my contemplations."[9]

Why not follow Edwards's example? Sing to God in private worship for the same reasons you sing to him in public worship. "It is good to sing praises to our God" (Ps. 147:1). Like Edwards, enjoy the goodness of singing praises to God every day, not just on Sunday.

---

[8] Dwight, "Memoirs," xiii.
[9] Ibid.

Solitude

It is no secret that Edwards was a private man and accused of being too withdrawn from society. Some of his habits for seclusion are understandable when we realize that his study, writing, and sermon preparation had to be done in the same house with a wife, eleven children, servants, and frequent guests. But even as a single man, Jonathan Edwards sought solitude, not merely to be more productive, but in order to meet with God. During his twentieth year, when he was in New York and in his first pastoral ministry, he often abandoned the bustle of the city and the attractions it might have had for an eligible bachelor so far from home. Writing of that time, Edwards recalls, "I very frequently used to retire into a solitary place, on the banks of Hudson's river, at some distance from the city, for contemplation on divine things and secret converse with God; and had many sweet hours there."[10]

Apparently this was a discipline by which he experienced much spiritual pleasure throughout his life. It seems to have been his daily habit—weather permitting—to ride the few blocks south from his house to the primary intersection in Northampton, there turn right on Main Street, go past the meetinghouse, and ride west of town two or three miles. On his way out and back he would pray, think, and sing. Typically he found a secluded spot to walk alone with God in the woods or along hillsides. He speaks of this as his regular practice in the *Personal Narrative*, which he wrote when he was thirty-five. As he begins the description of an experience two years earlier, he writes, "I rode out into the woods for my health . . . having alighted from my horse in a retired place, as my manner commonly has been, to walk for divine contemplation and prayer."[11]

While Edwards doubtless would have acknowledged his own propensity to privacy, he maintained that true grace inclined every Christian to be much alone with God:

> Some are greatly affected when in company; but have nothing that bears any manner of proportion to it in secret, in close meditation, prayer and conversing with God when alone, and separated from the world. A true Christian doubtless delights in religious fellowship and Christian conversation, and finds much to affect his heart in it; but he also delights

---

[10] Ibid., xiv.
[11] Ibid., xlvi.

at times to retire from all mankind, to converse with God in solitude. And this also has peculiar advantages for fixing his heart, and engaging his affections. True religion disposes persons to be much alone in solitary places for holy meditation and prayer. . . . It is the nature of true grace, however it loves Christian society in its place, in a peculiar manner to delight in retirement, and secret converse with God.[12]

Whatever may be said about Edwards's individual preferences for solitude, we cannot deny that Jesus himself frequently sought to be alone with the Father. Texts such as Matthew 14:23 and Luke 4:42 are similar to what we read in Mark 1:35: "In the early morning, while it was still dark, Jesus got up, left the house, and went away to a secluded place, and was praying there." Seeking God-focused solitude is a Christlike habit. Like Edwards, when we rightly practice the spiritual discipline of solitude, we not only conform to Christ's example, we encounter him.

Fasting

The frequency of references to the discipline of fasting in the literature by and about Jonathan Edwards may surprise those contemporary Christians who have seldom heard fasting mentioned in their own churches. He often referred to or called for congregational fasts, and for events as varied as military campaigns,[13] epidemic sickness,[14] and revival.[15] Eight months before he was fired, Edwards received the cooperation of the church in Northampton when he called for a Fast Day on October 26, 1749, "to pray to God that he would have mercy on this church . . . that he would forgive the sins of both minister and people."[16]

But these congregational fasts had a counterpart in Edwards's private spirituality. Samuel Hopkins tells us this, writing from the perspective of one who spent eight months in the Northampton pastor's home

---

12 Edwards, *Religious Affections*, in *Works*, ed. Hickman, 1:311-312.
13 "Edwards' sermon notes for April 4, 1745, are marked with the words, 'Fast for success in the expedition against Cape Breton'." Iain H. Murray, *Jonathan Edwards: A New Biography* (Edinburgh: Banner of Truth, 1987), 285.
14 Edwards's notes for a sermon on Psalm 65:2 in January 1736 are marked with the words, "Fast on occasion of the sickness at the East Ward." *The Works of Jonathan Edwards*, vol. 19, *Sermons and Discourses, 1734-1738*, ed. M. X. Lesser (New Haven, Conn.: Yale University Press, 2001), 803.
15 Jonathan Edwards, "Some Thoughts Concerning the Revival," in *The Works of Jonathan Edwards*, vol. 4, *The Great Awakening*, ed. C. C. Goen (New Haven, Conn.: Yale University Press, 1972), 515-521.
16 As quoted in Murray, *Jonathan Edwards*, 319.

in the early 1740s. While noting that much of Edwards's personal devotional life is shrouded in secrecy, he writes confidently that Edwards frequently fasted:

> Mr. Edwards made a secret of his private devotion, and therefore it cannot be particularly known: though there is much evidence, that he was punctual, constant and frequent in secret prayer, and often kept days of fasting and prayer in secret; and set apart time for serious, devout meditations on spiritual and eternal things, as part of his religious exercise in secret.[17]

Edwards thought that ministers, in particular, should discipline themselves to fast. In *Some Thoughts Concerning the Present Revival*, he said, "I should think ministers, above all persons, ought to be much in secret prayer and fasting, and also much in praying and fasting with one another."[18] But he certainly did not think that the blessings of fasting should be enjoyed only by the clergy, as his calls for congregational fasts demonstrate. Further evidence of his view that private fasting was a discipline for all Christians is seen in his letter to eighteen-year-old Deborah Hatheway, penned on June 3, 1741, in response to her request for spiritual counsel. Edwards advised her in a way consistent with his own practice: "Under special difficulties, or when in great need of, or great longings after, any particular mercy for yourself or others, set apart a day for secret prayer and fasting for yourself alone."[19]

In Matthew 6:16-18, Jesus taught his disciples about fasting and began the instructions with, "Whenever you fast . . ." Edwards understood these directions to apply to every Christian in every generation, including himself. His example in this discipline, like the Book upon which he based the discipline, is still valid.

Journal-Keeping

The diary (a term used synonymously here with "journal") of Jonathan Edwards opens with an entry on December 18, 1722, when he was nine-

---

[17] Samuel Hopkins, *The Life and Character of the Late Reverend Mr. Jonathan Edwards*, http://www.jonathanedwards.com/text/Hopkins/Hopkins.htm.

[18] Edwards, "Some Thoughts Concerning the Revival," 507.

[19] Jonathan Edwards, "To Deborah Hatheway," *The Works of Jonathan Edwards*, vol. 16, *Letters and Personal Writings*, ed. George S. Claghorn (New Haven, Conn.: Yale University Press, 1998), 94.

teen. It begins so abruptly that Sereno Edwards Dwight, a descendant
of Edwards who published in 1830 the first edition of his ancestor's
works, conjectures that there was an earlier section that may have
reached back to Jonathan's days of theological study at Yale (1720-
1722).[20] For all practical purposes, Edwards's diary concludes with an
entry on November 16, 1725. Inexplicably, there are but six brief entries
made over the next ten years.

Dwight is certain that Edwards never meant for his diary to be preserved and read by others. "Had it been with him at the close of his life,"
Dwight suggests, "it is not unlikely it might have been destroyed."[21] We
may be grateful to God that it was not.

The volume certainly qualifies as a spiritual journal, for it is far
more than the kind of diary that is a mere record of events. Yes, "it consists of facts," observes Dwight, as a diary of details and experiences
would do. But it's also comprised of

> solid thought, dictated by deep religious feelings. . . . It is an exhibition
> of the simple thinking, feeling, and acting of a man, who is unconscious
> how he appears, except to himself and to God; and not the remarks of
> one, who is desirous of being thought humble, respecting his own
> humility. If we suppose a man of Christian simplicity and godly sin-
> cerity to bring all the secret movements of his own soul under the clear,
> strong light of heaven, and there to survey them with a piercing and an
> honest eye, and a contrite heart, in order to humble himself, and make
> himself better; it is just the account which such a man would write.[22]

Sometimes he'd begin an entry with a single word, and then write
a paragraph explaining his spiritual condition. For example:

Wednesday, Jan. 2 [1723]. Dull.

Wednesday, Jan. 9. At night. Decayed.

Thursday, Jan. 10. About noon. Recovering.[23]

---

[20] Dwight, "Memoirs," xxiii.
[21] Ibid.
[22] Ibid., xxiii-xxiv.
[23] Ibid., xxiv.

He rebuked himself. "Saturday night, March 31. This week I have been too careless about eating."[24]

He rejoiced. "Saturday night, April 14. I could pray more heartily this night for the forgiveness of my enemies, than ever before."[25]

He could be mundane. "Wednesday night, Aug. 28. Remember, as soon as I can get to a piece of slate or something, whereon I can make short memorandums while traveling."[26] And again, "Sabbath morning, Sept. 8. I have been much to blame, for expressing so much impatience for delays in journeys, and the like."[27]

He could be sublime. "Wednesday, March 6. Near sunset. Regarded the doctrines of election, free grace, our inability to do anything without the grace of God, and that holiness is entirely, throughout, the work of the Spirit of God, with greater pleasure than before."[28]

Although Edwards apparently left off this diary, for the most part, by age twenty-two, his entries merely changed forms, and he remained to the end of his life an example to us of the discipline of journaling. For in the same year that he started his diary, the nineteen-year-old Edwards made his initial entry into what would become his "Miscellanies." These were typically paragraph or page-long meditations on biblical and theological subjects. And while these were not the places where he expressed his feelings or spoke of experiences, these journals stretched to 1,400 entries and 1,700 hundred pages. Before the end of the following year (1723), Edwards would start three more notebooks: "Notes on the Apocalypse," "The Mind," and "Notes on Scripture." He wrote in the latter volume until the end of his life, and it would eventually contain more than five hundred entries.

Jonathan Edwards believed in the value of preserving the insights given him by the illumination of the Holy Spirit. What he learned from Scripture or about Scripture, he did not want to lose. And even with his great mind, he knew that unless he recorded his thoughts, he wasn't likely to remember many of them.

---

[24] Ibid., xxvii.
[25] Ibid.
[26] Ibid., xxxi.
[27] Ibid.
[28] Ibid., xxvii.

Learning

Tracing Edwards's practice of the spiritual disciplines illustrates how it's common to engage in several of the spiritual disciplines simultaneously. Sometimes an objection to the enjoyment of the disciplines arises that there are too many for an ordinary person to practice. However, while we can isolate specific disciplines for the purpose of studying them, typically most are practiced in conjunction with other disciplines. We've already observed that almost daily Edwards withdrew to solitude where he would pray, meditate on Scripture, and sing in worship to God. In addition to these disciplines, he might be fasting all the while. So in the same experience he—and we—could be practicing no fewer than five different spiritual disciplines.

Another place where it's often difficult to separate one discipline from another in Edwards's life is his marriage of the disciplines of journaling and learning. Perhaps the majority of his pen work—sermon preparation, correspondence, and the completing of manuscripts for publication—would be termed simply "writing," not journaling. Still, as we noted in the previous section, Edwards was constantly writing notes, observations, and meditations about things he was learning in a journal of one type or another.

The two practices of journaling and learning began to intertwine in Jonathan's earliest days. Dwight remarks:

> Even while a boy, he began to study with his pen in his hand; not for the purpose of copying off the thoughts of others, but for the purpose of writing down, and preserving, the thought suggested to his own mind from the course of study he was pursuing. This most useful practice he commenced in several branches of study very early; and he steadily pursued it in all his studies through life. His pen appears to have been in a sense always in his hand.[29]

As evidence of this as a lifelong habit, Hopkins tells us again that "[Edwards] would commonly, unless diverted by company, ride two or three miles after dinner, to some lonely grove, where he would dismount and walk awhile—at such times, he generally carried his pen and ink with him, to note any thought that might be suggested."[30]

---

29 Ibid., xviii.
30 Ibid., xxxviii.

In the Beineke Rare Book and Manuscript Library at Yale is another fascinating pen-and-ink manifestation of Edwards's passion for God. In Folder 1251 of Edwards's manuscripts is a little notebook he called "Subjects of Enquiry." Paper was often scarce in places close to the frontier, but so zealous was Edwards to learn and retain his learning that he stitched scraps of dress patterns into a booklet no larger than a man's hand. It consists of twenty-two odd and irregularly shaped pieces folded in half to make forty-four pages. He also included what appear to be notes—perhaps in Sarah's hand—of announcements to be read in church, so he could write on the back of each small page. The first line in the volume explains that it is a place to record "Things to be particularly inquired into & written upon." Some of these were: "In reading the Old Testament observing its harmony with the new," and "Complete my enquiry about justification," and "Read Taylor on Romans," and "Compute the number of Christ's miracles."

Regarding Edwards's discipline of learning, Hopkins observed firsthand that:

> [Edwards] had an uncommon thirst for knowledge, in the pursuit of which, he spared no cost nor pains. He read all the books, especially books of divinity, that he could come at, from which he could hope to get any help in his pursuit of knowledge. . . . He applied himself with all his might to find out the truth: he searched for understanding and knowledge, as for silver, and dug for it, as for his treasures. Every thought on any subject . . . he pursued, as far as he then could, with his pen in his hand.[31]

Jonathan Edwards was blessed with one of the most formidable intellects in American history. But he sought to use it in obedience to the greatest commandment (Mark 12:28-30), as a means of pursuing and loving God. Edwards had an insatiably hungry mind, and he enjoyed all manner of learning, but he disciplined himself to give his best thoughts to the best of subjects—the pursuit and enjoyment of God.

Stewardship of Time

At the root of all discipline is the disciplined use of time. Without this one, there are no other disciplines. Edwards recognized this early on, and

---

[31] Hopkins, *The Life and Character of the Late Reverend Mr. Jonathan Edwards.*

thus three of the very first of his famous Resolutions—in this case, numbers 5-7—were on the stewardship of time:

> 5. Resolved, never to lose one moment of time, but to improve it in the most profitable way I possibly can.

> 6. Resolved, to live with all my might, while I do live.

> 7. Resolved, never to do anything, which I should be afraid to do if it were the last hour of my life.[32]

One of Edwards's best-known and most soul-searching sermons is on this very subject. In December 1734 he preached on "The Preciousness of Time and the Importance of Redeeming It."[33] Taking the words "redeeming the time" from Ephesians 5:16 as his text, Edwards reminded his listeners that time is the only brief preparation we have for all eternity. This time is short, it is passing, the remaining amount of it is uncertain, and whatever time is lost can never be regained. We will give an account to God of how we use our time, Edwards noted, and our precious time is so easily lost. In the most solemn section of the sermon, Edwards called his hearers to consider how people on their deathbed, and especially those in hell, long to have the time that we have at this moment, and how we ought to use our time as they would, if they had the opportunity.

Only one illustration is necessary to show how Edwards tried to live in light of the preciousness of time. Apparently Hopkins saw this on multiple occasions, and it demonstrates the diligence Edwards applied in every situation to improve the time.

> In solitary rides of considerable length, he adopted a kind of artificial memory. Having pursued a given subject of thought to its proper results, he would pin a small piece of paper on a given spot in his coat, and charge his mind to associate the subject and the piece of paper. He would then repeat the same process with a second subject of thought, fastening the token in a different place, and then a third, and a fourth, as the time might permit. From a ride of several days, he would usually bring home a considerable number of these remembrancers; and,

[32] Dwight, "Memoirs," xx.
[33] Edwards, "The Preciousness of Time," in *Works*, ed. Hickman, 2:233-236.

on going to his study, would take them off, one by one, in regular order, and write down the train of thought of which each was intended to remind him.[34]

Although he sought to redeem every precious moment of time in ways such as this, none of Edwards's biographers ever presents him as a hurried, breathless man, crashing through the day, always behind schedule. Moreover, we know he frequently took long rides with Sarah or alone and that he spent time with his eleven children and knew how to laugh with them. He lived this way because he believed it was Christlike to do so. Jesus frequently ministered for long hours and under great demands. But he, too, would often get alone with the Father, as well as spend time developing his relationship with those closest to him. He never misused a minute. We never read of him acting rushed. Jesus lived every moment for the glory of God and in the presence of God. And though Edwards did so imperfectly, he wanted to do the same. He found God worth seeking in every possible moment of life and by every God-given means—regardless of the cost. And there is much we can learn from him about this.

LESSONS FROM JONATHAN EDWARDS ON PURSUING A PASSION FOR GOD THROUGH THE SPIRITUAL DISCIPLINES

First, we need a lesson *about* lessons from Jonathan Edwards. In one sense, it's foolish to try to imitate Edwards. He was a genius. Moreover, let's make it clear that there are some things about Edwards that we *shouldn't* imitate, for he was a sinner too. But even though we cannot imitate his unique, God-given gifts and intellect, we can imitate his use and development of them.

Edwards teaches us to pursue a passion for God through the full range of the biblical spiritual disciplines.

He wanted to experience and enjoy God through as many God-ordained channels as possible. He didn't just read a chapter or two from the Bible and whisper a brief prayer of thanks, engaging in as few of the disciplines as possible without feeling guilty. Edwards viewed all the biblical spiritual disciplines as the divinely appointed means of experiencing the holy God he found so addictive to his soul. He took advantage

---

[34] Dwight, "Memoirs," xxxviii.

of every possible way, in the words of his sermon on Song of Solomon 5:1, to lay his soul "in the way of allurement."[35]

Listen to these words of Edwards from his sermon "The Christian Pilgrim" about the allurement he found in God:

> The enjoyment of him is our highest happiness, and is the only happiness with which our souls can be satisfied. To go to heaven, fully to enjoy God, is infinitely better than the most pleasant accommodations here: better than fathers and mothers, husbands, wives, or children, or the company of any or all earthly friends. These are but shadows; but God is the substance. These are but scattered beams; but God is the sun. These are but streams; but God is the fountain. These are but drops; but God is the ocean.[36]

All those indwelled by the Holy Spirit have desires that can be satisfied only in God himself. But how shall we satisfy these ever-thirsty longings for the ocean of God? The highways built by God to the ocean of himself are the spiritual disciplines.

If I wanted to go to the Pacific and enjoy its beauty and immerse myself in it, what should I do? I could stay in my house all my life and express my longings to experience the ocean but never feel its water on my skin. I must get on the highways that will take me to the ocean.

God has built highways by which those he has made alive can come and be satisfied with the ocean of himself. All of these highways (as I try to accommodate my imperfect analogy to perfect biblical truth) converge at Jesus Christ, the one bridge to the ocean of God the Father. These highways are the personal and interpersonal practices revealed in the Bible by which we may find and enjoy God. The highways do not exist for themselves. Our souls do not find satisfaction in the highways, but only in the ocean to which they take us.

It is God who makes us alive. It is God who has graciously built these highways to himself. It is God who gives us the ongoing thirst that this crystal-clear ocean alone can satisfy. It is God who entreats us with the invitations to come to him on these royal highways. It is God who

---

[35] Jonathan Edwards, "Sacrament Sermon on Canticles 5:1," sermon manuscript (1729), Beinecke Library, Yale University.

[36] Jonathan Edwards, "The Christian Pilgrim," in The Works of Jonathan Edwards, vol. 17, Sermons and Discourses, 1730-1733, ed. Mark Valeri (New Haven, Conn.: Yale University Press, 1999), 437-438.

gives us a spiritual affinity and enjoyment for the highways that take us to him. But we must get on the highways.

That's what Edwards disciplined himself to do, and in doing so became an example for us in how to pursue a passion for God.

Edwards teaches us concerning the need to pursue a passion for God through the spiritual disciplines regardless of our intellect or abilities.

Perhaps the most remarkable thing about Edwards is that he *was* disciplined. Because of his educational and intellectual advantages, he could have lowered the standards of his spiritual disciplines dramatically and still have been a capable pastor and admired spiritual leader. And no doubt this thought crossed his mind on occasion, for he had very little external accountability to maintain a spiritually disciplined life. He was by far the most brilliant and educated man at any gathering. How easy and excusable it would have been to coast intellectually and spiritually. This was especially true in those latter years in the backwoods outpost at Stockbridge. Despite all these temptations, Edwards never flagged in his discipline. In fact, he disciplined himself to do his best writing while at Stockbridge.

We've not been given Edwards's gifts. It's useless to encourage anyone to imitate Edwards's mental ability. We can, however, regardless of our intellectual capacity, imitate his discipline. We do not have to possess Edwards's intelligence to adopt his diligence. Regardless of how great or small our gifts or talents, our responsibility for 1 Timothy 4:7 remains: "Discipline yourself for the purpose of godliness." The spiritual disciplines are the means God has given to all of us as the way to pursue God and to experience the joys and pleasures of godliness.

Edwards teaches us to pursue a passion for God equally with head and heart through the spiritual disciplines.

If we seek for an explanation for the extraordinary blessing of God upon the ministry of Jonathan Edwards, I think we must do so in a way that shows that God was true to his own Word in 1 Timothy 4:16: "Pay close attention to yourself and to your teaching; persevere in these things, for as you do this you will ensure salvation both for yourself and for those who hear you." Edwards epitomizes the pursuit of the spiritual proportionality found in this command. He always sought to "pay close attention" equally to both sides of this spiritual equation—that is, to both devotion *and* doctrine, piety *and* theology, heart *and* head, heat *and* light, spirit *and* truth. His passion for God burned with a clear flame that was fueled by the pure truth of God. And just as God promised in this verse to bless the ministries of those who "persevere in these things," he has remarkably blessed the life and work of Jonathan Edwards with much enduring fruit.

In contrast to Edwards's example, most people seem to lean one way or the other, favoring devotion *or* doctrine, piety *or* theology. But strong piety will not excuse us from the study of theology, nor will a strong theology compensate for a lack of piety. Edwards models the fact that a real understanding of the truth of God will set the heart on fire, and that the heart set on fire by God will burn with a love for learning his truth. As it was with Edwards, sometimes the things of God should appear so beautiful to our minds that we can't help but study and meditate on them and so ravish our hearts that we want to weep or sing. What in all the world should delight our minds and ignite our hearts more than the things of God?

CONCLUSION

Historian George Marsden, in his 2003 biography, begins chapter 30 with a summary of Edwards's pursuit of a passion for God through a spiritually disciplined life:

> Edwards worked constantly to cultivate gratitude, praise, worship, and dependence on his Savior. Whatever his failings, he attempted every day to see Christ's love in all things, to walk according to God's precepts, and to give up attachments to worldly pleasures in anticipation of that closer spiritual union that death would bring.[37]

This is why Jonathan Edwards is worthy of being added to the list of spiritual heroes about whom we can say, "Remember those who led you, who spoke the word of God to you; and considering the result of their conduct, imitate their faith" (Heb. 13:7).

But as Edwards himself would remind us, ultimately his example as a spiritual leader has value only to the degree that he points us to his God. Merely human heroes often fail us, but there is One who never does, for the perfect and holy "Jesus Christ is the same yesterday and today and forever" (Heb. 13:8). In him alone is endless fascination, satisfaction, the forgiveness of sins, and eternal life.

---

[37] Marsden, *Jonathan Edwards*, 490.

6

How Jonathan Edwards Got Fired, and Why It's Important for Us Today

Mark Dever

Some of you, before you read the title to this chapter, or before you read the earlier chapters in this book, may not even have known that Jonathan Edward had been fired. He was fired by a vote of his congregational church. In July 1750 the members of his own congregation voted to sever the pastoral relationship between them. Only 10 percent of the church members voted to keep Edwards as their pastor. As Edwards put it to a friend a couple of weeks later, the "generality" of the church members voted to send him away.

But before he could be voted out, he had to be voted in.

In April 1725 the church in Northampton, Massachusetts, voted to find a colleague pastor for the ailing Solomon Stoddard, the so-called "Pope of the Connecticut Valley" and Jonathan Edwards's maternal grandfather. Edwards was first invited to preach there in August 1726. In November of that same year, Edwards was invited to settle in Northampton. He accepted the call to become the assistant and presumed successor of his Grandfather Stoddard at the church in Northampton, arguably the most important church center outside of Boston.

Stoddard was certainly one of the most celebrated ministers in New England. And it is at this point that Edwards's biography—and that of his family—gets so intertwined with ecclesiology and the purpose of this chapter. Back in 1662 the Congregational churches in New England had struck a compromise in order to give many of the rights of membership (which included, most importantly, having their own children baptized) to those who had made no profession of conversion. This would allow such people to enjoy all the privileges of church membership except for the Lord's Table. This was withheld from them. This became known as "the Halfway Covenant" and was bitterly opposed by Increase Mather and some others, but was finally generally accepted by the churches.

The church at Northampton had been founded by Increase Mather's brother, Eleazar Mather. It was one of the congregations that had *rejected* this Halfway Covenant. When Eleazar Mather died in 1669, he was immediately succeeded by Solomon Stoddard, who was himself a champion of the new Halfway Covenant. Stoddard took Mather's widow as his wife, and the church quickly took the new way advocated by Stoddard. Soon they had Covenant members (who gave evidence of conversion and were admitted to the Lord's Table) and non-Covenant members (who did not give evidence of conversion and were not admitted to the Lord's Table).

Within a few years something occurred that the plan's proponents had not foreseen—the non-Covenant members outnumbered the Covenant members. After some years of wrestling with this, in 1700 Stoddard suggested a fundamental change in the way that the Lord's Supper was given. He suggested that it should be expanded to include all of those members (regenerate and unregenerate) who wanted to partake, excepting only those whose lives were scandalous. "Mr. Stoddard's Way," as it was known, had been practiced for many years quietly in Northampton under his pastorate. Now he would make it known and advocate it.

Once again Increase Mather led the charge against this innovation. Stoddard published treatises in favor of his position, claiming that it might help in converting the unregenerate, and soon Stoddard's way became the practice of many, and perhaps most, of the New England churches. One can immediately grasp why it would be popular.

Now back to Edwards. In February 1727 Edwards was ordained a co-pastor of the church at Northampton, working alongside his grandfather. Two years later, on February 11, 1729, Solomon Stoddard died, and so Jonathan Edwards became the sole pastor of the most important congregation in western Massachusetts, with over 600 members. Stoddard's funeral was the very public occasion then for the beginning of Edward's solo pastorate. His first couple of years were spent quietly.

On July 8, 1731, Edwards preached a sermon in Boston entitled "God

Glorified in Man's Dependence," at the request of the Boston clergy. It was the regular Thursday lecture at First Church (largely attended by ministers), but it was special because it was also the week of commencement at Harvard College. Being invited to give this address, then, was the biggest honor of the whole series of lectures. It would be the best-attended lecture of the year. And this lecture promised to be a particularly interesting one for a number of reasons pertaining to the lecturer. First, the lectures were usually given by ministers from the Boston area; Edwards was from remote Northampton. Second, they were usually given by Harvard graduates; Edwards had not gone to Harvard, but to the new school, Yale (whose reputation was in serious question at the time). Third, Edwards was young—only twenty-eight at the time he was asked to give it. Fourth, he was the grandson of the famed Solomon Stoddard, who had often given this or some other important lecture in Boston. As Perry Miller described it, "The figure who stood before the congregation on this Thursday morning was the newly crowned successor of a rival principality, and the Boston clergy turned out to greet him as some privy council might greet the fledgling heir of a competing power."[1]

The lecture was deemed to be a success and was printed within a month; it was Edwards's first sermon to be printed. Its printed title was: *God Glorified in the Work of Redemption by the Greatness of Man's Dependence upon Him, in the Whole of It.*[2]

Edwards continued on in his ministry. He saw revivals in the work in Northampton during the next few years, most notably from December 1734 through the spring of 1735. The membership of the church increased by several score, and so in 1736-1737 they built a new meetinghouse to accommodate the increase. Edwards continued as pastor of this congregation for more than a decade, having an international reputation, until, in July 1750, the members of the church voted by a margin of 10 to 1 to dismiss him. Ten days later, Edwards preached his final sermon to them as their pastor.

The situations that led to his dismissal are a long story that has to do with everything from botched pastoral moves to disputes over salary, envy in the town, a perceived coolness and aloofness on the part of Mr. Edwards, and even long-standing tensions in his own extended family.

---

[1] Perry Miller, *Jonathan Edwards* (New York: William Sloane Associates, 1949), 13.
[2] *The Works of Jonathan Edwards*, vol. 17, *Sermons and Discourses, 1730-1733*, ed. Mark Valeri (New Haven, Conn.: Yale University Press, 1999), 200-219.

We could go on. The answer to "why" questions is almost always beyond human capacity to answer fully. Many of the particulars would be of interest only to academic historians or would take more space than the scope of this chapter allows.

At the very heart of the controversy that led to Edwards's being fired was church discipline and especially the question of who was to be admitted to the Lord's Table. Jonathan Edwards had come to disagree with his venerable grandfather, and the shock to the unity of the church was enough to send Edwards tumbling out of his pulpit, twenty-three years of spectacularly faithful and fruitful ministry notwithstanding.

Edwards had seven more years to live. They would mainly be spent in Stockbridge, a mission settlement further west in Massachusetts. The last few months of his life were spent in Princeton, New Jersey.

Edwards arrived in Princeton on February 16, 1758, and was formally installed as the President of the College that same day. One week later, February 23, he was inoculated for small pox, and after one month, lacking a day, on March 22, 1758, he died from it. Jonathan Edwards lived to be only fifty-four.

But in his brief life he had had the privilege of having a ministry of tremendous importance for a number of reasons. Not least among those reasons was his strong reassertion of the visible nature of the church, particularly reflected in his understanding of the Lord's Supper as an ordinance for believers.

THE SETTING FOR THE CONTROVERSY

The controversy surrounding Edwards's views on Communion had gone on for a couple of years, from 1748 until its resolution by his dismissal in 1750. The setting for the controversy was a church already frayed by tensions between the pastor and a few of the leading families. In what has been called the "Bad Book Case" in 1744—which George Marsden, in his magisterial recent biography of Edwards, has argued we should call the "young folks' Bible" case—Edwards had alienated (probably unnecessarily) a number of families by reading publicly the names of children whom he wanted to see concerning a certain scandal, thereby leaving the public impression that all of these children had behaved scandalously. In fact, all Edwards was really doing was asking that certain of the young people come to see him so that he could get information from them.[3] Pastors will understand the importance of such small mis-calculations, as well as their incalculable effects. Marsden describes Edwards as one "never given to excessive tact" and as having a person-ality that was "brittle" and "unsociable."[4]

Edwards continued to pastor the church and write prolifically, pro-ducing most notably *A Treatise Concerning Religious Affections* in 1746, and in 1747 *A Humble Attempt to Promote Explicit Agreement*, and in 1749 *An Account of the Life of Rev. David Brainerd.*

But it was in 1748 that dissension really seemed to take hold in Edwards's church.

Dealing with the difficulties of pastoral ministry became even more difficult for Edwards when, in 1748, his influential and supportive uncle, Col. John Stoddard, died. Various clergy who had been disaffected with Edwards for one reason or another began to feel more free to voice their dissatisfactions. The divisions in his own congregation were encouraged. The Hawleys and the Williamses had had differences with Edwards. Some matters of church discipline, perhaps poorly handled, had caused stresses and strains.

THE COMMUNION CONTROVERSY

It was against the backdrop of these existing tensions that the contro-versy over Communion broke out in earnest. In December 1748, Edwards told someone that they must profess Christianity before they could take Communion. This simple instruction reversed decades of practice. Stoddard had specifically opposed such requirements. Edwards was now quietly asserting his pastoral authority in a new direction.

The applicant talked to others about this and then refused to pro-fess being a Christian. He was happy to profess godliness, but not being a Christian. He withdrew his request for membership in the church.

Tongues wagged, and eyebrows were raised. In February 1749 Edwards proposed that he preach about this change in the terms of admission to Communion. He proposed preaching a series of sermons to teach the congregation. The leaders preferred that Edwards make his case in print, and so he did. In the meantime, in April, Mary Hulbert

---

[3] George M. Marsden, *Jonathan Edwards: A Life* (New Haven, Conn.: Yale University Press, 2003), 292–302.
[4] Ibid., 344, 349.

presented herself for Communion and membership, but Edwards and the Church Committee could not agree on whether she should make a profession of faith in order to do this, or whether such an action would prejudice the church. In order to break the impasse, Edwards bought time by offering to resign if the church would wait until after his defense of this change was written and published, so that they would have a chance to carefully consider his views. By a 15 to 3 vote the committee would not agree to it; so she was not allowed to join. The very fact that Edwards offered to resign signals something of how frayed the relationships had become.

In the midst of all this, it became clear that Edwards had come to disagree with the Halfway Covenant—the practice in New England churches of baptizing the infants of baptized, yet non-communicant church members. This only further alienated many of Edwards's church members, who felt that their own rights to church privileges were being threatened.

In a letter to John Erskine in Scotland, written on May 20, 1749, Edwards mentioned the controversy:

> A very great difficulty has arisen between my people, relating to qualifications for communion at the Lord's table. My honoured grandfather Stoddard, my predecessor in the ministry over this church, strenuously maintained the Lord's Supper to be a converting ordinance, and urged all to come who were not of scandalous life, though they knew themselves to be unconverted. I formerly conformed to his practice but I have had difficulties with respect to it, which have been long increasing, till I dared no longer proceed in the former way, which has occasioned great uneasiness among my people, and has filled all the country with noise.[5]

By August 1749 his new book had arrived in Northampton: *An Humble Inquiry into the Rules of the Word of God Concerning the Qualifications Requisite to a Complete Standing and Full Communion in the Visible Christian Church.*[6] That fall a secular meeting of citizens urged the church to separate Edwards either from his new principles or

---

[5] Jonathan Edwards to John Erskine (May 20, 1749), in *The Works of Jonathan Edwards,* vol. 16, *Letters and Personal Writings,* ed. George S. Claghorn (New Haven, Conn.: Yale University Press, 1998), 271.

[6] Jonathan Edwards, "An Humble Inquiry . . ." in *The Works of Jonathan Edwards,* ed. Edward Hickman, 2 vols. (1834; reprint, Edinburgh: Banner of Truth, 1974), 1:431-484.

from his congregation. In December a council of local ministers was convened to look into the case.

In February 1750 Edwards decided to lecture on his opinions on Thursday afternoons at 2 P.M. The sermons were well-attended by visitors, but not by his own people. And they were to no avail. There was a series of divisive church meetings throughout the spring, issuing in a meeting of a council of ministers from June 19-22, 1750. The council asked to know the congregation's mind on the matter, and in a specially called members' meeting, only 10 percent of the church's members voted for Edwards to remain as their pastor. The ministerial council then decided (by one vote) that the relations between Edwards and the congregation in Northampton should be dissolved. In effect, the council narrowly ratified what the congregation clearly desired.

Marsden sums the matter up this way:

> Without his clumsily managed reversal of direction on [the terms of admission to the sacraments], he would have remained pastor in Northampton. True, there were pent-up resentments that came pouring out when the occasion arose. Nonetheless, the question of admission to the sacraments was in itself a momentous issue, with potential to disrupt even a harmonious relationship between a pastor and a town.[7]

Perhaps if Edwards had introduced this more gradually, matters would have turned out differently, but we can only speculate.

On July 1, 1750, Edwards preached one of the most remarkable sermons that he—or any pastor to my knowledge—has ever preached. He preached his farewell sermon from 2 Corinthians 1:14 (KJV): "As also ye have acknowledged us in part, that we are your rejoicing, even as ye also are ours in the day of the Lord Jesus."[8] This sermon is remarkable for its gravity and tenderness, its love and certainty, and the evident deep trust in God expressed by its preacher. Strangely enough, Edwards (in what must have been a rather awkward situation) continued to live in the parsonage and to preach for them Sunday by Sunday at their request, until October 1751, fifteen months later.

The next year, 1752, from his home in Stockbridge, Edwards sent to the press the only other major work he published on this question:

---

[7] Marsden, *Jonathan Edwards*, 370.
[8] Edwards, "Farewell Sermon," in *Works*, ed. Hickman, 1:cxcviii-ccvii.

Misrepresentations Corrected, and Truth Vindicated in a Reply to the Rev. Mr. Solomon Williams's Book.[9] This was his answer to Solomon Williams, Edwards's cousin, who had written defending Stoddard's practice and the decision of the Northampton church. Of course, this controversy had been settled by the dismissal of Edwards, so it was not continuing to disturb Northampton. Nevertheless, Edwards thought that he must correct certain misrepresentations.

By the end of the century Solomon Stoddard's "converting ordinances" idea—the idea that prevailed in the church at Northampton over Edwards's objections—became virtually extinct. After his death, Edwards's ideas won out.

CONCERN FOR THE VISIBILITY OF THE CHURCH

In all of this, it is evident that Edwards's concern was a concern that had marked various parts of the Reformation and that was especially typical of the New England Puritan heritage he had received—the concern for the *visibility* of the church. By requiring those who are considered full members of the church to profess and demonstrate conversion, Edwards was hearkening back to the need for a clear distinction between the church and the world that had been so typical of the Puritan movement that had originally motivated so much of the settlement of New England. He was willing to put all of his personal convenience as a forty-six-year-old man, with a large (and therefore expensive to maintain) family on the line for what he understood to be faithfulness to Scripture on this particular matter.

As earlier separatists had maintained before him, Edwards understood that the visible church will always be mixed, and yet its purity was an asset to be cherished and improved. Its certain mixture was in no way an excuse for indifference or complacence about the moral purity of the church. In his sermons and particularly in his *Humble Inquiry*, Edwards advocated the simple idea that "none ought to be admitted to the communion and privileges of members of the visible church of Christ in complete standing, but such as are in profession and in the eye of the church's Christian judgment godly or gracious persons."[10] Edwards summoned the examples of the church in the New Testament, both in

---

[9] *Works*, ed. Hickman, 1:485-531.

[10] Jonathan Edwards, "An Humble Inquiry into the Rules . . . Concerning . . . Communion in the Visible Christian Church," in *The Works of Jonathan Edwards*, vol. 12, *Ecclesiastical Writings*, ed. David Hall (New Haven, Conn.: Yale University Press, 1994), 182.

the Acts and in the Epistles, as supporting his case. Based on texts such as 1 Corinthians 11:28, "Let a man examine himself . . . and so eat," Edwards argued that "It is necessary, that those who partake of the Lord's Supper, should judge themselves truly and cordially to accept of Christ, as their only Savior and chief good; for this is what the actions, which communicants perform at the Lord's table, are a solemn profession of."[11] The argument is straightforward enough.

WHAT LESSONS CAN WE LEARN FOR TODAY?

What are we today to learn from Edwards's stand? Why should this be so important that Edwards would be willing to be maligned and even fired over it? The main thing that I have been challenged about as I reflect on Edwards's resolve in this matter is the clarity with which he perceived that the church is to be visible; it is to be visibly the church.

We are to remember afresh that part of what we need to do is not simply try to make the church as accessible and comfortable as possible for the nonbeliever, but we must labor to make it as pure and holy as we can for all concerned—believers and nonbelievers, ourselves and others, the church, and even for the glory of God himself.

J. H. Thornwell, the great Southern Presbyterian theologian of the nineteenth century, noticed the churches in his day moving in a dangerous direction, a direction that he feared might compromise the very message of the church. In a letter written in July 1846, Thornwell warned:

> Our whole system of operations gives an undue influence to money. Where money is the great *want, numbers* must be sought; and where an ambition for numbers prevails, doctrinal purity must be sacrificed. The root of the evil is in the *secular* spirit of all our ecclesiastical institutions. What we want is a *spiritual* body; a Church whose power lies in the truth, and the presence of the Holy Ghost. To *unsecularize* the Church should be the unceasing aim of all who are anxious that the ways of Zion should flourish.[12]

Like the compromised church at Northampton, so too among evangelicals of our own day, somewhere along the way something has hap-

---

[11] Ibid., 256.
[12] J. H. Thornwell, in a letter dated July 24, 1846, quoted in Benjamin Morgan Palmer, *The Life and Letters of James Henley Thornwell* (Richmond, Va.: Whittet & Shepperson, 1875), 291.

pened to our ideas of church membership. And what touches membership touches the visibility of the church, and thereby the clarity and credibility of the gospel we preach in the world. Edwards seemed to understand this, and to understand its importance.

Evangelicals today may not have self-consciously entered into a Halfway Covenant. We may not be inviting non-Christians to Communion officially as they were in Edwards's day, but can anyone deny that membership in a church—the symbolic core of which is being regularly welcomed to the Lord's Table—is less meaningful today than it was a century ago? And if that is true, what kind of progress does that evidence, or portend, in sanctification? In evangelization? In missions? In bringing glory to our great Creator and Savior?

Is this a peculiarly American phenomenon, a leftover from the cultural dominance evangelical Christianity did in the past enjoy?

I read recently that the average Baptist church in England had seventy-three members and eighty-five in attendance (according to the 1989 English Church Census). In the U.S., the average attendance on Sunday morning among Southern Baptist churches was actually somewhat smaller—seventy—but still comparable. What was way out of line was this: Instead of having a slightly smaller membership—almost all of whom would be in attendance, with some visitors added in—the average U.S. Southern Baptist church has 233 members![13] Do you remember the line in the old spiritual "Ezekiel Saw the Wheel" that says, "Some go to church for to sing and shout, before six months they's all turned out"? That seems to happen, then, not just to some, but to most! And it's not just among Baptists. The statistics of denomination after denomination, local congregation after local congregation, evidence a laxness about church membership that undermines the gospel. Surely this is similar to the situation Edwards faced.

In Part 3 of Edwards's *Humble Inquiry,* Edwards asked why parents would be so concerned that their children have the signs and symbols—baptism and the Lord's Supper—and so evidently less concerned that they have the realities symbolized by them! Edwards wrote:

> What is the name good for, without the thing? Can parents bear to have
> their children go about the world in the most odious and dangerous

---

[13] According to *SBC Research Review* 6 (Fall 1996): 1.

state of soul, in reality the children of the devil, and condemned to eternal burnings; when at the same time they can't bear to have them disgraced by going without the honor of being baptized! A high honor and privilege this is; yet how can parents be contented with the sign, exclusive of the thing signified! Why should they covet the external honor for their children, while they are so careless about the spiritual blessing![14]

Edwards goes on like this for pages!

Perhaps for us today, it is not strictly that membership has become meaningless and that it doesn't matter, but that it has the wrong meaning, and that it matters wrongly. Today a high-affection, low-commitment idea of membership is common. That is, today it may mean much to "leave someone's membership" in a particular place, but such a membership in itself evidences no commitment whatever to attend the church or pray for its ministry, to give to the church or to work to forward the gospel through it. What we need is an exact reversal to take place. Ideas of membership should not be so associated with affection (I can love those who are not members of my church; I sometimes find that easier!) and linked more simply to commitment. Yes, make allowances for those who have recently moved, those who are invalids, those who are temporarily away for education or business or military service. But normalcy should be that a member of a church is in regular attendance and is evidently growing in love to God and man and in holiness of life.

Church discipline, too, should be reinvigorated to recover this winsome and hope-giving distinction that we Christians are to have from the world. Writing in the 1940s, New Testament scholar H. E. Dana said:

> The abuse of discipline is reprehensible and destructive, but not more than the abandonment of discipline. Two generations ago the churches were applying discipline in a vindictive and arbitrary fashion which justly brought it into disrepute; today the pendulum has swung to the other extreme—discipline is almost wholly neglected. It is time for a new generation of pastors to restore this important function of the church to its rightful significance and place in church life.[15]

---

14 Edwards, "Inquiry," 316.
15 H. E. Dana, *Manual of Ecclesiology*, rev. ed. (Kansas City, Mo.: Central Seminary Press, 1944), 244.

Again, why is discipline important? Why is Edwards's recovery of the idea of regenerate church membership important? Because the gospel matters! And because God has elected to move in human history in a corporate way. Did he send his Son uniquely? Yes. Did he raise up individual prophets and apostles? Yes. Does he gift his church with individuals as pastors and teachers, servants and workers of mercy? Yes. Does he save us as individuals? Yes. But that is not the whole story!

By the stand that Edwards took, even to the sacrificing of his own reputation, position, and welfare, he was only reflecting God's own concern as we see it on the pages of Scripture when he desires members of the church to be those who are manifesting and displaying the glory of God. How will the satanic slander against the Creator's character be refuted? Not merely by individual conversions, but by the church, as the society of the redeemed, the company of the elect, the trophy of God's grace, showing his love and grace, his justice and holiness to each other.

Why Should We Exclude People from Communion?

Why should we act, like Edwards, to exclude certain people from the Lord's Table in our own local churches? Why should we act to discipline or exclude people from Communion? We could give many reasons, but let me just give you five.

For the good of the individual disciplined. (See 1 Corinthians 5:5; Galatians 6:1; 1 Timothy 1:20; Titus 1:13.) The man in 1 Corinthians 5 was lost in his sin, thinking God was fine with his having an affair with his father's wife. The people in the churches in Galatia thought it was fine that they were trusting in their own works rather than in Christ alone. Alexander and Hymenaeus thought they were fine in blaspheming God. But none of these were! So out of our love for such people, we want to see church discipline practiced. We don't want to allow them to come to the Lord's Table, to enjoy the benefits of membership in our churches. We don't want to publicly affirm to them or to the watching world that they are pictures of what it means to savingly repent and believe. We don't want our church to encourage hypocrites who are hardened and confirmed, lulled in their sins. We do not want to live that kind of life individually or as a church. We don't want to see people who are not partakers of Christ by faith being treated as if they were! And we want this clarified for their own good![16]

For the good of the other Christians, as they see the danger of sin. When Paul wrote to Timothy in 1 Timothy 5:20, he said that if a leader sins, he should be rebuked publicly. That doesn't mean that anytime I, as the pastor of my church, do anything wrong, members of my church should stand up in the public service and say, "Hey, Mark, you were wrong when you did this." It means that when there is a serious sin (particularly that's not repented of), it needs to be brought up in public so that others will take warning by seeing the serious nature of sin. Even Solomon Stoddard understood that those who were "scandalous livers" were not to partake of the Lord's Table. Is there anything at your church that would inhibit the "scandalous livers" from taking the Lord's Supper?

For the health of the church as a whole. (See 1 Corinthians 5:6-8.) Again in 1 Corinthians 5, when Paul was pleading with them, he said that they shouldn't have boasted about having such toleration for sin in the church. He asked rhetorically, "Don't you know that a little yeast works through the whole batch of dough?" Here yeast represented the unclean and spreading nature of sin. So Paul said, "Get rid of the old yeast that you may be a new batch without yeast—as you really are. For Christ, our Passover lamb, has been sacrificed. Therefore let us keep the Festival"—that's the Passover supper—"not with the old yeast, the yeast of malice and wickedness, but with bread without yeast, the bread of sincerity and truth" (NIV).

For the Passover meal a lamb was slaughtered, and unleavened bread was eaten. Paul here told the Corinthians that the lamb (Christ) had been slaughtered and that they (the Corinthian church) were to be the unleavened bread. They were to have no leaven of sin in them. They as a whole church were to be an acceptable sacrifice. This would seem to mean that there was to be no partaking by those who were not Christians, who had not been forgiven by Christ.

Of course, such a reason to practice discipline doesn't mean that discipline is the point of the church. Discipline is no more the point of the church than medicine is the point of life. Sometimes you are necessarily

---

[16] Advocate this, and it will really show up whether people have only a subjective, psychologized understanding of the Christian faith or if they really understand the real danger that we are in objectively because of our sins.

consumed with it, but generally it is no more than that which allows you to get on with your main task; it is certainly not the main task itself. The main task of the church, which Jonathan Edwards well knew, is glorifying God by preaching the good news of Jesus Christ. And yet, along with that, for the health of the church as a whole, Edwards also knew that church discipline should be practiced, and only those who give evidence of conversion should be allowed to come to the Lord's Table. Only they should be members of our churches.

We should want to see discipline practiced in a church for the corporate witness of the church. (See 1 Corinthians 5:1; John 13:34-35; Matthew 5:16; 1 Peter 2:12.) This is a powerful tool in evangelism. People notice when our lives are different, especially when there is a whole community of people whose lives are different. The church is not a community of people whose lives are perfect, but whose lives are marked by genuinely loving God and loving one another. Conformity to the world in our churches makes our evangelistic task all the more difficult. As Nigel Lee of English Inter-Varsity once said, "We become so like the unbelievers they have no questions they want to ask us." May we so live that people are made constructively curious.

And finally, the most compelling reason we have to practice church discipline is:

For the glory of God, as we reflect his holiness. (See Ephesians 5:25-27; Hebrews 12:10-14; 1 Peter 1:15-16; 2:9-12; 1 John 3:2-3.) That's why we're alive! We humans were made to bear God's image, to carry his character to his creation (see Gen. 1:27). So it is no surprise that throughout the Old Testament, as God fashioned a people to bear this image for himself, he instructed them in holiness so that their character might better approximate his own (Lev. 11:44a; 19:2; Prov. 24:1, 25). This was the basis for correcting and even excluding some of the people in the Old Testament, as God fashioned a people for himself.

And that was the basis for shaping the New Testament church as well (see 2 Cor. 6:14—7:1; 13:2; 1 Tim. 6:3-5; 2 Tim. 3:1-5). In the passages already mentioned, we find that as Christians we are supposed to be conspicuously holy, not for our own reputation, but for God's reputation. So in Matthew 5 we see that we are to be the light of the world and that when people see our good deeds they are to glorify God (v. 16). Peter says the same thing: "Keep your conduct among the Gentiles honorable, so that when they speak against you as evildoers, they may see your good deeds and glorify God on the day of visitation" (1 Pet. 2:12). This is why God has called us and saved us and set us apart (Col. 1:21-22). What else should we look like if we bear his name? Paul wrote to the church at Corinth:

> *Do you not know that the unrighteous will not inherit the kingdom of God? Do not be deceived: neither the sexually immoral, nor idolaters, nor adulterers, nor men who practice homosexuality, nor thieves, nor the greedy, nor drunkards, nor revilers, nor swindlers will inherit the kingdom of God. And such were some of you. But you were washed, you were sanctified, you were justified in the name of the Lord Jesus Christ and by the Spirit of our God. (1 Cor. 6:9-11)*

From the very beginning, Jesus had sent his disciples out to teach people to obey all that he had taught (Matt. 28:19-20). God will have a holy people to reflect his character.

And then when you read the picture of the church at the end of the book of Revelation, you see it is this glorious bride that reflects the character of Christ himself. In chapter 21, and then in chapter 22, we read the words of Christ: "Outside are the dogs and the sorcerers and the sexually immoral and murderers and idolaters, and everyone who loves and practices falsehood" (22:15).

Taking 1 Corinthians 5 as a model, churches have long recognized church discipline as one of the boundaries that make church membership mean something. The assumption is that a church member is someone who can appropriately take Communion without bringing disgrace on the church, condemnation on themselves, or dishonor to God and his gospel (see 1 Cor. 11). Edwards understood better than his grandfather that it was not only moral uprightness but true spiritual life that is to be reflected in the church. It is by the collection of such spiritually alive people coming together that God is glorified as the church is made visible. It is through the church being made visible that the gospel is displayed. And the gospel glorifies God.

What was it Jesus said? "Let your light shine before others, so that they may see your good works and give glory to your Father who is in heaven" (Matt. 5:16). It is this shining, this visibility of the light of God's Word and of his hope for sinners that is the role of the church and that pastors should cultivate in churches—even if people resent it and misunderstand us, gossip about us and are cruel to us and our families, even if it costs us our jobs and our reputations—as it did Jonathan Edwards. But then, Edwards didn't live to please men but to please God.

I love the statement of David Hall about Edwards's conduct during the ministerial council's investigation of him, when they delivered the news that his relation with the Northampton congregation should be dissolved. This witness of Edwards's reaction at the time recorded, "That faithful witness received the shock, unshaken. I never saw the least symptoms of displeasure in his countenance the whole week but he appeared like a man of God, whose happiness was out of the reach of his enemies."[17]

This was Jonathan Edwards's vision of the visible church—visible for the glory of God. And it is a vision that we today should reaffirm. The church is to be constituted of believers, so that it will be visible for the glory of God. And that glory comes not by our exulting in our independence, but in our glorious dependence on God, and in creating distinct societies of love in a world of God-ignoring selfishness. God help us when our doctrine of the church stands to protect human pride and selfish individualism. God help us recover the true vision of the church— the vision that, by God's grace, Edwards really had—the vision of the church visibly shining and distinct from the world, radiantly distinct, visible for the glory of God!

---

[17] Marsden, *Jonathan Edwards*, 361.

7

TRUSTING THE THEOLOGY OF
A SLAVE OWNER

Sherard Burns

In his book *A Dream Deferred*, Shelby Steele writes that loneliness "is no doubt a risk that trails every effort to define one's beliefs. Most people could empty half of any room simply by saying what they truly believe."[1] I, like many of you, have felt this kind of "loneliness," and, in many ways for the cause of Christ and truth, I have come to expect it. When one deals with the issue of race or race relations, past and present, one enters into a realm of discussion that is tense, filled with emotion and assumptions and all kinds of feelings that make discussion difficult. But if endured, the discussion can often be fruitful. The content of this chapter deals with such an issue—namely, Jonathan Edwards and his understanding of slavery.

Nothing has been more of a stain on our history than the institution and cruelty of slavery in America. Try as one may to undermine its unspeakable evil, the present existence of varying worlds in the United States in particular (the world of the white, black, Hispanic, etc.) finds its roots in the mentality and social ideals that promoted and perpetuated slavery—namely, European ethnocentrism. The driving principle behind this institution was not simply economic prosperity, since to enslave anyone for financial gain one must first assume a moral right to enslave, as well as suppose the lack of freedom of those they would hold in bondage. Thus what formed the very heart of slavery was the belief that some had the authority to impose their rights on others in such a way that stealing men, women, and children from their native land, tearing families apart, and systematically dehuman-

---

[1] Shelby Steele, *A Dream Deferred: The Second Betrayal of Black Freedom in America* (New York: HarperCollins, 1994), 3.

izing them was condoned and rewarded. Hence merchandise was made of oppression.

One of the most troubling facts concerning slavery was its association with Christianity. Not only those who were deemed unregenerate and heathen owned slaves; those who professed to have met the true Liberator, Christ, also refused such liberty to men. This was then, and remains today, a difficult barrier for many to traverse. Yet it is our history, and if we affirm with the Scriptures that God is the Lord of history and long to honor Christ with the whole of our understanding of reality and desire to love one another as we ought, we must look through the lens of heaven if we are to make sense of it and glorify God in all things.

In preparing this chapter I wanted to understand how Edwards, with his intellect and theological understanding and love for God, could own slaves and do so till the day of his death. It was clear to me that in order for African Americans, or any other person of color, to hear and appreciate Edwards, that question had to be answered since it represents one reason for hesitation. I do not suppose that I will answer every question that will arise from the reading of this chapter. The topic is so vast and varied that it may raise additional questions that, I hope, will compel each of us to dig and find what is there to be explored and attained.

EDWARDS ON SLAVERY

The only known treatment by Edwards on this topic is his recently discovered "Draft Letter on Slavery."[2] In it we find not only his view on slavery, but also the rationale behind his condemnation of the slave trade. Its contents are not readily discernible due to the typical style employed by Edwards as he sought to get his mind around a topic or an issue. Kenneth Minkema writes:

> The draft is typical of Edwards' habits of letter writing. In preparing many of his letters, particularly those of an important nature, Edwards first sketched out major points and transitions in an elliptical, stream-of-consciousness manner on a scrap of paper and then wrote the letter in full on good foolscap.[3]

---

[2] Jonathan Edwards, "Draft Letter on Slavery," in *The Works of Jonathan Edwards*, vol. 16, *Letters and Personal Writings*, ed. George S. Claghorn (New Haven, Conn.: Yale University Press, 1998), 71-76.

[3] Kenneth Minkema, "Jonathan Edwards on Slavery and the Slave Trade," *William and Mary Quarterly* 54 (October 1997): 823.

As of today, no fuller treatment of this draft has been discovered, if indeed it ever existed.

THE OCCASION OF THE DRAFT

On the occasion of this draft, Edwards biographer George Marsden writes:

> Some parishioners at the church in Northfield . . . had denounced their pastor Benjamin Doolittle, for owning African slaves. The accusation was only one part of larger controversy between Doolittle and part of his congregation, led by a number of older men in the town. The "disaffected brethren" accused Doolittle who had been their pastor since 1716, of making exorbitant salary demands. . . . Some of the discontent arose from suspicions that Doolittle had Arminian leanings and that he was cool toward awakenings. At the moment, however, the controversy over slaveowning had come before the Hampshire Association, and Edwards was chosen to draft a response.[4]

The writing of this draft reveals several things about Edwards and his view on slavery. First of all, it is interesting that Edwards would even consider writing in defense of a man who opposed him theologically and who held opposing views with regard to awakenings. Noting this oddity, Marsden comments: "That he would do so is striking because he probably shared the suspicions that Doolittle had unorthodox and Old Light leanings."[5] The implication is that Edwards was engaged in theological compromise on this issue. The evidence of this is recognized when one considers the fact that "Doolittle was reputed to be an anti-Calvinist 'Arminian,' and in other contexts, would have been Edwards' staunch foe."[6] If what Marsden writes is accurate—namely, that Edwards knew of Doolittle's theological persuasions and negative feelings toward awakenings—we come to see how socially ingrained and acceptable the oppression of Africans in America had become. That Edwards would defend Doolittle, a man who opposed everything he stood for theologically, on this issue of slavery betrays a more immediate concern with

---

[4] George M. Marsden, *Jonathan Edwards: A Life* (New Haven, Conn.: Yale University Press, 2003), 256.
[5] Ibid.
[6] Harry S. Stout and Kenneth Minkema, "The Edwardsean Tradition and Antebellum Slavery" (www.law.yale.edu/outside/pdf/centers/sc/Stout_Minkema.pdf), 2.

the existence of the institution of slavery than with theological consistency.

This compromise demonstrates the impact that a culture and its accepted norms can exert upon the church. That a man of Edwards's learning and convictions could defend Doolittle on the issue of slavery demonstrates the ongoing battle the church wages with the cultural ethics in which it exists and the ethics of the home for which it strives. "Here, as in other places, we see how experience could shape and transform theology in most scientific ways."[7]

R. C. Sproul has said that when he disagrees with the giants of the Christian faith, he does so with fear and trembling. I feel the same way as I write this concerning Edwards. It is a difficult thing to posit that Edwards compromised theologically when what we have known of him in virtually every other case is theological precision and conviction. Yet the facts remain. However, though such compromise happened, we must be careful to remember that, though he was a brilliant thinker, he, like all of us, still fought against the remaining effects of sin. This should not leave us thinking only of the culture's influence over Edwards but should raise in our own minds the question of whether or not some of our assumptions and perceptions are culturally driven rather than theologically driven. If a man of great learning and religion such as Jonathan Edwards could be driven by culture's influence, how much more might many in the church today, who are not given to the same biblical and theological precision as Edwards, be similarly influenced?

A second observation gleaned from Edwards's draft concerns what did *not* prompt him to write. It seems doubtful that Edwards would have *ever* written anything on the subject, since what occasioned the writing of the draft was not his own internal promptings concerning slavery and the slave trade but a controversy that had become prevalent in his day. Stout and Minkema comment:

> . . . he threw theological differences to the side and stood shoulder to shoulder with Doolittle. . . . So it was that Edwards, the Calvinist, promoter of revivalism, found himself in the ironic position of defending an Arminian, Old Light critic of the awakenings on an issue he never cared to address before.[8]

---

[7] Ibid.
[8] Ibid.

This being the case, what was it that compelled Edwards to defend and side with an Arminian slave owner and write about a subject that, supposedly, he never cared to discuss? The prime motivation behind Edwards's action was the reality that he himself owned slaves. It was not that he felt a great burden against the atrocities of slavery, if indeed he knew them at all, nor that there was great desire to see the institution abolished and men gain the freedom that he and others like him enjoyed as gifts from God.

> By many accounts Edwards was America's greatest religious thinker and, according to Perry Miller, was "so far ahead of his time that our own can hardly be said to have caught up with him." Unfortunately, Edwards' progressivism did not extend to the question of slavery. In fact, Edwards was a slave owner who purchased a number of slaves in the course of his lifetime . . . he bought his first slave in the auctions at Newport, Rhode Island, the major northern hub of the Atlantic slave trade.[9]

Minkema writes: "[I]n 1731 they purchased three: Joseph, Lee and a woman named Venus. . . . [L]isted in the inventory of his estate in 1758, [was] a 'negro boy' named Titus."[10]

Whatever Edwards knew about slavery did not affect his participation in it. Stout and Minkema write:

> [What] we now know of the brutalizing dehumanization of the slave market did not faze him. . . . Apparently, Edwards was so at home with the institution of slavery, and the status that it conferred on aristocratic clergymen, such as himself, that he never really questioned its central tenets. . . . That any congregation would feel justified in censoring and removing their pastor over the issue of slavery was an affront to Edwards' aristocratic sensibilities and sense of clerical status.[11]

While some have argued that he was ambivalent on this issue of slavery, the fact that he owned slaves until his death without any record of granting their freedom upon his death makes such an idea difficult to embrace. In his draft he "acknowledged [slavery's] inequities and dis-

---

[9] Ibid., 2.

[10] Minkema, "Jonathan Edwards on Slavery and the Slave Trade," 825.

[11] Stout and Minkema, "The Edwardsean Tradition," 2.

turbing implications,"[12] yet continued to endorse and sanction its legitimacy. If by *ambivalent* we refer to Edwards's wholesale view of slavery and the slave trade, this may be true. Edwards embraced slavery along with others, but unlike most, he denounced the slave trade (as we shall see below). This position "represents a transitional stage in the development of antislavery thought among elites between complete advocacy of slavery and the immediatism of his first generation, New Divinity disciples."[13]

In Edwards's day "slave-owning was an elite practice. . . . A significant number of ministers owned slaves as a symbol of social status."[14] Slavery had become so embedded in the fabric of society and so necessary for the prosperity of man and country that any confrontation to its legitimacy was to call into question an accepted way of life. So intertwined was the condoning of slavery by the church that "Edwards . . . perceived that such railings against the minister could be to the great wounding of religion."[15] Driven by a dual reality—namely, that he owned slaves and knowing that a threat to the slaveholding of any one minister was a threat to the slaveholding of any minister—Edwards dismissed theological differences and defended Doolittle, the Arminian.

EDWARDS'S DEFENSE OF SLAVERY

Edwards was a masterful logician, and this ability is seen in the manner in which he defends slavery. "In characteristic fashion, Edwards began his defense with an unrelenting offense, charging the congregation with hypocrisy and an unbecoming resistance to clerical superiority."[16] Against such Edwards argued:

> How ill does it suit for a man to cry out of another for taking money that is stolen, and then taking of it of him that wherein the injustice consists. If the slaves are unjustly theirs, then their slavery is unjustly theirs, and of this they are partakers of. All the difference there can be, is that they are not so immediate partakers, that it is a step farther off. . . . Their argument, if it carries anything, implies that we ought

---

[12] Minkema, "Jonathan Edwards on Slavery and the Slave Trade," 825.
[13] Ibid.
[14] Ibid., 826.
[15] Marsden, *Jonathan Edwards*, 256.
[16] Stout and Minkema, "The Edwardsean Tradition," 3.

not to be partakers at all. If they don't mean so, but only mean by so many steps, they would do well to fix the number of steps. And besides, they don't know but that they are partakers as immediately as we. They may have their slaves at next step. Let them also fully and thoroughly vindicate themselves and their own practice in partaking of negroes' slavery, or confess that there is not hurt in partaking in it, or else let 'em cease to partake in it for the future, one of the three. For if they still continue to cry out against those who keep negro slaves as partakers of injustice in making them slaves, and continue still themselves notwithstanding to be partakers of their slavery, let 'em own that their objections are not conscientious, but merely to make difficulty and trouble for their neighbors.[17]

The argument is clear and consistent. Those who were opposing slavery were at the same time benefiting from what they opposed by continuing to profit from slave labor. "In this way they are partakers of a far more cruel slavery than that which they object against in those that have slaves."[18] From the quote above, Edwards conceived of three options these opposers could take.

One option would be for them to take slaves for themselves. In light of the conflict between Edwards and the opposers of slavery, this may appear to be an odd option, but in the mind of Edwards, to oppose slavery and yet to continue to benefit from and not condemn the slave trade was hypocrisy. Thus, "calling for the cessation of slaveholding while continuing to participate indirectly in the slave trade implied a never ending increase of enslaved people."[19] In such a case Edwards held that "They may have their slaves at next step."[20]

A second option would be to admit that there was nothing morally evil in slave owning. This argument is dependent on the argument of the first option. If the slave trade necessitated slave owning, those who continued to benefit from the trade did not have to take slaves themselves but should, by reason of logic, close their mouths from speaking any further opposition.

A third option would be to refuse to benefit from slave labor and slave trading altogether. This was perhaps the most consistent position

---

[17] Edwards, "Draft Letter on Slavery," 72–73.

[18] Ibid., 72.

[19] Minkema, "Jonathan Edwards on Slavery and the Slave Trade," 827.

[20] Edwards, "Draft Letter on Slavery," 72.

that the opposers could take, but at the same time it was difficult to almost impossible since "The whole economy of New England . . . depended on products produced by African slavery (a key part in New England's trade was with the slave economies of the Caribbean)."[21]

What happened as a result of this draft with Doolittle and those who opposed him is not readily known. What we do know is that Edwards delivered an undeniably decisive blow to the arguments of those who opposed the institution by highlighting the contradictions inherent in their arguments. These same contradictions pointed out by Edwards, however, are evident in his own logic in denouncing the slave trade.

DENOUNCING THE SLAVE TRADE

Edwards held that the slave trade was being continued on faulty grounds—namely, seeing God's allowance of Israel to plunder the Egyptians before the Exodus as a parallel and justification for the slave trade.[22] That is, in the mind of slavery's defenders, the Exodus formed the basis and rationale for taking slaves. For Edwards, however, to take people from their land and to hold them in bondage was an unjustifiable atrocity since it "would have a much greater tendency to sin, to have liberty to disfranchise whole nations."[23] Minkema writes:

> He used the word "disfranchise" to describe the practice, by which he meant depriving individuals of the freedom, rights, and privileges they enjoyed in their native country. Thus he presented the question "whether Scripture warranted the enslavement of non Christians" and answered negatively. He queried "if God's observing & Giving Leave for a thing prove it is not unreasonable in its own nature." Again, the implied answer was "No." One cannot, he held, make a "special" injunction to God's people (whether Israel of old or Christians under the New Testament) into an "Established Rule." "A special precept for a particular act is not a Rule. . . ." For example, in Deuteronomy 15:6 God allowed Israel to plunder the Egyptians before the Exodus, but this, Edwards stated, "is quite a different thing from Establishing it as a rule that his People might borrow and not pay in all ages."[24]

[21] Marsden, *Jonathan Edwards*, 258.
[22] Minkema, "Jonathan Edwards on Slavery and the Slave Trade," 827.
[23] Edwards, "Draft Letter on Slavery," 73.
[24] Minkema, "Jonathan Edwards on Slavery and the Slave Trade," 827.

Edwards also argued against the trade on the basis of what it means to love one's neighbor and examined who, in fact, "neighbor" refers to.

> [Edwards] took particular exception to a narrow definition of "Neighbor" as identifying only fellow believers. If neighbors were limited to Christians, then any sort of immoral behavior toward others was permissible. "This," Edwards commented, "makes the SS. [Scriptures] Contradict it self." Such a circumscribed definition of neighbor negated the moral law, which Christians were obliged to follow regardless of where they lived.[25]

The slave trade, according to Edwards, was against the moral law of God since it imposed on the liberties of men in their native land and, at the root of its execution, was a belief that such persons were not neighbors and thus did not deserve the love commanded in the law of God. Those who would condone the trade were "partakers of a far more cruel slavery than that which they object against in those that have slaves."[26] While Edwards was right in his understanding of the cruelty of the trade, he did not carry the same logic to his understanding of slavery. The argument used to debunk the critics of slavery—namely, that to participate in the trade was to necessitate the institution—now stood in the face of Edwards. To condone slavery contradicts condemning the trade since the existence of slaves in the States is owing to rejection of the moral law and also the fact that the institution demands the trade.

The dichotomy in all of this is that Edwards would "oppose the overseas trade, even though he had hitherto purchased his slaves through it."[27] Thus, to condemn the trade and at the same time to participate in the selling and buying of slaves was a glaring contradiction.

An illustration of this can be seen in a man who condemns the transporting of illegal drugs by cartels all over the world into the U.S. and at the same time is an active participant in the buying and distribution of those drugs in America. No one, except other drug dealers, could ever buy such logic since the one (selling and buying drugs) necessitates the other (the transporting of drugs to the U.S.). It is on this basis that many after Edwards, including Edwards, Jr., Samuel Hopkins, and

---

[25] Ibid., 828.
[26] Edwards, "Draft Letter on Slavery," 72.
[27] Stout and Minkema, "The Edwardsean Tradition," 3.

Lemuel Haynes, sought the cessation of not only the institution but the trade as well.

From where we sit today, looking back at that period of history and the subsequent influence that the thought of Edwards would have on America, it seems that with one strike of a pen, perhaps, Edwards could have exerted a radical influence on the way we view and understand race in American society. But he, like many before him and after him, did not rise to the occasion on this issue.

Another noteworthy point concerning the primacy of culture in slaveholding is the view of Edwards toward African and Native Americans. Marsden writes:

> Even though Edwards regarded African and Native American civilizations as vastly inferior to Christendom, especially since these heathen peoples had suffered so long under Satan's rule, he thought they were very equal to Christian nations both in their rights and potentialities. In his sermons on *The History of the Work of Redemption* . . . he assured the Northamptonians that although these peoples now lived almost like the beasts in some respects, it would not always be that way. In the millennium era . . . "[It] may be hoped that then many of the Negroes and Indians will be divines, and that excellent books will be published in Africa, in Ethiopia, in Turkey—and not only very learned men, but others that are more ordinary men, shall then be very knowing in religion." [28]

Edwards, Jr., son of Jonathan and a noted abolitionist, "grappling with his own family's history and slave ownership . . . sought to exonerate them," including his father, "by pleading at once their Christian sincerity and their ignorance."[29] Though arguments may and perhaps could abound against such reasoning, understanding Edwards's view on revelation as being progressive, this may well be true. While Edwards could very well believe something different than what is stated, we find nothing but words of equality as he understood equality in his day.

"We are made of the same human race," [Edwards] had written in a note on Job 31:15[30] . . . perhaps soon after he became a slave-

---

[28] Marsden, *Jonathan Edwards*, 258.

[29] Stout and Minkema, "The Edwardsean Tradition," 15.

[30] "Did not he who made me in the womb make him? and did not one fashion us in the womb?" (KJV).

owner. "In these two things," he wrote, "are contained the most forcible reasons against the master's abuse of his servant, viz. that both have one Maker and that their Maker made 'em alike with the same nature."[31]

Interestingly enough, the logic Edwards used to diffuse the arguments of those who condemned Doolittle and others for owning slaves was not used in the seeming contradiction of Edwards—condemning the trade and yet owning slaves, keeping the trade alive, at least in the sense that his behavior in no way was a deterrent to others who might desire to purchase slaves.

HOW COULD HE OWN SLAVES?

In an effort to help make sense of how Edwards could own slaves, Marsden calls us to "consider Edwards' attitudes towards slavery in the context of his hierarchical assumptions . . . where it was assumed that higher orders of society would have servants to perform domestic and farm labor."[32] Before we can adequately move to any conclusions concerning Edwards and slavery, we must battle the natural inclination of removing Edwards from his historical-cultural context and then viewing him through our modern assumptions. Perhaps for some in the African-American community this kind of cultural imposition has hastened judgment without due consideration for that kind of cultural understanding to which Marsden calls each of us.

In coming to the aid of his fellow minister and in owning slaves himself, another question that arises is, how could such behavior be justified by a man whose vision of God was as glorious as any in America? Robert J. Cameron, in his book *The Last Pew on the Left*, comments:

> The only reasonable explanation for intellectual ministers like Edwards . . . owning slaves and preaching that slaves were not to seek to be free, is the pervasive, perpetual, subtle influence of the sin nature possessed by all. . . . Could it be that these men were more interested in maintaining their lifestyles and justifying the tranquility and economic growth of the colonies . . . than they were in carrying out the Great

---

[31] Marsden, *Jonathan Edwards*, 258.
[32] Ibid., 255-256.

Commission, or assisting their congregations in the transformation of their minds?[33]

As stated above, Jonathan Edwards was a sinner saved by the grace of God, who still battled with the remaining effects of his fallen condition. This in no way stands to exonerate him for the role he played in sustaining slavery; rather it brings into perspective the way in which sin can have effect in our lives.

In the cosmic sense of reality, owning slaves is no different from any other sin, in that all sin is against God, and all of us are capable of the greatest of evils were God to release his restraining hand for his eternal purposes. What is interesting, however, is that while we must see sin as the cause of Edwards's behavior, Edwards himself never called what he and his other colonists were doing "sin." To Edwards, slavery was a necessary evil that served some positive good in the natural order that God had decreed—a thought his disciples would take up some years following his death. Yet if Edwards was wrong, it is not his God or his theology that is to blame—only his sin.[34] Reformed theology did not produce a heart to own slavery.

A second way to understand how Edwards could own slaves is a matter of his own heritage. The only life that Edwards knew was one in which the enslavement of Africans was an acceptable practice. A rather lengthy quote from Minkema will demonstrate this point.

> As a clergyman and a member of the social elite, Edwards was representative of the slaveowning class in New England. . . . Many of Edwards' relatives and friends owned slaves as a symbol of social status. Alternatively, they used slaves to augment their often tardy salaries by hiring them out as day laborers. Jonathan's father, Timothy, owned a slave named Ansars. His wife, Sarah Pierpont Edwards, sought to purchase slaves of her own. The reverend Timothy Woodbridge of Hartford, Connecticut, owned an Indian boy and African slave; Elisha Williams of Wethersfield, Connecticut, rector of Yale College from 1726 to 1739, owned an Indian woman. Both of these men were relatives of Edwards. In Massachusetts, such prominent ministers as

---

[33] Robert J. Cameron, *The Last Pew on the Left: America's Lost Potential* (Layfayette, La.: Prescott Press, 1995), 82.

[34] I am grateful to John Piper for this insight.

Edward Holyoke, president of Harvard College, and Nathan Webb of
Uxbridge were slave-owners.[35]

By no means is this to be a justification for Edwards's slaveholding, but
it is an attempt to set him in his proper context. Marsden cautions us
against the natural inclination to view men of history from our own contexts, stating that we should think

> about Edwards as an *eighteenth-century* figure and about how that
> context should shape [our] understanding of him . . . it would be a fail-
> ure of imagination if we were to start out by simply judging people of
> the past for having outlooks that are not like our own. Rather, we must
> first try to enter sympathetically into an earlier world and to under-
> stand its people. Once we do that we will be in a far better position
> both to learn from them and to evaluate their outlooks critically.[36]

The grounds for such cultural imposition centered around two
"ethical" premises of slave owning: (1) They were to be treated
humanely, and (2) they were to be Christianized.

First, Edwards held that slaves could be rightly owned *if they were
treated humanely*. On the assumption of humane treatment Edwards
could not be found at fault. There is in fact no record of any abuse or
ill treatment by Edwards toward his slaves. "In 1740, Jonathan and
Sarah cosigned to guarantee the financial support of 'Jethro Negro and
his wife Ruth,' who were manumitted in the will of Sarah's step
mother."[37]

It is true, perhaps, that the majority of northern slave owners
treated their slaves with much more respect and dignity, though still not
as fellow image bearers of God, than their southern counterparts did.
Having said that, while humane treatment was a justification for slavery, it was not at all a valid one. Throughout history that has been the
dominant cry of the white church in seeking to minimize the horrific
consequences of slavery, even in our day, appealing that many were
treated well. In response, listen to the words of one of Edwards's disciples to whom he was most connected (his son):

---

35 Minkema, "Jonathan Edwards on Slavery and the Slave Trade," 826.
36 Marsden, *Jonathan Edwards*, 2.
37 Ibid., 255.

Should we be willing, that the Africans or any other nation should purchase us, our wives and children, transport us into Africa and there sell
us into perpetual and absolute slavery? Should we be willing that they
by large bribes and offers of a gainful traffic should entice our neighbors to kidnap and sell us to them, and that they should hold, in perpetual and cruel bondage, not only ourselves, but our posterity through
all generations? Yet why is it not as right for them to treat us in this
manner, as it for us to treat them in the same manner? Their colour
indeed is different from ours. But does this give us the right to enslave
them? The nations of Germany to Guinea have complexions of every
shade from the fairest white, to the jetty black: and if a black com-
plexion subject a nation or an individual to slavery; where shall slavery begin? Or where shall it end.[38]

Edwards, Jr.'s statement is better grasped by an illustration to the
point. Let's say that someone came to your home and took away your
child. For years you searched and after much agony found her location
and her captor. You then say to him that you are going to press charges
against him because he kidnapped your child, broke up your family, and
caused much grief and despair. To your charge he responds, "But I
treated her well." It is doubtful that this would be an acceptable explanation to drop the charges and continue life, business as usual.

This is what Edwards, Jr., is asking, and the tone of his argument
suggests that the slaveholders—none in that day, and for certain no
right-minded person in our day— would be satisfied with the claim that
their kidnapped loved one was treated humanely. The issue is not how
slaves were treated, but the fact that they were slaves in the first place.
While Edwards held that the slave trade was cruel and an abomination
to God, those who followed him would condemn both slavery and the
trade as great evils and causes of divine retribution from God upon the
nation—namely, the Revolutionary War.

On a similar note, Hopkins added that if slavery was not abolished
in America, the practice would "practically authorize any nation or people, who have the power to do it, to make [them] their slaves."[39]

Second, Edwards held that slaves could be owned *if they were*

[38] Jonathan Edwards [Jr.], *Injustice and Impolicy of the Slave Trade and of the Slavery of Africans . . .
A Sermon* (New Haven, Conn.: Thomas and Samuel Green, 1791). The entire text can be read online
at the National Digital Library: http://memory.loc.gov.
[39] David S. Lovejoy, "Samuel Hopkins: Religion, Slavery, and the Revolution," *The New England
Quarterly* 40 (June 1967): 235.

Christianized, which has been long stated as the reason God ordained slavery. To his credit, Edwards not only preached to the Africans but included them in the membership of his church.

> In his own effort to convert slaves, Edwards in his regular preaching did not draw metaphysical differences between races. He exhorted both, "black and white" to "hearken to the call of Christ." Christ he declared, "Condescends to take notice of serv[an]ts & people of all nations[;] he Condescends to poor negroes."[40]

There were nine full communicant African-American members of his Northampton church; "[Six] of these, including the Edwardses' slave Leah, were products of the awakening . . . and became communicants in 1736. Around this time the church admitted two Indian members, Mary and Phoebe Stockbridge."[41]

Nothing is said of their status in the church, or whether they were allowed to sit with the whites in the congregation. On the one hand, from what we know of history, broadly speaking, we can deduce that they were excluded in many ways. Yet on the other hand, Edwards was faithful, as he saw faithfulness to this issue, to the blacks of his day by way of evangelism.[42] Having said that, whatever the case may be with regard to Edwards and his evangelizing of slaves, we are always brought back to the reality that is at the heart of this entire chapter: the institution of slavery and its unjustified existence as it was expressed in America.

There is an inherent contradiction in offering Christ to men and women whom you hold in bondage, against their own will, and on the basis of man-stealing. Murray J. Harris, in his book *Slaves of Christ*, states:

> If we may generalize, ancient writers about slavery, assuming the inevitability and necessity of slavery for the well being of society,

---

40 Minkema, "Jonathan Edwards on Slavery and the Slave Trade," 829.

41 Marsden, *Jonathan Edwards*, 258.

42 Note the title of a recently transcribed, previously unpublished sermon by Edwards: "All Mankind of All Nations, White and Black, Young and Old, Is Going in One or the Other of These Paths, Either in the Way That Leads to Life or the Way That Leads to Destruction," in *The Blessing of God: Previously Unpublished Sermons of Jonathan Edwards*, ed. Michael D. McMullen (Nashville: Broadman & Holman, 2003), 225-230. This sermon was given to the Indians at Stockbridge, but his concern to mention "white and black" suggests that evangelism of African-Americans was an important consideration for him.

focused their attention not on the slave's gaining or regaining of physical independence but on the need for spiritual freedom in the midst of physical servitude. Although the body may be enslaved, the spirit or the mind remains free, while the spirit of many free people is enslaved to passions. But this was not the emphasis of Christianity. For the early Christians, whether slave or free, both body and spirit belong to the Lord (1 Cor. 6:15, 17) and slavery to him constituted true freedom.[43]

Here I am compelled to make some comments concerning the difference between sanctioned slavery in the Bible and the institution of slavery in America. When people discuss slavery, they do so with preconceived ideas, assuming that others hold the same definitions and understandings of the words that create those ideas.

The argument that says slavery was not evil because the Bible does not say slavery is evil is not sound, since it relies upon a number of assumptions that turn out to be untrue. One is that the slavery in America modeled the sanctioned slavery in the Bible. But that is not the case. Rather than asking, "What does the Bible say with regard to rightfully owning slaves?" we should first ask, "What does the Scripture *prohibit* in the owning of slaves?" Harris helps us on this issue, stating that the Scriptures forbid "the exploitation of the slave for monetary gain" and "the kidnapping of persons for slavery and trafficking in slavery."[44]

Harris cites the incident in Acts 16 where Paul had cast the evil spirit out of the slave girl who mocked Paul and the gospel. Luke writes:

> As we were going to the place of prayer, we were met by a slave girl who had a spirit of divination and brought her owners much gain by fortune-telling. She followed Paul and us, crying out, "These men are servants of the Most High God, who proclaim to you the way of salvation." And this she kept doing for many days. Paul, having become greatly annoyed, turned and said to the spirit, "I command you in the name of Jesus Christ to come out of her." And it came out that very hour. But when her owners saw that their hope of gain was gone, they seized Paul and Silas and dragged them into the marketplace before the rulers. (Acts 16:16-19)

---

[43] Murray J. Harris, *Slave of Christ: A New Testament Metaphor for Total Devotion to Christ* (Downers Grove, Ill.: InterVarsity Press, 1999), 62.
[44] Ibid.

Harris comments:

> Although Paul's action precipitated his arrest and imprisonment along
> with Silas (16:19-24), Luke's report of the episode does not suggest the
> inappropriateness of Paul's action, but rather the opposite; the abuse
> of the slave was repudiated. This is also clear, by implication, from
> those passages where slaves-owners are directed to treat their slaves
> justly and fairly.[45]

This kind of exploitation, which, by implication, is condemned in
Acts 16, was a central tenet of American slavery, and the evidence for
such is not scant. Yet with regard to the church, we see the same
exploitation of men and women for monetary gain. When churches were
unable to give full compensation to their pastors, they would often hire
out their slaves in an effort to meet their financial obligations. America
prospered and became what it is today in large part due to the labor of
Africans, and many who prospered were professing Christians. The land
of the free was built on the backs of chained and shackled Africans who,
though they labored to make it what it was, enjoyed little, if any, of its
fruits. The most desired of fruits was freedom.

The second aspect that Harris cites is that of man-stealing and slave
trafficking. Here he makes reference to 1 Timothy 1:9-11, but focuses
on the word translated "enslavers." The only use of this term is in this
passage, and the word "refers to someone who sells slaves . . . and in
particular to someone who kidnaps people for sale as slaves." Harris
also adds the penalties for such persons stating that "Paul is alluding to
the eighth commandment, 'You shall not steal' (Ex 20:15), which applies
to persons as well as things. Exodus 21:16 prescribes the death penalty
for the kidnapper (cf. Deut 24:2). That is, while both Testaments assume
the practice of slavery, both repudiate kidnapping and dealing in
slaves."[46]

We return to the question of what the Bible prohibits in sanctioned
slavery. While we may grope to understand the practice of slavery in the
Bible, it seems clear that the very actions and practices prevalent in
American slavery are the same actions prohibited by the Bible. While the
penalty of death sanctioned in the Old Testament for such practices may

---

[45] Ibid., 53.
[46] Ibid., 54.

seemed to have passed over America, one may justifiably wonder whether the damning effects of homosexuality on the culture and its evil rise within the hallowed walls of the church and countless other catastrophic realities in our land count as evidence for the wrath of God on America because of the unspeakable evils of slavery. Much can be debated on this issue.

What these two prohibitions show is that the form of slavery in America was contradictory to the Bible and was therefore evil. While Edwards may have seen slavery as being justified on the basis of Christianization and humane treatment, some of his followers—namely, Edwards, Jr., Samuel Hopkins, and Lemuel Haynes—believed differently. Hopkins believed that "the millennium was to commence with the defeat of Satan's followers . . . among whom Hopkins counted slave traders and slaveholders."[47]

The negativity of American slavery, however, is not seen simply in its opposition to Scripture, but also in the social sins it encouraged. "Hopkins clearly defines slavery as a sexual sin, a lustful and lewd version of selfishness. 'Lust' was, indeed, the cause of slavery, Hopkins maintained."[48] Quoting Edwards, Jr., John Saillant writes, "Slavery 'tends towards lewdness' since a 'planter with his hundred wenches' is like a Sultan in his seraglio.' The evident issue of this sexual sin, also known as amalgamation, was generations of mulattoes in America."[49]

Slavery was and still is a blemish upon America. Even after its abolition the residual effects are evident in the culture at large and regrettably within the church. As an African American who loves Reformed theology and Jonathan Edwards and who desires to see these truths embraced by all, especially those within the African-American context, I have to make sense of this hypocrisy. Edwards was only a small part of a much larger picture of Reformed thinkers and preachers. The theology I love so much is tainted with stains of slavery, and my heroes—one of which is Jonathan Edwards—owned my ancestors and cared not to destroy the institution of slavery.

---

[47] John Saillant, *Black Puritan, Black Republican: The Life and Thought of Lemuel Haynes* (New York: Oxford University Press, 2003), 99.

[48] Ibid., 97.

[49] Ibid.

WHY READ EDWARDS?

The question that many have posed over the years is: Why should I read a white man's theology? Why should I care or even consider that what he says is accurate when he missed something that was seemingly obvious and evil? Why should I give my attention to the ideas and constructs of men who constructed a reality of segregation and superiority that held in check the advancement of Africans in America and treated them like brutes and beasts and less than human? Why should I care about a theology that, on the surface, seems to devalue every cultural expression of Christianity indigenous to African Americans? One of the most important answers is that Edwardsean Calvinism formed the basis of early American abolitionism.

> His position [condoning slavery and condemning the slave trade] . . . represents a transitional stage in the development of antislavery thought among elites between complete advocacy of slavery and immediatism of his first-generation, New Divinity disciples.[50]

While the major promoter of such a transition was Samuel Hopkins, others like Edwards, Jr., and Lemuel Haynes shared in his passion to see slavery and the trade eradicated. These men took their cue from Edwards's understanding of what he called "disinterested benevolence," which to him was love toward "Being in General" or "God and his Creatures."[51] To Edwards, this love was the very basis of our expression of love toward our neighbor; not a love full of self-interest, but one that is inclined to the good and happiness of others.

> . . . disinterested benevolence . . . meant to Hopkins an unselfish goodness not just to mankind in general or even to one's enemies, but primarily to those who needed benevolence most, that is, the oppressed of mankind. And who, of all beings, asked Hopkins, were most oppressed and most needed universal good will but the Negroes whose slavery was an offense to Christian benevolence.[52]

Some have written that Hopkins went dangerously beyond his mentor in extending this concept of benevolence in ways Edwards, sup-

---

[50] Minkema, "Jonathan Edwards on Slavery and the Slave Trade," 825.
[51] Lovejoy, "Samuel Hopkins," 232.
[52] Ibid., 233-234.

posedly, did not intend. Hopkins, wanting to give imminent expression to what appeared to be purely aesthetic, other-worldly thought, sought to flesh out the social implications of Edwards's teaching by showing its leaning toward abolitionism. Whatever one may say of Hopkins's use of Edwards on this issue, what cannot be questioned is Hopkins's unswerving commitment to the view of God's supremacy and the theology upon which it was expressed. Saillant explains how New Divinity ministers drew upon this understanding of disinterested benevolence:

> [D]ivine benevolence required, Edwards reasoned, the damnation of the unregenerate, since God could not have consistently loved himself and his creation at the same time as he accepted sinners into heaven. Sin became, then, a providential means of revealing divine benevolence, since God had designed evil as the occasion of the damnation of the unregenerate and the revelation of his glory and goodness.[53]

Saillant, quoting Hopkins, continues: "'God makes the sin . . . the occasion and Means of His own Glory.' God 'over-ruled sin' . . . in the sense that deeds that individuals intended as evil were used by God as the occasion of good."[54]

The framework for such a belief was justified in two biblical accounts: the story of Joseph and the crucifixion.

Joseph was sold into to slavery by his brothers, rose to power and honor, and in the end held the very lives of his relatives who sold him into slavery in his hands. The grand statement of that account is Genesis 50:20: "As for you, you meant evil against me, but God meant it for good, to bring it about that many people should be kept alive, as they are today."

We see the same in the crucifixion of Christ: By his death many were made alive and brought near to God. The pleasure of God in the crushing of his Son displays the paradoxical happiness of God in that crushing, since by it he was glorified and sin defeated. He took what men intended for evil and made it, by design, for his glory and our good.

The response of many southern Presbyterians to Edwardseanism constitutes additional evidence that the seeds of abolitionism flowed through the theology of Edwards.

---

[53] Quoted in Saillant, *Black Puritan, Black Republican*, 87.
[54] Ibid.

Due to the influence of "Edwards and his school," its relationship to abolitionism, and its influence in the New School branch of the Presbyterian church, southern Presbyterian theologians became increasingly concerned to distance themselves from Edwards and his followers.[55]

Columbia Seminary, a bastion of Reformed orthodoxy, found itself embroiled in controversy, having come under much suspicion of its orthodox commitments when

> many of the first students later became New School in their sympathies. . . . As one editorial writer in the Columbia newspaper questioned, "Is [Columbia Seminary] as free from all suspicions of a taint of the new divinity, and of abolitionism as a Southern school ought to be?"[56]

While other aspects of southern Presbyterians' objections of Edwards lay on theological grounds (believing that Edwards was too innovative and free with theological speculation), it is not denied that another problem they held against Edwardseanism was its seeds of abolitionism.

While the New Divinity disciples were in unanimous agreement concerning the cruelty and evil of slavery, and that the theology of Edwards with its centrality of the sovereignty of God was a means to combating its survival, there was one point at which such unanimity crumbled. Saillant writes: "Members of the New Divinity school were among the first Americans to publish against the slave trade and slavery, yet were also among the first to propose expatriation of freedmen and freedwomen to Africa."[57]

By the mid-1770s, two distinct approaches would emerge.

> One approach emphasized the connections between blacks and whites, envisioning a day when both races would be united as equals in America. The other approach emphasized the distance between blacks

---

[55] Sean Michael Lucas, "'He Cuts Up Edwardsism by the Roots': Robert Lewis Dabney and the Edwardsian Legacy in the Nineteenth-Century South," in *The Legacy of Jonathan Edwards: American Religion and the Evangelical Tradition*, ed. D. G. Hart, Sean Michael Lucas, and Stephen J. Nichols (Grand Rapids, Mich.: Baker, 2003), 202.

[56] Ibid., 203.

[57] Saillant, *Black Puritan, Black Republican*, 83.

and whites, envisaging the end of the slave trade and slavery yet also promoting the expatriation of blacks from North America.[58]

While they all shared an understanding that the immediate effects of abolitionism were the spiritual and physical freedom of the Africans, it was their understanding of the long-term solution that created separation. To Hopkins and Edwards, Jr., the long-term solution was expatriation. While they conceived of freedom for the Africans, they had not intended that such freedom be exercised in the colonies, fearing a number of things, most notably intermarrying and retribution. Haynes, on the other hand, "argued that the slave trade and slavery were designed by God to further the appreciation felt by black and white alike for liberty, education and social harmony."[59]

With such a division among the sole promoters of abolitionism all claiming Edwards as their theological defense, a question that would naturally be raised is: Which strand of abolitionism would be a logical expression of Edwards? Another way to approach the subject is to ask: If Edwards were alive during the days of such events as the American Revolution, which of the New Divinity disciples best represents his thoughts consistently?

Understanding Edwards's view of the Millennium and his subsequent understanding of the progressiveness of revelation and its effects on peoples and nations, I am persuaded that the strand of Edwardseanism that understood slavery as God's means of displaying unity among the races is consistent Edwardseanism. While Lemuel Haynes, the African-American New Divinity disciple, did not readily agree with Hopkins and others within the New Divinity school that God used the slave trade and slavery for the Christianization of Africa,

> he was unable to disagree . . . in a *theological* fashion. Haynes pointed to a vision of blacks and whites united affectionately and equally in American society—a vision that he believed God was offering to Americans through the suffering of slaves. Just as theologians . . . put the abolition of the slave trade and slavery on a par with the Reformation, Haynes put the sufferings of slaves on par with the

---

[58] Ibid., 96.

[59] Ibid., 86. The nature of this chapter is not meant to explore the intricacies of these two strands of Edwardsean abolitionism, but I commend John Saillant's scholarly work, *Black Puritan, Black Republican* (especially chapter 3), for a well-documented treatment on the subject.

Revolution as means to a further liberty and accord between the races. God was using the evil of the slave trade and slavery to emphasize the goodness and beauty of a free and benevolent society.[60]

I offer two reasons for the idea that that consistent Edwardseanism led to such a conclusion. The first is Edwards's feelings towards African Americans and Native Americans and his allowing them not simply to attend but also to become full members in the church. This is no small matter, certainly when you consider the history of African Americans and their experiences within white, Protestant churches. It is not recorded whether or not these persons were allowed to sit among the majority in church, but that such were able to become full communicants and treated as equals is no small thing.

A second reason for my conclusion is his ministry to Native Americans.

> Though Edwards' mind never changed on slavery, it did change over another colonial shame: the treatment of Native American Indians, which included their enslavement. While serving as a missionary to the Mahican and Mohawk Indians at the Stockbridge mission in Massachusetts, Edwards had the occasion to witness the cruel exploitation of the Indians firsthand. This experience prompted him to work actively on behalf of the Indians, often in opposition to selfish Englishmen, including some direct relatives.[61]

What is it that makes a man once driven by cultural norms and familial dynamics to behave counterculturally and in opposition to his family? One answer is *experience*. This was a tremendous factor in Edwards's theological and social development. Because he witnessed the evils and corruption toward the Native Americans, he fought for them and against his own time. One wonders if such a shift would have occurred had he been privy to the horrors of the slave trade. Stout and Minkema comment:

> That Edwards saw no contradiction between "winking" at domestic slavery but not winking at the slave trade is curious, but characteristic also of many of his clerical peers. Perhaps the explanation lies in their

---

[60] Saillant, *Black Puritan, Black Republican*, 103.
[61] Stout and Minkema, "The Edwardsean Tradition," 5.

experiences with the slaves. Having never witnessed the ultimate bru-
talities of the institution, and clean in their conscience that they witnessed and preached to their slaves, they were at peace with it. By
accepting domestic slavery as a "necessary evil" not unlike a just war,
Edwards could remain at ease with his domestic slaves as long as he
tutored them in the truths of Christianity.[62]

In my reflection on Edwards and this thought of experience, and
after reading of his subsequent change of heart and mind after witness-
ing the horrible treatment of the Native Americans, I am inclined to
think that Edwards, had he understood the atrocities of the slave trade,
would have changed his position on slavery. I realize that no one can
know this for certain, but had Edwards lived to see the hypocrisy of the
Revolution—men seeking to be free from the rule and dominion of the
crown, yet denying Africans the same freedom for which they fought—
I am inclined to believe that he would have considered such to be
hypocrisy.

How Do We Listen to Edwards?

By asking how we give Edwards a hearing, I am thinking more of what
kind of mental construct must be present in the minds of anyone who
wants to understand Edwards in spite of his shortcomings. The only true
answer to this question has manifold implications: *we must embrace the
sovereignty of God.*

The aim of this chapter is neither to exonerate Edwards nor to condemn him. The aim is to love his God. The God whom Edwards
preached was the God of the Bible; he is sovereign over all things and
events in the universe, even the sin of slavery.[63]

The difficulty that such a belief may pose is its seeming exoneration
of the perpetuators of slavery on the basis that it was God's design.
However, evil is not justified because God, in his mysterious ways,
ordains for it to be. Two events in the Scriptures illustrate this point. The
death of the Lord Jesus Christ was, as the Scripture declares, "according to the definite plan and foreknowledge of God" (Acts 2:23).

And still, in the same voice and context, a paradox is created with

---

62 Ibid., 4.
63 This is the conclusion of Job, specifically in 1:20-22; 2:11; and 42:11, as reflection is given to the
nature and cause of his suffering.

the stating of a seemingly contradictory truth, namely: "you crucified and killed [him] by the hands of lawless men" (Acts 2:23).

The death of Christ was by the hand of God, as Isaiah says in Isaiah 53:10: "Yet it was the will of the LORD to crush him; he has put him to grief." At the same time we know that it was by the hands of men that Christ suffered. The sovereign hand of God does not stand in opposition to the responsibility of men. God crushed Christ by the hands of sinful men, so that even though he is in control of all events, men are held accountable.

It is with this understanding that we can hold that while slavery falls under God's sovereign control, the perpetuators of slavery and those who profited from the slave trade are not excused by the admission of this fact. Instead, the opposite may be the case. It is the sovereignty of God in slavery that may stand to implicate such human agents, since it is God at work even in their deeds, for the good of his name. Hopkins and others saw the horrors of the Revolutionary War as the punishment of God because of slavery. This is the context in which we must labor, as Christians, to hear and understand anything regarding slavery and draw our conclusions thereof. Embracing this reality does not call for an intellectual or emotional abandoning of history, living and behaving as if slavery never happened; rather it is an attempt to place history within its right context—namely, as subservient to the will and decrees of the Sovereign King.

What the trials of God have to teach us, with regard to slavery and racism, is not only a demonstration of the continual effects of sin, but more importantly, racism, seen by the godly through the grid of God's sovereignty and our everlasting joy in him only, is to be a reminder to us that we are not home yet. Trials are to teach us to be looking and reaching for that eternal city, to be seeking the joy that is certain to follow such faithfully endured trials (see Jas. 1:1-2; 2 Cor. 4:16-18).

Perhaps, as pilgrims in this world, our history and present-day sufferings are making us uncomfortable in this world so that we might long for heaven. Perhaps a radical way to view suffering is not to grapple and argue, as many seem to do, for a piece of the American pie, but rather to see such hindrances as reminders that you—we—are not yet home. Fight for social justice? By all means! Yet fight as a citizen of heaven, not as one who thinks that this earth and America's economy is the end-all.

This, I know, is not easy to digest, especially if you are African American and you witness, whether in others' lives or in your own, the residual effects and implications of days gone by. Though I have studied this and taught it many times, it is not easy to write, and it is difficult to communicate in some contexts. Yet we all desire to be driven and shaped by the truth and are willing, I hope, to lay everything at the foot of divine revelation and to allow such to construct a mentality that holds sway by its creeds and ethics over that of our own culture. This in no way calls anyone to deny culture, but it expresses the tension in which we live, certainly as African Americans, as we seek to make sense of our history in America in light of the Word of God.

The reality of this tension is captured in a provocative statement made by a friend of mine, Ken Jones, pastor of Greater Union Missionary Baptist Church in Compton, California. In a discussion we had regarding this issue some years ago, Pastor Jones commented that "the challenge of the African American within the Reformed context is that we are called to embrace the theology of our oppressors and to reject the theology of our liberators."[64] This means that the odd and ironic position of the African American who seeks to be shaped by orthodox theology must reject, in many respects, the theology of a Martin Luther King, Jr., and embrace the theology of a Jonathan Edwards or Robert Dabney. While I admire Dr. King for his work and efforts in fighting for the freedom of African Americans in this country (my freedom), I am not hesitant to note that he will not offer much help in theological precision. While, on the other hand, Edwards never held the mantle as social liberator, his theology will saturate a man in orthodoxy.

As an African American, I know daily the pressures of being in a predominantly white society. Yet how I approach that society, the grid by which I engage that society, is more telling than anything else. God cannot be sovereign over some things and yet not in control of others. This is no justification for abuse or racism, for such perpetuators will have their day of reckoning. But the eradication of racism today, as would be the case with slavery then, will not come about through programs, but by means of a God-centered and God-entranced view of reality. We must not be governed by the political persuasion of today, but

---

[64] For a more extensive treatment on this topic see Anthony Carter's *On Being Black and Reformed: A New Perspective on the African-American Experience* (Phillipsburg, N.J.: P&R, 2003).

governed by the sovereign reign and rule of God. Whatever we may think of Edwards, one thing is for certain: He left the American church with the necessary theological truths to kill racism in our hearts and to be conquerors of it in the church.

In light of that, though we fight and should fight the residue of such hatred in our day, the reality is that the desire to be theologically orthodox today means we must add to our shelves books by dead white men who owned slaves. All of our heroes have clay feet. Jonathan Edwards was not a perfect man, and he did not get everything right, nor did he stand for all the right things. Neither do any of us. His blind spots and sins are pointers to our own blind spots and sins. To ask for grace and mercy on our own sins is, by logical implication, to be ready and willing to extend it to Edwards.

PART THREE

EXPOSITIONS OF
EDWARDS'S MAJOR
THEOLOGICAL WORKS

8

THE GREAT CHRISTIAN DOCTRINE (*ORIGINAL SIN*)

Paul Helm

Edwards was not conscious of differing essentially from the reformed tradition with respect to the entrance of sin into the world. He simply went deeper into the matter and got into deeper difficulty thereby. His problems were not different from others, but the others tended to let sleeping dogs lie.

JOHN GERSTNER

INTRODUCTION

Jonathan Edwards was a tense, highly focused, and very intelligent man, a person of many parts. Ambitious too, while reserved and austere, as he himself recognized. Not just a preacher and revivalist, as he has come to be known to us through evangelical tradition,[1] but a theologian, a philosopher, and a scientist. Part of the romance—or tragedy—of Edwards's life is that he took it upon himself to play radically different roles at one and the same time. But he seems to have played each of these roles with characteristic thoroughness and commitment.

So it was at Stockbridge (where he moved in 1751) during the years in which he composed *The Great Christian Doctrine of Original Sin.*[2]

---

[1] In the introduction to his study of Samuel Rutherford, John Coffey notes how the Rutherford of evangelical piety of the nineteenth century, the Rutherford of the *Letters*, and the Rutherford of a few quaint sermons offers a highly selective and even distorted picture of Rutherford the man. See John Coffey, *Politics, Religion and the British Revolutions: The Mind of Samuel Rutherford* (Cambridge: Cambridge University Press, 1997). The same could be said of Jonathan Edwards, who to generations was known only as the author of the *Life of David Brainerd*, of the *Religious Affections*, and of two sermons, "Sinners in the Hands of an Angry God" and "God Glorified in Man's Dependence."

[2] Its full title is *The Great Christian Doctrine of Original Sin Defended, Evidences of Its Truth Produced, and Arguments to the Contrary Answered* (1758). Page references provided in the main text are to volume 3 of *The Works of Jonathan Edwards*, ed. Clyde A. Holbrook (New Haven, Conn.: Yale University Press, 1970).

At the same time that he was still feuding with people from the Northampton church from which he had recently (in 1750) been dismissed, he was preaching to the Indians and fearfully preparing for war with other Indians (for a time Stockbridge became a stockade), while at the same time attempting to gain their confidence.[3] More significantly for us, Edwards—who at that time endured an illness that "exceedingly wasted my flesh and strength, so that I became like a skeleton"[4]—was also composing two of the three great treatises for which he will ever be remembered as a theologian. The first of the three, *The Religious Affections*, appeared in 1746, while the second, *The Freedom of the Will*, was published in 1754, followed by *Original Sin*, published posthumously in 1758.

Another way of saying that Edwards was a man of many parts is to say that he addressed diverse audiences. While he was preaching to the Indians and attempting to have them taught English, and continuing to recriminate with people connected with the Northampton pastorate, Edwards was endeavoring to address a wider audience—not merely his fellow ministers in New England, nor even the Reformed constituency that included his English and Scottish correspondents and the churches that they represented, but (as he hoped and believed) the wider intellectual world of the eighteenth century.[5]

For Edwards was nothing if not confident in his own God-given abilities to address the deepest currents of thought of his century. It has become a commonplace of contemporary Edwards scholarship to stress that he used many of the tendencies of the "advanced" thought of his time, the "late improvements in philosophy" as he called them (385)— John Locke's philosophy, Sir Isaac Newton's science—to reinforce the conservative theological position of his Puritan and Reformed forebears. The very ideas that in the minds of others strengthened latitudinarian

---

[3] The mixture of emotions felt by the Edwards family during this period is vividly portrayed by George M. Marsden in chapter 24 ("Frontier Struggles") of *Jonathan Edwards: A Life* (New Haven, Conn.: Yale University Press, 2003), 395-413.

[4] Jonathan Edwards in a letter to John Erskine, in "The Memoirs of Jonathan Edwards," *The Works of Jonathan Edwards*, ed. Edward Hickman, 2 vols. (1834; reprint, Edinburgh: Banner of Truth, 1974), 1:clxv.

[5] One of the great merits of Gerald McDermott's *Jonathan Edwards Confronts the Gods: Christian Theology, Enlightenment Religion, and Non-Christian Faiths* (New York: Oxford University Press, 2000) is that it makes plausible the view that Edwards's basic intellectual concern, in his various polemical works, was with the Unitarian outlook of deism and with the presuppositions that gave rise to it. The book is somewhat spoiled, however, by the overly rosy picture it paints of Edwards's view of non-Christian religions.

tendencies, in the mind of Edwards were put to work to reinforce his own Puritan heritage not only against its obvious opponents, but even in the face of the writings of those, such as Thomas Ridgeley and Isaac Watts, whom Edwards recognized as valued members of his own tradition, but whom he thought of as waverers (410).

However, what he did have in common with his radical opponents—men such as John Taylor of Norwich, whom we shall meet a little later on—was a confidence in human reason. Not because he believed that it was the only reliable source of human knowledge, but because he believed that it was God-given, and that properly used it corroborated and undergirded the teaching of God's special revelation, the Bible. On Edwards's view, as we shall see in more detail later, in the Fall God had not so much disabled reason as isolated it from mankind's original "supernatural" endowment. Reason was capable of functioning properly, and in the right hands it was capable of confirming the teaching of Scripture or at least providing data that were consistent with it. It is entirely in keeping with this outlook that Edwards should devote a chapter of *Original Sin* (*OS* in what follows) to considering objections against the *reasonableness* of the doctrine of original sin (394). Such an approach was characteristic of the eighteenth century.

But in endeavoring to carry out such a program it was never Edwards's intention to leave everything as it was in the world of Reformed and Calvinistic theology. To say that he was an innovator is too strong. But he was a re-formulator of those ways of expressing Reformed theology that he thought were outdated (outdated by the latest thought, that is) or unhelpful in other ways. We shall consider some of his innovations later.

We can see Edwards's confidence in reason in the very structure of *OS*. It is a three-part defense of the doctrine of original sin: from the empirical evidence of human evil (most of Part One), from Scripture (Parts Two and Three), and from reason (most of Part Four and some of Part One). I suppose that if Edwards had been asked to rank Scripture, reason, and experience in order of importance for theology, he would undoubtedly have ranked Scripture first. But he would have thought that the choice that we were offering him was rather unnecessary, and indeed superficial. For it is evident from his patterns of thought elsewhere—for example, in his earlier treatise on free will—that he saw each of the three as complementing each other. For if the doctrine of original sin (or his particular understanding of human action) is God's truth, then we might expect to see evidence of its consequences in personal and social life, and perhaps even to demonstrate the incoherence of rival doctrines. If mankind is made in the image of God, and reason is a divine gift, then we should be able to show that some doctrine about the human will or about the propagation of sin, understood from Scripture, is in accordance with human reason, or that it is at least not *repugnant* to reason, as Edwards might himself have put it. (It is important to note that at no point does Edwards think that reason can independently prove the truth of the doctrine of original sin. But it can, he thinks, corroborate it by appealing to human experience and by answering objections to it devised from human reason.)

We must not allow ourselves to paint too romantic a picture of Edwards in Stockbridge. As we have noted, he wrote *OS* while feuding with the Northamptonites, helping to defend Stockbridge against attack (by having soldiers billeted in the Edwards home, for example), and trying to teach and preach to the Indians there. One can imagine the distractions and interruptions, though it would be wrong to conclude that these necessarily frustrated him. After all, Edwards believed that Stockbridge was the place where he ought to be, for following the troubles in the pastorate at Northampton he had waited for the chance to go there. And so we must suppose that though often waylaid by the goings-on at the frontier and diverted by the machinations of the Williams clan—the family that had played a major part in having Edwards ousted from Northampton—he believed that what he was doing with the Indians mattered every bit as much as fine-tuning his thoughts on original sin.

It would also be inaccurate to think that Edwards wrote *OS* from scratch in a few months amidst the cares of Stockbridge. Readers of Edwards's writings have for years been aware of his *Miscellanies,* the continuous, on-the-hoof notebook entries of his own thought, records of what he read, speculative asides, and the like.[6] Recent scholarship, notably the outstanding work of Professor Thomas Schafer, has confirmed not only the voluminous, lifelong extent of these *Miscellanies,*

---

[6] In the Yale edition of *The Works of Jonathan Edwards*, see, for example: *The "Miscellanies," a-500,* ed. Thomas A. Schafer (1994); *The "Miscellanies," 501-832,* ed. Ava Chamberlain (2000); *The "Miscellanies," 833-1152,* ed. Amy Plantinga Pauw (2002); *The "Miscellanies," 1153-1360,* ed. Douglas A. Sweeney (2004).

but also the fact that Edwards composed many of his later writings by incorporating chunks of them, as well as passages from his sermons (and also material from what he called his "Book of Controversies"[7]), directly into the text of whatever work was in progress. So it would be misleading to suppose that Edwards sat down in Stockbridge one evening with a blank page before him having decided to write a book on sin. Rather, we must see OS as the accumulation of a life's work of reflection on this and on kindred topics and see Edwards composing the work by actively incorporating his voluminous notes and jottings.

However, it does seem that in the case of OS Edwards was galvanized into action by what he feared the impact of John Taylor of Norwich's view on sin might be.[8] John Taylor was an example of "radical Dissent" of the sort that became increasingly common when, under the influence of Locke and others, Puritan orthodoxy quickly waned. What Edwards feared was the importing of Taylorian ideas from old England into New England. So OS is a polemical work in which from start to finish Edwards critically engages with Taylor (and to a lesser extent with another eighteenth-century challenger, George Turnbull[9]). Further, unlike *Religious Affections*, but very much like *The Freedom of the Will*, OS contains little or no references to Puritan writers, and only a few to continental Reformed theologians. Rather Edwards appeals to thinkers, such as the philosophers Francis Hutcheson and John Locke, whom his opponents Taylor and Turnbull respected. This reinforces the view that in both these works Edwards was endeavoring to be read and respected beyond the confines of New England Puritanism.

In what follows we shall try to distill Edwards's positive position by reengaging with what is necessarily a dated controversy. We shall draw out Edwards's views by briefly reviewing the most significant sections of each of the first three parts of OS. But since the distinctiveness of what he thought largely emerges in the course of the objections he considers in Part Four, we shall pay particular attention, later on, to that part.

---

[7] For details of the sources of the work and the manner of its composition, see Clyde Holbrook's Introduction to the Yale edition of OS (1-101).

[8] John Taylor (1694-1761), a Lancastrian by birth, was a Presbyterian minister in Norwich, England, 1733-57. He became a teacher at Warrington Academy until his death. His *Scripture Doctrine of Original Sin, Proposed to Free and Candid Examination* was published in 1738.

[9] George Turnbull (1698-1748) taught for a time at Marischal College, Aberdeen. His *Principles of Moral Philosophy* was published in 1741, and *Christian Philosophy* the following year.

The Argument of Part One

The form of the argument of Part One is as follows. Edwards notes that all men and women without exception "run into" moral evil. Furthermore this evil is very evil, it occurs immediately, it is continuous and progressive, and its effects remain even in the best of men, those who enjoy the benefits of God's regenerating grace. Humanity is depraved, and the means adopted for the reformation and regeneration of human evil have had comparatively little effect. (One may wonder whether Edwards's estimate of the relatively small impact of the gospel on human evil was affected by his own disillusionment with the revivals of the Great Awakening, and particularly by what had happened so recently in Northampton, which in the revivals had been a "a city set on a hill.")

Edwards intends this survey of evidence to have a cumulative effect on the mind of the reader. One line of evidence reinforces each of the other lines in turn. So what is the best explanation of the evidence? Could it be that all human beings of all ages and cultures turn out this way simply as a matter of fact? That each individual case of human evil has its own separate explanation? Is it not more plausible to suppose that there is one underlying explanation of this exceptionless universality?[10] Edwards offers this analogy:

> If it be observed, that those trees, and all other trees of the kind, wherever planted, and in all soils, countries, climates and seasons, and however cultivated and managed, still bear ill fruit, from year to year, and in all ages, it is a good evidence of the evil nature of the tree: and if the fruit, at all these times, and in all these cases, be very bad, it proves the nature of the tree to be very bad. And if we argue in like manner from what appears among men, 'tis easy to determine, whether the universal sinfulness of mankind, and their all sinning immediately, as soon as capable of it, and all sinning continually, and generally being of a

---

[10] According to Douglas Moo, this is precisely the question that the interpreter of Romans 5:12 is faced with, the sense to be given to, "and in this way death came to all men, because all sinned" (NIV). What is the connection between Adam's sin and the sin and death of all? Is the latter in imitation of Adam? Or is it through the sinful nature that comes from Adam and that caused all people to sin (the so-called mediate theory of imputation)? Or rather is the sinning in question sinning in and with Adam? This is the view that Moo "tentatively" opts for. "The point is rather that the sin here attributed to the 'all' is to be understood, in the light of vv. 12 a-c and 15-19, as a sin in some manner identical to the sin committed by Adam. Paul can therefore say both 'all die because all sin' and 'all die because Adam sinned' with no hint of conflict because the sin of Adam is the sin of all." Douglas J. Moo, *Romans 1-8* (Chicago: Moody, 1991), 338.

wicked character, at all times, in all ages, and all places, and under all possible circumstances, against means and motives inexpressibly manifold and great, and in the utmost conceivable variety, be from a permanent internal great cause. (191)

Of particular interest in this section is Edwards's consideration of several evasions, which in some cases anticipate the objections that he will consider in Part Four. These evasions have the status of counter-hypotheses, of other ways of accounting for the universal and deep sinfulness of the human race. The first is this. Scripture teaches that sin entered a world that was "very good." There was a first sin. What is the explanation for that? By definition, that sin cannot have been inherited. So if one sin may not have been inherited, may not all sins not have been? May not the sin of each one of us be like the sin of Adam in this respect, that we are the originators of it? To which Edwards replies that the first sin of Adam did not come about from a fixed disposition but was "transient" (193). For Edwards an action is transient if it is not the expression of a settled habit. Edwards argues that Adam's first sin was transient in this sense, but that it produced fixed dispositions to evil in himself and those "in" him. This appeal to the transient source of Adam's first sin will return to haunt Edwards later on in the argument.

But may not the cause of the sin in each human being be that person's free will (Evasion 2) (194)? To which Edwards replies: If the free will in question is the power to choose either good or evil as the chooser sees fit (a position that he had vehemently argued against in his treatise on the freedom of the will, but that he now allows for the sake of the argument), how is it that the result of this exercise of freedom is not something like a 50-50 incidence of good and evil?

But (Evasion 3) why may not the universality of sin be the result of the influence on the race of bad examples (196)? But, Edwards asks, how does it come about that there are so many, uniformly many, bad examples? Why were the children of Noah, who had a good example to follow, so wretchedly disappointing? How is it that efforts at the reforming of manners, or of the reviving of religion are so soon and so deeply dissipated?

When England grew very corrupt, God brought over a number of pious persons, and planted 'em in New England, and this land was planted

with a noble vine. But how is the gold become dim! How greatly have
we forsaken the pious examples of our fathers! (198)

And look at how the example of supreme goodness, Jesus Christ, was
treated.

But (Evasion 4) may not the prevalence of sin be accounted for by
the influence of the "animal passions" (201)? The trouble with this suggestion, Edwards says, is that it proves too much, since it looks to make
God, who created us with a sensual nature, the author of evil.
(Throughout OS Edwards is particularly exercised over the question of
God's authorship of evil: discussion of the problem recurs a number of
times, and Edwards devotes a chapter of Part Four to rebutting the idea.)
And what about Adam at the first, and what about Jesus? How do we
then account for Christ's sinlessness?

The final evasion is that human nature is in a state of permanent pro-
bation or trial, and it is of the nature of a trial that we combat vice in
order to promote and solidify virtue. Hence, it is argued, the presence of
vice is needed for the development of virtue in the human race.[11] Edwards
replies with his characteristic acuteness: Either the presence of temptation
accounts for sin and evil, in which case the temptation is itself sinful and
evil, or it does not, in which case how does it account for evil at all?

Edwards has not quite finished. In the concluding chapter of this
part he argues that original sin is proved by the fact that we all, including many infants, die. In the light of the current theological preoccupation, if not obsession, with the Holocaust, leading to the development
of "Holocaust theologies," the following words of Edwards are, to say
the least, cautionary:

> How inconsiderable a thing is the additional or hastened destruction,
> that is sometimes brought on a particular city or country by war, com-
> pared with that universal havoc which death makes of the whole race
> of mankind, from generation to generation, without distinction of sex,
> age, quality or condition, with all the infinitely dismal circumstances,
> torments and agonies which attend the death of old and young, adult
> persons and little infants? (208)

---

[11] Such a view is the source of modern evolutionary, "soul-making" theodicies such as that of John
Hick, *Evil and the God of Love*, rev. ed. (London: Harper & Row, 1978).

In this part Edwards is chiefly rejecting the views of his two principal adversaries, Taylor and Turnbull, quoting them in their own words, at length, and then rebutting them. He is meeting them on their own territory and answering them with their own weapons, with general observations and rational argument. Although the discussion is dated, Edwards has the advantage that his opponents both held, with him, to the historicity of the biblical account of the Fall. Had Edwards been arguing today, he would have had to start further back, so to speak, but there is no reason to think that his argument would not have been similar in structure.[12] The debate is also dated by the fact that there is no reference to later theories, to the unconscious, or to the place of the economic or social order in promoting evil. Yet it is not hard to imagine how Edwards could have transposed his argument that the universality and depth of human sin is due to the presence in us all of original sin to meet these later views.

THE HEART OF THE WORK

Parts Two and Three of the work are the heart of Edwards's positive exposition. Here he deals with Scripture in his usual trenchant way. In Part Two he chiefly has in view two main passages, the first three chapters of the book of Genesis (chapter 1) and Romans 5:12ff. (chapter 4). Sandwiched in between are sets of observations on relevant passages of the Old Testament (chapter 2) and on similarly relevant passages of the New Testament (chapter 3). Part Three has two chapters offering evidence of original sin from the accomplishment and application of redemption. We shall look at what Edwards has to say in chapters 1 and 4 of Part Two and both chapters of Part Three.

1. Genesis 1—3

As in *The Freedom of the Will*, so here Edwards denies that virtue arises from choice. Rather he maintains that virtuous actions arise from prior virtuous dispositions. Adam must have had an original God-given endowment of virtue—that is, original righteousness. How could he otherwise have been righteous? So Adam's sin of taking the fruit must have occurred in the life of a man who was "perfectly righ-

---

[12] Note, in this connection, Edwards's interesting remarks on "human nature" and "mankind" (231-232).

teous, righteous from the first moment of his existence; and consequently, created or brought into existence righteous"[13] (228). More
generally:

> Human nature must be created with some dispositions; a disposition
> to relish some things as good or amiable, and to be averse to other
> things as odious and disagreeable. Otherwise, it must be without any
> such thing as inclination or will. It must be perfectly indifferent, with-
> out preference, without choice or aversion towards anything, as agree-
> able or disagreeable. (231)

This, Edwards thinks, is borne out by the Genesis narrative. Until
Adam sinned, he was both happy and good. Had he been left alone,
without virtue, in a position of neutrality, then (as Edwards puts it) "the
curse was before the fall" (233). The Garden would not have been prepared as a fit environment for a virtuous man but would have acted as
bait to lure the morally "neutral" Adam into sin. Edwards's concern to
protect God from the charge that he is the author of sin surfaces once
again.

Section 2 discusses the "eternal death" with which Adam was
threatened. Section 3 takes us to the heart of Edwards's treatment, for
here he considers whether what Genesis teaches implies that Adam was
not to be considered a mere individual but was the "first father . . . of
mankind in general" (245). He maintains that the language of Genesis
1—3 is replete with references to Adam as "father," father of the race.
Taylor had claimed that the threat to Adam was of "mere" mortality as
an individual (246). Some of Edwards's reasoning here is weak, as he
himself seems to acknowledge, as when he rather lamely states (251)
that the sentence to Adam ("unto dust thou shalt return," KJV) includes
his posterity, "as is confessed on all hands." But of course Taylor himself was not willing to confess this. Is not Edwards trying to get out of
these passages more than is in them? For a corporate view of Adam,
would he not have been better simply to rely on Romans 5 and 1
Corinthians 15?

---

[13] It is instructive to compare this with John Calvin's description of unfallen Adam as "weak, frail and
liable to fall." *A Defence of the Secret Providence of God*, trans. Henry Cole, in *Calvin's Calvinism*
(London: Sovereign Grace Union, 1927), 274. Compare *Institutes* I.15.8.

2. *Romans 5:12ff.*

Edwards is certainly on stronger ground when he turns, in chapter 3 and especially chapter 4 of Part Two, to the New Testament, particularly (of course) to Romans 5:12 and the following verses. He holds strongly to the parallel between Adam and Christ (344ff.). For the present-day reader one drawback of Edwards's exposition is that it is a series of reactions to Taylor's views. For example, Taylor held that the death threatened to Adam was mere physical death. Edwards responds by arguing that Paul means by "death" here what he means by "death" throughout Romans. Taylor claims that the apostle merely taught that Adam was the first transgressor, while Edwards argues, surely correctly, that Paul has in view a much more "corporatist" view of the relation between Adam and his posterity and insists strongly on the parallel between Adam as the head of the race and Christ as the head of the church. In his interpretation of Paul's words in Romans 5, Edwards is particularly strong in his emphasis on what he calls the "causal particles." When Paul says that it is "*through* the offense of one," "*by* one that sinned," "*by* one man's offense," "*by* the offense of one" (KJV), these expressions "signify some connection and dependence, by some sort of influence of that sin of one man, or some tendency to that effect which is so often said to come *by* it" (310). The expressions call for some explanation, which Taylor purposely evades.

Throughout this discussion it is Edwards's aim to counter Taylor's individualistic interpretation of the fall of Adam with one that stresses the solidarity of the race in Adam. In my view this is one of the strongest parts of Edwards's overall case in OS.

So Edwards holds that Scripture teaches that there is solidarity between Adam and the human race, so that when Adam—created, as Edwards claims, in original righteousness (223)—fell, he sinned not simply as an individual, setting a bad example for the race, nor was the effect of his sin simply to infect his progeny with sin, as a person may infect her unborn child with HIV, but in sinning Adam was punished and the race was punished because in some sense the race was "in" Adam. In so saying Edwards is simply echoing the teaching of the church, and particularly that of the Augustinian tradition that he inherited through the Puritans. For the Christian church has always held and explicitly taught since the time of St. Augustine (who drew on what Paul wrote in Romans 5) that when infants are born, they do not arrive holding a position of ethical or spiritual neutrality.[14] Rather they are born as children of Adam, sinning because Adam sinned and also bearing the guilt that Adam bore through his disobedience to the Lord when placed in the Garden of Eden. And they are innately sinful and guilty because they fell "in" Adam.

Edwards lived in a strongly individualistic century (as he came increasingly to see and to deplore). Both socially and morally, emphasis was placed on the individual person, on his powers to accept or reject God's grace and in these ways to possess the power to distance himself from God. So there came to be less and less recognition of original sin and of the corporate view of the human race that it implied. As we have seen, Edwards argued that boys and girls did not became sinful by the actions of their parents. (This, after all, evaded the question of why their parents behaved in that way.) Rather, sinful actions occur because of what happened to the race when Adam fell. Adam's "first disobedience" had an effect not only upon Adam, but also upon all who were "in" Adam, as Paul put it. He "brought death into the world and all our woe."[15] That is, when boys and girls knowingly do wrong things, from wrong motives, they do so not only or simply on their own account but because they are in some way implicated in Adam's first sin.

How are they implicated? Not simply because they are the biological offspring of Adam and so inherit his bad character. (For no one holds that Scripture teaches that the Fall resulted in a genetic change in Adam.) Rather, they are implicated because they are "in" Adam not merely in a biological sense, Adam being their first father, but in a more immediate and direct sense. Adam was not simply their first father, bearing a more distant but essentially similar position to their father and grandfather, but he was a unique figure. He was the head of the race. Evidence of this is provided by the fact that although Eve was the first person to sin, according to Paul it is "in Adam" that "all die" (1 Cor. 15:22).

How is the headship of Adam to be understood? Edwards was faced

---

[14] Augustine's views can be found, for example, in his work *On the Merits and Forgiveness of Sins, and Baptism*. "All then sinned in Adam, when in his nature, by virtue of that innate power whereby he was able to produce them, they were all as yet the one Adam" (3:14) (St. Augustine, *Writings Against the Pelagians*, in *Library of the Nicene and Post-Nicene Fathers*, ed. Philip Schaff [reprint, Grand Rapids, Mich.: Eerdmans, 1971], 5:74). It was Augustine who first coined the expression *original sin*. For a sympathetic account of Augustine and a defense of his view, see W. G. T. Shedd, *History of Christian Doctrine* (Edinburgh: T & T Clark, 1872), 2:77ff.

[15] John Milton, *Paradise Lost*, Book i, line 1.

with two competing accounts. One, going back to Augustine, laid stress on the oneness of the human race in its first father Adam. He encapsulated the race. When he was created, the race was created, and so all the subsequent members of the race, including you and me, were "in" him. Just as, according to the letter to the Hebrews, Levi was in the loins of his father Abraham when Abraham paid tithes to Melchizedek (Heb. 7:9), and so in effect he himself paid those tithes, so we were all in the loins of our father Adam and so were one with Adam. This was because Adam was not just an individual person but was in himself the whole race in essence. Put rather more drastically, on this view you and I were Adam, and so in virtue of that oneness with him, when he sinned we sinned because there is an inescapable unity between Adam and the race of which he was the first father.

On this view it does not matter that we do not think or feel or remember that we were in or with Adam. The idea of the solidarity of the race in Adam is not propounded as a social or psychological theory but as a metaphysical reality, as that reality which was at the first constituted by God.[16] This is the so-called *realist interpretation* of the Fall, championed by Augustine, by Anselm, by some of the Reformers and Puritans, by one or two moderns since (notably W. G. T. Shedd[17] and A. H. Strong[18]), but not, as we shall see, by Jonathan Edwards himself.

The alternative view, which came into prominence with the rise of Reformed theology, and especially of the so-called Federal or Covenant theology, sees the relation between Adam and the race not as a real one (the race being in Adam and acting in him and so, with him, responsible for what he did) but as a *representative relation*. Adam is viewed as an individual just as you and I are individuals, but (as it happens) he was the first individual. And he was appointed by the Lord to be the representative of each member of the race, just as a Member of Parliament is taken to represent his constituents, even those constituents who have not voted for him in a General Election. Adam represents the race not because it is in his very nature to do so (the realist view), but because he was given this representative role by his Lord. So when he sinned, he did

---

[16] So it is not a case of the shame that a son may feel at the actions of his father and may "take responsibility" for them, nor of "corporate responsibility" in the sense in which a firm can be held accountable for the actions of its officials.

[17] W. G. T. Shedd, *Dogmatic Theology* (1881; reprint, Grand Rapids, Mich: Zondervan, 1969), 2:42-44.

[18] A. H. Strong, *Systematic Theology* (Old Tappan, N.J.: Fleming H. Revell Co., 1907), Part V, Section V.

so not only as an individual but also on behalf of those whom he represented; and when he fell, they fell too, in virtue of that representative arrangement.

I think it is fair to say that Edwards also rejected or repudiated this view.[19] So what position did he take? In order to find an answer to this question we must turn to Part Four of *OS*, where he considers objections to the doctrine of original sin. Here we find what many have regarded as Edwards's innovations.

EDWARDS'S INNOVATIONS

Edwards's distinctive position is drawn out in answer to objections (381ff.). We shall consider two of these answers.

1. *The Occurrence of the First Sin*

Here Edwards's concern is dominated by the charge to which (as we have already noted) he seems especially sensitive, that the orthodox view of original sin makes God the author of sin. We have already seen how he approaches this question of Adam's first sin by stressing its "transience." Sin did not arise from a "settled principle," since Adam was created good.

In creating Adam, God not only made him a man but endowed him with virtue.

> The case with man was plainly this: when God made man at first, he implanted in him two kinds of principles. There was an *inferior* kind, which may be called *natural*, being the principles of mere human nature; such as self-love, with those natural appetites and passions, which belong to the nature of man, in which his love to his own liberty, honor and pleasure, were exercised: these when alone, and left to themselves, are what the Scriptures sometimes call *flesh*. Besides these, there were *superior* principles, that were spiritual, holy and divine, summarily comprehended in divine love; wherein consisted the spiritual image of God, and man's righteousness and true holiness; which are called in Scripture the *divine nature*. These principles may, in some sense, be called *supernatural*, being (however concreated or connate,[20]

---

[19] References by Edwards to "federal heads" (e.g., 259-260) must not mislead us into thinking otherwise. The expression as used here simply refers to the covenant role of Adam and by itself has no implications for the relation of Adam to his posterity.

[20] That is, given at birth, though not strictly speaking an essential part of human nature.

yet) such as are above those principles that are essentially implied in, or necessarily resulting from, and inseparably connected with, *mere human nature*. (381-382)[21]

For Edwards, a person could be essentially a human being, lack the Holy Spirit, and so not possess the image of God. Holiness and true righteousness, the image of God, are not part of man's essential nature. Adam was "naturally" a "mere" man, he had all the properties of human nature, but he was, in addition, "supernaturally" a virtuous person, because of this original endowment of righteousness and true holiness (381-382). But when he sinned, his supernatural endowment was (penally) removed, and he reverted to "natural" manhood, a prey to selfish desires, etc. Edwards sees the answer to the charge that original sin makes God the author of sin to lie in this "two tier" view of Adam's original condition. Mankind's nature would (were it to be left to its own resources) inevitably be corrupted by becoming selfish and God-defying. But the "supernatural" influences with which the pre-Fall pair were endowed (the image of God in them) preserved them in holiness. These superior principles were removed (by divine judgment) when man sinned.

> These divine principles thus reigning, were the dignity, life, happiness, and glory of man's nature. When man sinned, and broke God's Covenant, and fell under his curse, these superior principles left his heart: for indeed God then left him; that communion with God, on which these principles depended, entirely ceased; the Holy Spirit, that divine inhabitant, forsook his house. (382)[22]

As a consequence, left to his own unsupported nature, the course of man's life immediately became sinful, a condition that was both natural (i.e., universal, and a consequence of the possession of human nature) and penal (386). As a result, so Edwards concludes, God is not the author of sin even though he is responsible for continuing the sinful race in being after the Fall (387). God permits sin by withdrawing the super-

---

[21] Holding these views, it becomes easier to see how Edwards could retain confidence in fallen human reason. For the Fall was for him essentially moral and spiritual. From what he says, it seems that human reason escapes fairly unscathed. This also has a bearing on his distinction between "moral" and "natural" ability and inability in *Freedom of the Will*.

[22] Does Edwards believe that the Holy Spirit left the house *after* the sin of Adam or *before* it? His language in the passage just quoted seems deliberately to avoid answering this question.

natural virtues; he does not positively cause Adam to sin; and so he is not the author of Adam's sin, and so not the author of sin. Edwards claims that since in other theological systems (such as Taylor's) God permits Adam's sin, his own system is in no worse case than theirs.

Whether or not this argument of Edwards in fact succeeded in rebutting Taylor's charge about the divine authorship of sin, it leaves him with a major problem. It is hard to see how he could have been satisfied with this theory or have been confident that it would convince opponents such as Taylor that God is not the author of sin. For either mankind sinned while still in possession of these supernatural principles, with all the virtuous influence they afforded, in which case it is hard to make the occurrence of the Fall plausible, or alternatively, if the Fall could occur while Adam had such principles and was under their influence, then they were hardly "supernatural" in the sense that Edwards intends, for they did not succeed in preserving him. In any case, Edwards is stuck with his earlier claim that the first sin was "transient." How, if it was transient, did it arise in the mind and heart of a person endowed with supernatural virtue so as to turn him from the path of obedience? John Gerstner avers that since in Edwards's view this supernatural addition was none other than the Holy Spirit himself—the presence of whom must keep man from falling, and whose influence could not be overpowered by a mere human decision, since Adam in fact fell—"this divine super-added 'gift' must have been a mere offer."[23] But this is pure surmise. Edwards does not say it is an offer, and the powerful language he uses regarding the actual presence of the Spirit strongly suggests otherwise.

If at this point Edwards were to stress the transience of the first sin (which he does not) and also to stress that Adam was created in such a condition as to turn his back on these supernatural principles, so making the Fall certain, then it is hard to see how this arrangement safeguards God from being the author of sin. Either way, Edwards has done little by this innovation to cast light on the mystery of the entrance of sin into a world made good by God.[24]

Whether or not Edwards's theory could account for the Fall, or at least be seen to be consistent with it, it does have one advantage. It offers

[23] John H. Gerstner, *The Rational Biblical Theology of Jonathan Edwards*, 3 vols. (Powhatan, Va.: Berean/Orlando, Fla.: Ligonier, 1992), 2:273.

[24] As Clyde Holbrook notes, Edwards's account leaves him "mired in difficulty" (51), and John Gerstner refers to his inability to extricate himself "from the pit he has dug" (*The Rational Biblical Theology of Jonathan Edwards*, 2:314).

an account of how it is that fallen, humankind possesses a settled disposition to do evil. That disposition immediately arises from the dominant effects of the "lower" nature that asserts itself in wicked ways once the supernatural virtues have departed.

2. The One-ness of the Race in Adam[25]

We need now to give more detailed attention to the account that Edwards provided of the oneness of the race in Adam. It was suggested earlier that he was not satisfied either with the "realist" Augustinian position on the relation of Adam to his posterity, nor with the "representative" view beloved of classical Covenant theology. So what was his own view?

As a result of his deep conviction about the immediate dependence of the creation upon the Creator, Edwards developed a unique account of the relation between Adam and his progeny as part of his overall defense of the reasonableness of the Christian doctrine of original sin in Part Four of *OS*. In chapter 3 of this Part he offers what can best be described as a daring (if not rather rash) metaphysical excursus in an attempt to answer "that great objection against the imputation of Adam's sin to his posterity . . . that such imputation is unjust and unreasonable, inasmuch as Adam and his posterity are not one and the same" (389). How, if Adam is distinct from his progeny, can it be fair to impute his sin and its consequences to them? It is at this point that Edwards appeals to the philosophy of John Locke. Edwards was a lifelong devotee of Locke's philosophy, but no doubt he hoped that by citing Locke here he was appealing to an authority whom Taylor respected.

He replies to the objection by offering a "metaphysical" explanation of the nature of things, including their identity through time. According to this alternative, rather radical explanation, there is no such thing as strict or numerical identity through time. I am no more nor less strictly identical to Adam than I am to an earlier phase of myself. For both Adam and I are dependent things, and such unity as I have with an earlier phase of myself, or with Adam, is a unity constituted solely by the will of God.

---

[25] Some of the material in this section is adapted from "A Forensic Dilemma: John Locke and Jonathan Edwards on Personal Identity," in *Jonathan Edwards, Philosophical Theologian*, ed. Paul Helm and Oliver D. Crisp (Aldershot, Hants/Burlington, Vt.: Ashgate, 2003), 45-49.

> A father, according to the course of nature, begets a child; an oak, according to the course of nature, produces an acorn, or a bud; so according to the course of nature, the former existence of the trunk of the tree is followed by its new or present existence. In the one case, and the other, the new effect is consequent on the former, only by the established laws, and settled course of nature; which is allowed to be nothing but the continued immediate efficiency of God, according to a constitution that he has been pleased to establish. (401)

A thing's "new and present existence" is therefore an existence that is numerically distinct from its immediate past existence. Nothing can exist for more than a moment; the fact that nature, the temporally continuous order of things, is as orderly as it is, is due solely to the wisdom and power of God, not to the inherent natures of things that he has created. Not only was I (i.e., the present "me") not around when Adam existed, I was not around yesterday or a moment ago. So if I'm to be held responsible for some of what went on yesterday (as seems reasonable), why may I not also be implicated in what Adam did?

It is in connection with this defense of the reasonableness of the doctrine of original sin that Edwards utilizes what Locke had written on identity in his *Essay Concerning Human Understanding*. He begins by adopting a Lockean approach to what he calls sameness or oneness among created things, as for example, in the following:

> A tree, grown great, and an hundred years old, is one plant with the little sprout, that first came out of the ground, from whence it grew, and has been continued in constant succession; though it is now so exceeding diverse, many thousand times bigger, and of a very different form, and perhaps not one atom the very same. . . . So the body of man at forty years of age, is one with the infant body which first came into the world, from whence it grew; though now constituted of different substance, and the greater part of the substance probably changed scores (if not hundreds) of times. . . .
>
> And if we come even to the *personal identity* of created intelligent beings, though this be not allowed to consist wholly in that which Mr. Locke supposes, i.e. *same consciousness*; yet I think it can't be denied, that this is one thing essential to it. (397-398)

Turning from plants to people, Edwards starts with the Lockean account of personal identity through time, according to which same consciousness is necessary for personal identity. That is, persisting personal identity requires having the same enduring consciousness. But this cannot be the whole story for Edwards because it is obvious that you and I do not have the same consciousness that Adam had. As we shall shortly see, although he followed Locke in general, Edwards understands this sameness in a rather different way from Locke. For it is here that Edwards's idea of creaturely dependence upon God, mentioned earlier, comes to play a crucial role in his argument.

Both in his account of plants and of people Locke had argued that their identity through time consists in a succession of overlapping parts, generated by the growth of a plant or (in the case of people) by temporally continuous mental organization, memories, trains of thought, and the like. From this it is a short step—but perhaps for Edwards a fatal step—to argue that (since, as he believed, nothing exists for more than a moment) identity is a succession of *non*-overlapping parts, a view particularly attractive to him given his strong view of creaturely dependence. Since according to Edwards nothing creaturely can exist for more than a moment, nothing can overlap or be overlapped. However, according to Edwards a succession of momentary parts, qualitatively similar in important respects, is treated both by ourselves and (more importantly) by God as if it were numerically one thing. That's all the identity through time that there is and can be.

Edwards was concerned to stress, against the deists, for whom God's power was mediated through the law-like dispositions given to created things, that God's power was *immediately* exercised upon his creation, on all aspects of it equally. Here is Edwards in full cry against Deism:

> That God does, by his immediate power, *uphold* every created substance in being, will be manifest, if we consider, that their present existence is a *dependent* existence, and therefore is an *effect*, and must have some *cause*: and the cause must be one of these two: either the *antecedent existence* of the same substance, or else the *power of the Creator*. But it can't be the antecedent existence of the same substance. For instance, the existence of the body of the moon at this present moment, can't be the effect of its existence at the last foregoing moment. For not only was what existed the last moment, no active cause, but

wholly a passive thing; but this also is to be considered, that no cause can produce effects in a *time* and *place* in which itself is *not*. . . . From these things, I suppose, it will certainly follow, that the present existence, either of this, or any other created substance, cannot be an effect of its past existence. The existences (so to speak) of an effect, or thing dependent, in different parts of space or duration, though ever so *near* one to another, don't at all coexist one with the other; and therefore are as truly different effects, as if those parts of space and duration were ever so far asunder: and the prior existence can no more be the proper cause of the new existence, in the next moment, or next part of space, than if it had been in an age before, or at a thousand miles distance, without any existence to fill up the intermediate time or space. Therefore the existence of created substances, in each successive moment, must be the effect of the *immediate* agency, will, and power of God.

. . . God's *preserving* created things in being is perfectly equivalent to a *continued creation*, or to his creating those things out of nothing at *each moment* of their existence. If the continued existence of created things be wholly dependent on God's preservation, then those things would drop into nothing, upon the ceasing of the present moment, without a new exertion of the divine power to cause them to exist in the following moment. (400-402)

So God can constitute the race as one individual, extended through time and space by his re-creating, upholding power.[26] Adam is not a representative of the rest of us. But nor was Augustine correct in surmising that the race is "seminally" present in Adam and so one in him. According to Augustine the oneness of the race in Adam arises from the nature of things. But for Edwards the unity in question does not come from the nature of things but is one arranged by God, by his "arbitrary constitution."[27]

There has been some difference of opinion regarding Edwards and what he thought was the relation of Adam's sin to the sins of his posterity. The main line of Reformed theologians have favored a doctrine of immediate imputation: that in view of the representative relation with which Adam stood to his posterity, the guilt of his first sin was imme-

---

[26] It is because of his emphasis on the progression of the race through time that Edwards's view of the unity of the race does not commit him either to the view that each of us is strictly identical with each other, nor that our sin is imputed to Adam.

[27] As Shedd notes, *Dogmatic Theology*, 2:32. Nevertheless Shedd held that Edwards's view tends to that of Augustine (80).

diately imputed to them. It was reckoned to them, and they were judged guilty because of it. But others have favored a less direct view of imputation—namely, that the posterity of Adam is judged guilty, not on account of Adam's sin, but on account of the sinfulness that they have inherited through Adam. This is a derived imputation, so-called mediate imputation.

Some, such as Charles Hodge,[28] have reckoned that from some of the things that Edwards says in *OS* he must have favored mediate imputation. For instance, from these words:

> Therefore I am humbly of opinion, that if any have supposed the children of Adam to come into the world with a *double guilt*, one the guilt of Adam's sin, another the guilt arising from their having a corrupt heart, they have not well conceived of the matter. The guilt a man has upon his soul at his first existence, is one and simple: viz. the guilt of the original apostacy, the guilt of the sin by which the species first rebelled against God. This, and the guilt arising from the first corruption or depraved disposition of the heart, are not to be looked upon as two things, distinctly imputed and charged upon men in the sight of God. Indeed the guilt, that arises from the corruption of the heart, as it remains a confirmed principle, and appears in its consequent operations, is a distinct and additional guilt: but the guilt arising from the first existing of a depraved disposition in Adam's posterity, I apprehend, is not distinct from their guilt of Adam's first sin. (390)

Others, such as B. B. Warfield[29] and John Murray,[30] have believed, on the basis of other evidence from *OS*, that Edwards was in the Reformed mainstream, favoring immediate imputation.

But this difference of opinion and the way in which some theologians have tried to resolve it, by paying detailed attention to certain phrases that Edwards uses,[31] is based upon a somewhat odd procedure. For given Edwards's unique position on the unity of the race, on God's reckoning the myriad members of the human race to be one with Adam, it should be clear that he must be committed to the strictest form of immediate imputation, since according to Edwards you and I and every-

---

[28] Charles Hodge, *Systematic Theology* (London: Thomas Nelson and Sons, 1871), 2:207ff.

[29] B. B. Warfield, "Edwards and the New England Theology," in *Studies in Theology* (New York: Oxford University Press, 1931), 530.

[30] John Murray, *The Imputation of Adam's Sin* (Grand Rapids, Mich.: Eerdmans, 1959), 56ff.

[31] Ibid., 57ff.

one else are each constituted one with Adam. And so his guilt must be ours. Indeed "immediate imputation" is perhaps too *weak* an expression to convey Edwards's view accurately. For according to him there is no question of guilt being reckoned from one person (Adam) to another (for example, to you and me) since we are each one with Adam. We are one with him and so are guilty of his sin, since his sin is our sin. As B. B. Warfield put it, since Edwards thinks that "all mankind are one as truly as and by the same kind of divine constitution that an individual life is one in its consecutive moments," Adam and his posterity are one "in the strictest sense" possible in the case of things that persist through time, a sense in which that unity is conferred by God's arbitrary will.[32]

It ought to be borne in mind that on Edwards's view, though each of us is constituted one with Adam, God has not in the same sense constituted us one with each other, with either our progenitors or our contemporaries. This is because we can be constituted one with Adam in a way in which we cannot with each other, not even with our own parents. They bear exactly the same relation to Adam as we do. They are constituted one with Adam, as we are, but we are not constituted one with each other. Nor, though we are one with Adam, is our guilt imputed to him. Why is this? The short answer is: because of the arbitrary constitution of God. A longer answer may be: because Adam is the original phase of the human race, and we are later phases, like later branches from the original stock of a tree. So any later phase is related in the same fundamental way to the original phase. And all the arrangements that we have just mentioned are constituted so by a supremely wise fiat. Despite our earlier claim that Edwards distanced himself from the Augustinian view of Adam's relation to his posterity, perhaps the rather selective way in which, according to Edwards, divine wisdom has chosen to configure the unity of the race suggests a vestigial attraction to that position. Or is Edwards simply making an appeal to the arbitrary will of God at each such point? It is not easy to tell.

Edwards's view of personal identity through time and of the unity and identity of the race through time is undoubtedly extravagant. His idea that each thing exists only for a moment seems bizarre, to say the

[32] Warfield, "Edwards and the New England Theology," 530. See also Gerstner, *The Rational Biblical Theology of Jonathan Edwards*, 2:328 ("It is not a doctrine of imputation, mediate or immediate"), and especially Oliver Crisp, "On the Theological Pedigree of Jonathan Edwards' Doctrine of Imputation," *Scottish Journal of Theology* 56 (2003):1-20.

least, though it would be wrong to deduce from this doctrine alone that Edwards thought that God is the only true cause in the entire universe. Presumably even things that exist for a moment may exercise their causal powers for that moment. Yet Edwards has one charming (if rather long-winded) aside that suggests that he thinks of his remarks on the oneness of the race more as a hypothesis than as a settled truth. He says:

> On the whole, if any don't like the philosophy, or the metaphysics (as some perhaps may choose to call it) made use of in the foregoing reasonings; yet I cannot doubt, but that a proper consideration of what is apparent and undeniable in fact, with respect to the dependence of the state and course of things in this universe on the sovereign constitution of the supreme Author and Lord of all, "who gives none account of any of his matters, and whose ways are past finding out," will be sufficient, with persons of common modesty and sobriety, to stop their mouths from making peremptory decisions against the justice of God, respecting what is so plainly and fully taught in his Holy Word, concerning the derivation of a depravity and guilt from Adam to his posterity; a thing so abundantly confirmed by what is found in the experience of all mankind in all ages. (409)

In other words, if you object to Edwards's philosophical reasoning here, and if you are a sufficiently modest and sober person, you will be content to take refuge in the sovereignty of God. We can be sure that this sentiment, while perfectly consistent with Edwards's own theological outlook, would hardly have satisfied Taylor of Norwich! Unless Taylor favors Edwards's "metaphysics," then this response to his objections will hardly convince him.

SUMMING UP

We have seen that Edwards presents the case for the "great Christian doctrine" of original sin by drawing on the evidence from experience (including that provided by Bible history), from the biblical teaching about the human race's relation to Adam, and from the weakness of many of the arguments of opponents of the doctrine. These strands of inquiry, when drawn together, combine to provide a powerful cumulative case for the solidarity of the race in the sin of Adam and of their guiltiness in him.

The Christian doctrine of original sin, and Edwards's defense of it, invites us to think of human sin in a way that cuts across much contemporary Christianity where the focus is on the individual, not on the human race, and where sin, in order to be sin, must be consciously identified as such by the sinner. But on Paul's or Augustine's or Edwards's view, sin is race-deep, arising in historical circumstances different from our own, from Adam with whom we are "one." Human wickedness arises from depths that are beyond conscious awareness. For such human wickedness there is no natural cure—certainly not from efforts made to repent and reform of conscious sin—but only a God-given cure through union with the last Adam, Jesus Christ.

We have also seen that for Edwards the writing of OS in the trying and testing circumstances of Stockbridge in the 1750s was not an academic exercise. He was engaged in sustained polemic against the individualistic and moralistic interpretation of the gospel propounded by John Taylor and others, whose writings in his view embodied the worst features revealed in the dawning of a new age. In this situation Edwards was faced with a classic dilemma. He could simply restate the doctrine of original sin in a formulaic way, or he could attempt to take the argument into the enemy's territory by offering arguments that are intended to convince him of the truth of this "great Christian doctrine."

Being both a creative and courageous person Edwards inevitably chose the latter strategy, the one adopted by all the great apologists of the Church from Athanasius onwards. It is the program of faith seeking understanding, of endeavoring to gain a better grasp of revealed truth by drawing out the "good and necessary" consequences of Scripture in the light of some opposed view or other, often by using the language of the opposition, and doing so in the heat of argument.[33] This project has proved invaluable in the development of theological understanding across the centuries. But it has its dangers, especially when it is practiced, as Edwards practiced it, in an "age of reason." The danger is that the taunts of the opposers will tempt the defender of the faith not only to express and epitomize the teaching of Scripture in language familiar to the opposition, but to be seduced into thinking that it is the job of the Christian theologian to offer explanations of biblical doctrine like a sci-

---

[33] For further discussion, see Paul Helm, *Faith and Understanding* (Grand Rapids, Mich: Eerdmans, 1997).

entist offering an explanation of experimental data or like a detective clearing up a crime.

There is reason to think that Edwards did not altogether escape this danger. It seems that by his extravagant idea of the unity and identity of the human race through time, as well as his distinctions between transient and abiding principles of human character, and between natural and supernatural features of human nature, he endeavored to offer explanations of deeply mysterious features of the human condition: the solidarity of the human race in sin and the entrance of sin into a world created good by God. I think that he thought he could lessen the mystery.

There is a fine line to be drawn between true theological creativity and theological rationalism. Such was his concern to safeguard the deposit of the faith against its detractors that Edwards stretched his great intellectual gifts almost to the breaking point, but his failure to provide an increased understanding of these aspects of the faith serves only to underline their deeply mysterious character. The faith is mysterious at such points not because it is intrinsically incoherent or paradoxical, but because a comprehensive understanding of it is beyond the grasp of finite minds. In Jonathan Edwards's endeavor to push theological understanding to the limits, and perhaps beyond the limits, there are, as in other aspects of his life, both heroic and tragic features.[34]

ANNOTATED BIBLIOGRAPHY

Crisp, Oliver D. *The Metaphysics of Sin*. Aldershot, Hants/Burlington, Vt.: Ashgate, forthcoming.
   A book-length treatment of Edwards's understanding of sin.

Gerstner, John. *The Rational Biblical Theology of Jonathan Edwards*. 3 vols. Powhatan, Va.: Berean/Orlando, Fla.: Ligonier, 1992.
   A massive and massively sympathetic treatment of Edwards's theology.

Helm, Paul. *Faith and Understanding*. Grand Rapids, Mich.: Eerdmans, 1997.
   A discussion of the place of reason in the development of theologi-

---

[34] Thanks are due to Oliver Crisp for his helpful comments on an earlier draft.

cal understanding. It contains a number of "case studies," including one on Edwards's views of personal identity.

— —. "A Forensic Dilemma: John Locke and Jonathan Edwards on Personal Identity." In *Jonathan Edwards, Philosophical Theologian*, edited by Paul Helm and Oliver D. Crisp, 45-49. Aldershot, Hants/Burlington, Vt.: Ashgate, 2003.
A comparison between the views of John Locke and Jonathan Edwards on personal identity and personal responsibility.

McDermott, Gerald. *Jonathan Edwards Confronts the Gods: Christian Theology, Enlightenment Religion, and Non-Christian Faiths*. New York: Oxford University Press, 2000.
Valuable particularly for its treatment of Edwards's relation to Deism.

Quinn, Philip. "Disputing the Augustinian Legacy: John Locke and Jonathan Edwards on Romans 5:12-19." In *The Augustinian Tradition*, edited by Gareth B. Matthews, 233-250. Berkeley, Calif.: University of California Press, 1999.
An interesting comparison between Locke's and Edwards's understanding of the Pauline parallel between Adam and Christ.

Storms, Sam. "Is Imputation Unjust? Jonathan Edwards on the Problem of Original Sin." *Reformation & Revival Journal* 12 (Summer 2003): 61-69.
A short, punchy account of Edwards's view treading much of the ground of the present essay.

Warfield, B. B. "Edwards and the New England Theology." In *Studies in Theology*, 515-538. New York: Oxford University Press, 1931.
An invaluable brief introduction to Edwards's theological thought and its immediate influence in New England.

9

THE WILL: FETTERED YET FREE (*FREEDOM OF THE WILL*)

Sam Storms

Jonathan Edwards was right. If the concept of libertarian freedom can be established, Calvinist theologians (he called them "reformed divines") will have lost all hope of defending their view of "original sin, the sovereignty of grace, election, redemption, conversion, the efficacious operation of the Holy Spirit, the nature of saving faith, perseverance of the saints, and other principles of . . . like kind."[1]

To understand "libertarian" freedom and the threat it poses to evangelical orthodoxy, we must look closely at the title to Edwards's treatise. *Freedom of the Will* is merely shorthand for the more cumbersome, *A Careful and Strict Inquiry into the Modern Prevailing Notions of That Freedom of the Will, Which Is Supposed to Be Essential to Moral Agency, Virtue and Vice, Reward and Punishment, Praise and Blame.*[2] Edwards's purpose was clearly to address a "prevailing" concept of human freedom that was thought to be foundational to moral accountability. Stephen Holmes is correct in reminding us that "Edwards' fundamental question in this book is ethical: what conditions must obtain for an action to be worthy of praise or blame? . . . He is concerned to establish those things that must be the case concerning human decision for such decision to be meaningfully analyzable ethically."[3] In other

---

[1] *The Works of Jonathan Edwards*, vol. 3, *Original Sin*, ed. Clyde A. Holbrook (New Haven, Conn.: Yale University Press, 1970), 376.

[2] All citations from Edwards's treatise will be from *Freedom of the Will*, ed. Paul Ramsey (New Haven, Conn.: Yale University Press, 1973 [fourth printing]), originally published in 1957 as the first in the projected twenty-seven-volume edition of Edwards's works, and hereafter cited within the text by page number only. Edwards began the actual drafting of the treatise in August 1752; it was ready for publication in 1753. This is somewhat misleading, however, in that Edwards had written extensively on the will in the *Miscellanies*, his private theological notebook, beginning as early as 1723.

[3] Stephen R. Holmes, "Strange Voices: Edwards on the Will," in *Listening to the Past: The Place of Tradition in Theology* (Grand Rapids, Mich.: Baker, 2002), 87-88.

words, it is "that freedom of the will which is supposed to be essential to moral agency," i.e., libertarian freedom, against which Edwards launches his considerable theological and philosophical skills.[4]

Sad to say, though, notwithstanding Edwards's efforts, the understanding of human freedom that he "sought to stop in its tracks is now so pervasive as to be axiomatic everywhere except amongst philosophers, who are aware there is an argument to be had, and those theologians who are prepared to risk incomprehension and dismissal as anachronistic by daring to mention such offensive (but traditional) notions as predestination, special providence and the sovereignty of God."[5] I have made a similar point in an article that addresses the use of libertarian freedom among so-called contemporary "open theists."[6] Clark Pinnock is representative of the latter and defines libertarian freedom or the power of contrary choice as follows:

> What I call "real freedom" is also called libertarian or contra-causal freedom. It views a free action as one in which a person is free to perform an action or refrain from performing it and is not completely determined in the matter by prior forces—nature, nurture or even God. Libertarian freedom recognizes the power of contrary choice. One acts freely in a situation if, and only if, one could have done otherwise. Free choices are choices that are not causally determined by conditions preceding them. It is the freedom of self-determination, in which the various motives and influences informing the choice are not the sufficient cause of the choice itself. The person makes the choice in a self-determined way. A person has options and there are different factors influencing us in deciding among them but the decision one takes involves making one of the reasons one's own, which is anything but random.[7]

My purpose in this essay is threefold. First, I will briefly unpack Edwards's devastating critique of libertarianism,[8] one that I am con-

---

[4] One cannot help but think of Paul Ramsey's comment in his editorial introduction to the volume on freedom of will: "This book alone is sufficient to establish its author as the greatest philosopher-theologian yet to grace the American scene" (2).

[5] Holmes, "Strange Voices," 88.

[6] C. Samuel Storms, "Prayer and the Power of Contrary Choice: Who Can and Cannot Pray for God to Save the Lost?" *Reformation & Revival Journal* 12 (Spring 2003): 53-67.

[7] Clark Pinnock, *Most Moved Mover: A Theology of God's Openness* (Grand Rapids, Mich.: Baker, 2001), 127.

[8] For a more extensive interaction with Edwards's arguments against libertarianism, see my *Tragedy in Eden: Original Sin in the Theology of Jonathan Edwards* (Lanham, Md.: University Press of America, 1985), 176-206.

vinced has yet to be successfully refuted. Second, I will reconstruct Edwards's concept of the will. Although some have found it to be intolerably complex,[9] it is actually quite simple and forthright once one grasps the meaning of several important terms he employs. Third, and finally, I want to address the most problematic element in Edwards's theology of the will—the fall of Adam and the entrance of evil into the human race. For all the biblical cogency of his concept of the will, Edwards argues himself into a philosophical predicament that gives all the appearance, his protests notwithstanding, of making God the author of sin. More on this below.

EDWARDS AND LIBERTARIANISM

The libertarians[10] whom Edwards encountered insisted that the will must exercise a certain sovereignty over itself whereby it determines or causes itself to act and choose. Whereas the will may be influenced by antecedent impulses or desires, it always retains an independent power to choose contrary to them. The will is free from any necessary causal connection to anything antecedent to the moment of choice.

Edwards finds this argument both incoherent and subject to an infinite regress. He points out that for the will to determine itself is for the will to act. Thus the act of will whereby it determines a subsequent act must itself be determined by a preceding act of will or the will cannot properly be said to be *self*-determined. If libertarianism is to be maintained, every act of will that determines a consequent act is itself preceded by an act of will, and so on until one comes to a *first* act of will. But if this first act is determined by a preceding one, it is not itself the first act. If, on the other hand, this act is *not* determined by a previous act, it cannot be free since it is not *self*-determined. If the first act of voli-

---

[9] Conrad Wright ("Edwards and the Arminians on the Freedom of the Will," *Harvard Theological Review* 35 [October 1942]) contends that "whatever else its publication may have done, it produced a state of incredible intellectual confusion. Edwards's followers part of the time did not understand him; his opponents often found themselves in a maze of contradictions; and the historian is fortunate if he can finish a reading of the documents with a confident understanding of the arguments and a clear picture of the real issues involved" (241). Mark Twain called Edwards's treatise an "insane debauch" marked by "the glare of a resplendent intellect gone mad" (*Mark Twain's Letters*, ed. A. B. Paine, 2 vols. [New York, 1917], 2:719-720, as cited in Henry F. May, "Jonathan Edwards and America," in *Jonathan Edwards and the American Experience*, ed. Nathan O. Hatch and Harry S. Stout [New York: Oxford University Press, 1988], 23).

[10] Those whom Edwards chose as representative of the libertarian position were Daniel Whitby (1638-1726), an Anglican divine; Thomas Chubb (1679-1747), a deist; and Isaac Watts (1674-1748), a hymn-writer who more closely approached Edwards's general theological position than the other two.

tion is not itself determined by a preceding act of will, that so-called first act is not determined by the will and is thus not free.

Edwards's point is that if the will chooses its choice or determines its own acts, it must be supposed to choose to choose this choice, and before that it would have to choose to choose to choose that choice, and so on *ad infinitum*. Therefore, the concept of freedom as self-determination either contradicts itself by positing an unchosen (i.e., non-self-determined) choice or shuts itself wholly out of the world by an infinite regress.

To avoid this conundrum, some libertarians argue that acts of will come to pass of themselves without any cause of any sort. They simply happen, spontaneously and inexplicably. But nothing is causeless, except the uncaused First Cause, God. To argue for volitional spontaneity would render all human choice random and haphazard, with no reason, intent, or motive accounting for its existence. If human acts of will are not causally tethered to human character, on what grounds does one establish their ethical value? How may one be blamed or praised for an act of will in the causation of which neither he nor anything else had a part? Furthermore, how can one explain a diversity of effects from a monolithic no-cause? If there is no ground or cause for the existence of an effect, what accounts for the diversity of one effect from another? Why is an entity what it is and not otherwise if not because of the specific nature of the cause that produced it?

Yet another option for the libertarian is to argue that one chooses in the absence of a prevailing motive. The will chooses between two or more things that are allegedly perfectly equal as perceived by the mind. The will is altogether indifferent to either (or any) of the objects of choice, yet determines itself toward one without being moved by any preponderating inducement.

But this is to say that the will chooses something instead of another at the same time it is wholly indifferent to both. But to choose is, by definition, to prefer. Whatever is preferred thus exerts a preponderate influence on the will. How can the will *prefer* A over B unless A appears *preferable*? Says Edwards:

> How ridiculous would it be for anybody to insist, that the soul chooses one thing before another, when at the very same instant it is perfectly indifferent with respect to each! This is the same thing as to say, the

soul prefers one thing to another, at the very same time that it has no preference. Choice and preference can no more be in a state of indifference, than motion can be in a state of rest, or than the preponderation of the scale of a balance can be in a state of equilibrium. (207)

How could a man be praised for preferring charity to stinginess, for example, if both deeds were equally preferable to him, or more accurately, lacking any preferability at all? Do we not praise a man for giving generously to the poor because we assume he is of such an antecedent character that such a deed appears more preferable to him than withholding his money? If there is nothing about the man that inclines him to prefer generosity, if the act of giving money is no more preferable to him than the act of withholding it, is he worthy of praise for giving?

Neither will it do to contend that freedom consists not in the act of the will itself but in a determining so to act. The operative sphere of freedom, on this suggestion, is simply removed one step farther back and is said to consist in causing or determining the change or transition from a state of indifference to a certain preference. "What is asserted," said Edwards, "is, that the will, while it yet remains in perfect equilibrium, without preference, determines to change itself from that state, and excite in itself a certain choice or preference" (208). But this determination of the will, supposedly indifferent, is open to the same objection noted above. Neither is it feasible to locate the sphere of freedom in a power to suspend the act of will and to keep it in indifference until there has been opportunity for proper deliberation. For is not the suspending of volition itself an *act* of volition, subject to the same strictures already stated? And if it is not an act of volition, how can liberty of will be present in it? I concur with Edwards that the idea of freedom consisting in indifference is "to the highest degree absurd and contradictory" (208).

Finally, Edwards's opponents would often assert that all acts of will are contingent events. They are not in any sense necessary. They could as easily not happen as happen. Nothing necessitates their occurrence. This argument is driven by the belief that if an event is necessary, it is morally vacuous. Only an act of will that could as easily have not occurred as occurred is an act worthy of the predicate "free" and subject to praise or blame. Edwards's response to this argument is multifaceted and beyond the scope of this essay. Be it noted that I have elsewhere addressed his argument from divine foreknowledge and the necessity the latter imposes on all events.[11] But Edwards's most important response to the argument from contingency is found in the distinction he makes between *natural* necessity and *moral* necessity. More on this below.

EDWARDS ON AUTHENTIC FREEDOM

If all events, including acts of will, have a cause or are determined by something, what is it that determines the will? Edwards argues that "it is that *motive*, which, as it stands in the view of the mind, is the strongest, that determines the will" (141, emphasis mine). By motive Edwards means the whole of that which moves, excites, or invites the mind to volition, whether that be one thing alone or several in conjunction. Motive is not itself desire, "but rather the totality of whatever awakens desire in us when apprehended."[12] Thus volition or choice is never contrary to the greatest apparent good. "The choice of the mind never departs from that which, at that time, and with respect to the direct and immediate objects of that decision of the mind, appears most agreeable and pleasing, all things considered."[13]

But if the choice of the mind, to use Edwards's terms, "never departs" from that motive that appears strongest, does not this impose a *necessity* on all acts of will? Yes, but it is a necessity that arises within and proceeds from the will, rather than one that is imposed from without and is contrary to it. The former Edwards calls "moral necessity" and the latter "natural necessity." I will return to this critical distinction momentarily.

If it is assumed that the will, to use Edwards's language, always is as the strongest motive, what is it that constitutes any supposed motive *to be* the strongest in the mind's eye? What is the cause of the state or condition of the mind that results in one motive being strong and another weak in the moment of perception? The answer to this question

---

[11] See my chapter "Open Theists in the Hands of an Angry Puritan: Jonathan Edwards on Divine Foreknowledge," in *The Legacy of Jonathan Edwards: American Religion and the Evangelical Tradition*, ed. D. G. Hart, Sean Michael Lucas, and Stephen J. Nichols (Grand Rapids, Mich.: Baker, 2003), 114-130.

[12] Hugh J. McCann, "Edwards on Free Will," in *Jonathan Edwards: Philosophical Theologian*, ed. Paul Helm and Oliver D. Crisp (Aldershot, Hants/Burlington, Vt.: Ashgate, 2003), 35.

[13] Ibid., 147.

leads us to Edwards's doctrine of constitutional depravity, or the doctrine of original sin.

Given a constitutional bias (i.e., inborn disposition or inclination) toward evil and unbelief, every motive that confronts the mind will appear good, agreeable, and strong only so far as it corresponds to (or tends to invite) an evil and vicious inclination. Likewise, every motive that has no strength or tendency to incite or induce an evil mind will be weak and hence ineffective to the will or any supposed consequent external action. Thus, given the reality of constitutional depravity, or a fixed bias of mind, only that which appears agreeable to that quality of mind will issue in external action, and every external action will simply be the effect of said bias. This is merely to say that Edwards's concept of the will is a function of his doctrine of original sin. Conrad Wright is surely correct in the following:

> The whole controversy would have been vastly simplified if the Arminians had recognized clearly that Edwards' treatise was not wrong, but irrelevant [or perhaps a better word would be, secondary]. They should have dismissed the Freedom of the Will, and concentrated on the treatise on Original Sin which complemented it. Moral necessity without total depravity loses all its sting.[14]

I will return to this point in the last section of this essay.

In the above citation, Wright referred to *moral necessity*, an idea without which Edwards's concept of the will is incoherent. Moral necessity refers to "that necessity of connection and consequence, which arises from such *moral causes*, as the strength of inclination, or motives, and the connection which there is in many cases between these and such volitions and actions" (156). By way of contrast, *natural* necessity is that which "men are under through the force of natural causes" (156), such as physical compulsion or torture or threat of pain or lack of opportunity. The "moral causes" noted by Edwards are

---

14 Conrad Wright, "Edwards and the Arminians on the Freedom of the Will," 252. See the discussion by Allen C. Guelzo in his *Edwards on the Will: A Century of American Theological Debate* (Middletown, Conn.: Wesleyan University Press, 1989), 47-50, as well as his article, "The Return of the Will: Jonathan Edwards and the Possibilities of Free Will," in *Edwards in Our Time: Jonathan Edwards and the Shaping of American Religion*, ed. Sang Hyun Lee and Allen C. Guelzo (Grand Rapids, Mich.: Eerdmans, 1999), 87-110.

internal to the person choosing—a like or dislike; a moral imperative that is held in high esteem; a sense of some advantage to be gained by moving one way or the other. Natural causes are external—a gun held to my head or a locked prison door. . . . Edwards can insist that a free choice is one which is caused only by moral causes, a constrained choice [i.e., one lacking authentic freedom] is one caused, in part at least, by natural causes.[15]

If a person should choose evil in consequence of that necessity which is external to his will and imposed upon him by constraint of natural forces, he is absolved from moral responsibility. But if he behaves unlawfully because of a necessity that is *in* his will and consistent with it, he is surely to blame. Far from undermining moral accountability, this is foundational to it, for do we not highly praise that person whose compassion arises from a deep-seated disposition or propensity for the welfare of others, and do we not condemn that person whose cruelty is the fruit of an entrenched and malicious character? Hugh McCann's explanation is lucid and to the point. Freedom, he notes,

> concerns the relation between willing and its consequences, with whether decision and volition are able to issue in the behavior chosen. Where we are able to do as we please, so that a choice to do A would result in our A-ing, we have free will. The opposite of this is not causation, which Edwards holds operates throughout, but rather *constraint* or *restraint*, whereby we are either forced to do what we do not will, or prevented from doing what we do or might will. This kind of necessity—Edwards sometimes calls it "natural necessity," to distinguish it from the moral variety—excuses. A prisoner in a locked cell can neither be praised nor blamed for not leaving. But moral necessity does not. However determined his will may have been in committing the crime that brought him to his cell, the prisoner deserves to be there.[16]

Or to illustrate yet again, if a man confined to a wheelchair by paralysis does not *move* to deliver a woman from attack, he is not morally culpable. But if he does not *care* that she is attacked, he is. Or if he is *not*

---

15 Stephen R. Holmes, *God of Grace and God of Glory: An Account of the Theology of Jonathan Edwards* (Grand Rapids, Mich.: Eerdmans, 2000), 153.
16 McCann, "Edwards on the Will," 36.

confined and is physically capable of saving her but chooses to look the other way, he is deserving of contempt.

An odd incident that illustrates this distinction occurred not long ago in the state of Pennsylvania. A man who robbed a bank by telling an employee that he had a bomb strapped to his body was later apprehended by police. He pleaded with them for help, insisting that the bomb had been placed there by someone else who threatened to detonate it if he did not comply. Sure enough, at the precise moment the "robber" said the bomb would explode, it did—on national television, no less. Assuming this man was in no way inclined to theft, his choice to "rob" the bank was constrained. His will was subject to a natural necessity by factors over which he had no control. Had he survived and his claim substantiated, a court of law would most certainly have declared him not guilty. On the other hand, had it been proven that he lied about the bomb and that his decision to rob the bank was his own, arising from the greed or anger or rebellion of his heart, he would be fully deserving of whatever penal sanctions attach to such a crime.

Edwards's point is that there is a natural inability, arising from a natural necessity, that exonerates a person from praise or blame. But there is also a moral inability, arising from a moral necessity, that actually establishes culpability. If I fail to save a drowning child because I cannot swim (a natural inability), I am subject to a natural necessity and thus blameless. If I refuse to save a drowning child because I don't care (a moral inability), I am subject to a moral necessity and deserving of condemnation. When Martin Luther stood before the Diet of Worms in 1521 and declared, "Here I stand. I can do no other," it wasn't because his legs were incapable of carrying him out of the presence of his accusers. His "inability" to do anything other was the "necessary" product of a will that "freely" defied the Roman Catholic Church.

This is the same understanding that we find in Calvin, who chides those who fail to distinguish between necessity and compulsion. He points, as does Edwards, to the necessity that God always does what is good. "But suppose," says Calvin, "some blasphemer sneers that God deserves little praise for His own goodness, constrained as He is to preserve it. Will this not be a ready answer to him: not from violent impulsion [or what Edwards would call natural necessity], but from His boundless goodness [i.e., moral necessity] comes God's inability to do evil?"[17] He concludes that "if the fact that he *must* do good [emphasis mine] does not hinder God's free will in doing good; if the devil, who can do only evil, yet sins with his will—who shall say that man therefore sins less willingly because he is subject to the [moral] necessity of sinning?"[18] The point of this distinction between necessity and compulsion, then, is that

> man, as he was corrupted by the Fall, sinned willingly, not unwillingly or by compulsion; by the most eager inclination of his heart, not by forced compulsion; by the prompting of his own lust, not by compulsion from without. Yet so depraved is his nature that he can be moved or impelled only to evil. But if this is true, then it is clearly expressed that man is surely subject to the [moral] necessity of sinning.[19]

So let me summarize. Foundational to Edwards's theory is that nothing comes to pass without a cause, including all acts of the will. The cause of an act of will is that motive which appears most agreeable to the mind. The will, therefore, is determined by or finds its cause and ground of existence in the strongest motive as perceived by the mind. The will, therefore, always is as the greatest apparent good is. The will is neither self-determined nor undetermined but always follows the last and prevailing dictate of the understanding. The act of will is necessarily connected in a cause/effect relationship with the strongest motive as perceived by the mind and cannot but be as the motive is. This type of necessity is moral, lies within the will, and is one with it. It is a necessity wholly compatible with praise and/or blame. If, on the other hand, the will is acted upon by external factors contrary to its desires, the individual is exempted from responsibility. Freedom is simply the opportunity one has to act according to one's will or in the pursuit of one's desires. This notion of freedom, contends Edwards, is not only compatible with but absolutely essential to moral responsibility.

---

[17] John Calvin, *Institutes of the Christian Religion*, ed. John T. McNeill (Philadelphia: Westminster, 1975), II.3.5.
[18] Ibid.
[19] Ibid.

EDWARDS AND THE PROBLEM OF EVIL

As I briefly noted earlier, the fundamental issue is not whether the strongest motive has a causal influence on the will, but what it is that causes any supposed motive *to be* highest in the mind's view. What is the cause of the state or temper of mind that results in one motive being strong and another weak in the moment of perception? Since every effect must have a cause, either man or God is the uncaused initial cause of the disposition or state of mind from which issue evil actions. If the will is not self-determined, it must be determined by God. But this would appear to make God the direct and efficient cause of moral evil. Edwards explicitly denies the latter and accounts for the existence of evil by appealing to the notion of divine *permission*:

> There is a great difference between God's being concerned thus, by his *permission*, in an event and act, which in the inherent subject and agent of it, is sin (though the event will certainly follow on his permission), and his being concerned in it by *producing* it and exerting the act of sin; or between his being the *orderer* of its certain existence, by *not hindering* it, under certain circumstances, and his being the proper *actor* or *author* of it, by a *positive agency* or *efficiency*. (403)

But if Edwards is to exonerate God, he must define divine permission as the absence of any causal influence in the inception of a sinful disposition. But to do so results in either asserting no cause for the evil disposition of the mind (spontaneity) or allowing the person to be his own cause (self-determination), both of which are contrary to his entire treatise.

We are left with this question: Why and how did Adam sin? The first transgression was either self caused, spontaneous, or caused by some act of God. James Dana, Edwards's chief critic,[20] insists that Edwards "must either maintain the positive energy and action of the deity in the introduction of sin into the world, or else admit that it arose from a cause in the mind of the sinner—in other words, that he was self-determined."[21]

To understand Edwards's response to this criticism we must consider his view of the nature of Adam and his will as created antecedent

---

[20] James Dana, *An Examination of the Late Reverend Edwards' 'Enquiry on Freedom of Will'* (Boston: Daniel Kneeland, 1770); and *The "Examination of the Late Rev'd President Edwards' Enquiry on Freedom of the Will," Continued* (New Haven, Conn.: Thomas and Samuel Green, 1773), hereafter cited as *Examination Continued.*

[21] Dana, *Examination Continued*, 59.

to the Fall. Edwards articulated his view in response to John Taylor,[22] who argued that the Reformed doctrine of original sin demanded that human nature at some time be corrupted by a positive influence or infusion of evil, either from God or the individual. Edwards countered by insisting that

> the absence of positive good principles, and so the withholding of a special divine influence to impart and maintain those good principles, leaving the common natural principles of self-love, natural appetite, etc. (which were in man in innocence) leaving these, I say, to themselves, without the government of superior divine principles, will certainly be followed with corruption, yea, and total corruption of the heart, without occasion for any positive influence at all.[23]

Edwards conceived of the creation of Adam as follows:

> When God made man at first, he implanted in him two kinds of principles. There was an *inferior* kind, which may be called *natural*, being the principles of mere human nature; such as self-love, with those natural appetites and passions, which belong to the nature of man, in which his love to his own liberty, honor and pleasure were exercised.[24]

Besides these, he continues,

> there were *superior* principles, that were spiritual, holy and divine, summarily comprehended in divine love; wherein consisted the spiritual image of God, and man's righteousness and true holiness; which are called in Scripture the *divine nature*.[25]

The superior principle was designed by God to rule the natural and thus maintain psychical and physical harmony in the being of Adam. However, "when man sinned, and broke God's Covenant, and fell under his curse, these superior principles left his heart: for indeed God then left him."[26] But if these principles did not leave *until* Adam sinned,

---

[22] For a thorough analysis of Taylor's treatise, see my *Tragedy in Eden: Original Sin in the Theology of Jonathan Edwards*, 31-70. Much of what follows has been adapted from that book.
[23] Edwards, *Original Sin*, 381.
[24] Ibid.
[25] Ibid.
[26] Ibid., 382.

their absence cannot be the cause of sin. Communion with God, on which the existence of the superior principles in Adam and their domination of the lower principles depended, ceased only *after* he had transgressed.

Edwards says, "it was of necessity, when once man had sinned, that original righteousness should be taken away; . . . It was impossible therefore, but that original righteousness must be taken away *upon man's sinning.*"[27] The consequence for Adam was this:

> The inferior principles of self-love and natural appetite, which were given only to serve, being alone, and left to themselves, of course became reigning principles; having no superior principles to regulate or control them, they became absolute masters of the heart. The immediate consequence of which was a *fatal catastrophe*, a turning of all things upside down, and the succession of a state of the most odious and dreadful confusion.[28]

Were it necessary, Edwards believes it an easy task to demonstrate

> how every lust and depraved disposition of man's heart would naturally arise from this *privative* original, . . . Thus 'tis easy to give an account, how total corruption of heart should follow on man's eating the forbidden fruit, though that was but one act of sin, *without God's putting* any evil into his heart, or *implanting* any bad principle, or *infusing* any corrupt taint and so becoming the *author* of depravity.[29]

Here is the problem: If total corruption of heart *followed* the initial transgression, and was therefore not its cause but its consequence, how did Adam sin? Edwards insists that "only God's *withdrawing*, as it was highly proper and necessary that he should, from rebel-man, being as it were driven away by his abominable wickedness, and men's *natural* principles being *left to themselves*, this is sufficient to account for his being entirely corrupt, and bent on sinning against God."[30]

But since Adam's fall preceded and resulted in the withdrawal by God of the superior principle in his soul, thereby assuring only that

---

27 "Miscellanies," no. 374, in *The Works of Jonathan Edwards*, vol. 13, *The "Miscellanies," a-500*, ed. Thomas A. Schafer (New Haven, Conn.: Yale University Press, 1994), 446 (emphasis mine).

28 Edwards, *Original Sin*, 382.

29 Ibid., 383.

30 Ibid.

Adam would persist in sin, but not explaining the cause of its initial appearance, and since Edwards has previously dismissed the suggestion that Adam's first act of volitional rebellion was self-determined or spontaneous, why did, or rather, *how could* Adam sin?

Edwards consistently affirms that the withdrawal from Adam of divine influence was *subsequent to* his transgression. The departure of God's sustaining grace was in consequence of something Adam, not God, did. Adam's nature became corrupt, says Edwards, prior to and therefore apart from any action on the part of the Deity. How then did Adam sin? Was it in consequence of some antecedent disposition in his nature as created? No, for Adam was created upright and inclined to righteousness. Edwards does suggest in one place that "it was meet [fitting], if sin did come into existence, and appear in the world, it should arise from the imperfection which properly belongs to a creature, as such, and should appear so to do, that it might appear not to be from God as the efficient or fountain" (413). But any imperfection in the creature, as such, can only reflect badly on the Creator.

Might not this evil disposition be the effect of a sinful act of will by Adam, rather than antecedent to it? But how could Adam have come by a wicked will if he was created holy? Such an act of will cannot be self-determined nor have emerged spontaneously. Is, then, Thomas Schafer correct in saying that "Edwards' doctrine of the will, required alike by his theology and his metaphysics, breaks on the impossible task of accounting for both original righteousness and the fall"?[31]

Once Edwards has exempted God from any direct causal influence in the initial transgression of Adam, he simply has no way of explaining how the first man, being righteous, could generate an act of rebellion, and this notwithstanding the positive presence and sustaining influence of divine grace! The only antecedent cause in Adam sufficient to a volitional effect is that upright and holy disposition with which he was endowed by God from the beginning of his existence. However, such a disposition could, by Edwards's own admission, yield only such acts that partake of the quality of the cause (or motive) whence they proceed. Thus Edwards's scheme is capable only of explaining how Adam might continue to sin but not how he might *begin* to sin.

If Adam's sin, like all events, demands a cause sufficient to the effect,

---

[31] Thomas A. Schafer, "The Concept of Being in the Thought of Jonathan Edwards" (Ph.D. diss., Duke University, 1951), 228.

either Adam by self-determination or God by direct interposition is the morally responsible efficient of that first transgression. A divine decree to permit the Fall merely asserts that God determined not to hinder it *should* it occur. It does not sufficiently explain why or how it did in fact occur. In several of his "Miscellanies" Edwards addresses this point. For example:

> Adam had a sufficient assistance of God always present with him, to have enabled him to have obeyed, if he had used his natural abilities in endeavoring it; though the assistance was not such as it would have been after his confirmation, to render it impossible for him to sin.[32]

But why did he not use his natural abilities if they were created righteous? If they were not righteous, then they were either evil or indifferent. If evil, then God is the cause of sin for having directly created Adam in that condition. If indifferent, then how could they yield an ethically blamable action? Edwards has already argued that an indifferent cause cannot explain an immoral (or moral) effect.

In the same paragraph he contends that "man might be deceived, so that he should not be disposed to use his endeavors to persevere; but if he did use his endeavors, there was a sufficient assistance always with him to enable him to persevere."[33] But to what in Adam, as created, would temptation have appealed? What in Adam was subject to being deceived to sin if, as argued, Adam was created righteous? And if righteous, how could any temptation have any strength to evoke a sinful response? By Edwards's own reasoning, the will always is as the greatest apparent good. But by virtue of that original righteousness with which Adam was initially endowed, no evil motive could ever appear good or have any tendency to evoke or excite the mind. The mind, being by nature inclined to righteousness, will find suitable or pleasing only such motives as are morally compatible with it. Should it be suggested that God permitted Adam to be confronted with a temptation (motive) he knew Adam was too weak to resist in that condition in which God had created him, then it is God, not Adam, who is to blame for the sin that necessarily followed.

---

[32] "Miscellanies," no. 501, in *The Works of Jonathan Edwards*, vol. 18, *The "Miscellanies," 501-832*, ed. Ava Chamberlain (New Haven, Conn.: Yale University Press, 2000), 51.
[33] Ibid.

216 A God-Entranced Vision of All Things

Adam, says Edwards, was created upright and thus from the moment of his first existence preferred what is good and righteous. Consequently, to use Edwards's own terminology, for Adam, who presently prefers good, to at present prefer evil is for him to prefer at present what is at present not preferable. Edwards himself insisted that this is logically absurd. But to predicate of Adam a preference for evil at precisely the moment he prefers good is to affirm just that. On the basis of what Edwards himself has said, the only way for Adam at present to prefer the opposite (i.e., evil) of what is at present preferred (i.e., good) is for God to directly alter or influence his present preference. To admit this, however, is to concede the objection that Edwards's concept of causal determinism of the will makes God the author of sin.

Edwards is not unaware of this problem and addresses it this way:

> If it be inquired how man came to sin, seeing he had no sinful inclinations in him, except God took away his grace from him that he had been wont to give him and so let him fall, I answer, there was no need of that; there was no need of taking away any that had been given him, but he sinned under that temptation because God did not give him more.[34]

But how did he sin even with what God *had* given him, if what he had was righteous? Edwards continues:

> He did not take away that grace from him while he was perfectly innocent, which grace was his original righteousness; but he only withheld his confirming grace. . . . This was the grace Adam was to have had if he had stood, when he came to receive his reward. This grace God was not obliged to grant him . . . . and so the sin *certainly* followed the temptation of the devil. So that, as to the sin of mankind, it came from the devil.[35]

By this Edwards means, as he says again in "Miscellany 436," that God gave Adam "sufficient" grace but not "efficacious" grace to resist temptation. But why does Edwards infer from the absence of efficacious grace that sin "certainly" followed from the temptation? As I have already argued, even in the absence of confirming or efficacious grace there is nothing in Adam causally sufficient to explain the effect (i.e., his

---

[34] "Miscellanies," no. 290, in *WJE*, 18:382.
[35] Ibid. (emphasis mine).

sin). If by creation he is in such a condition that, antecedent to God's withdrawal of divine influence, he necessarily sins, then God is most certainly the efficient and morally responsible cause of the transgression.

Neither will it do to say that Adam fell because his will was overpowered by the immoral and deceptive influence of Satan. This suggestion is problematic for two reasons. First, it would mean that Adam fell by a *natural* necessity, which Edwards has argued exempts one from moral responsibility. Second, this would only push the problem of evil back a step such that every question heretofore asked of Adam and his transgression would be asked of Satan and his.

This is the dilemma that prompted James Dana to conclude that, on the whole, Edwards's doctrine,

> while it acquits the creature from all blame, impeacheth the Creator as the positive cause and source of the revolt of angels and mankind, and ultimately fixeth all the criminality in the universe on him. How infinitely reproachful must that scheme of doctrine be, which involveth so horrid and blasphemous an imputation on the supreme creator and governor of the universe.[36]

Dana's solution to the problem, however, is likewise plagued with an insurmountable difficulty. Nothing that the Arminian can say about the contingency or self-determining power of the will can serve to explain with any less difficulty how a sinful inclination could arise in the heart of him who was created holy and upright. Nor will it suffice to argue (as did Pelagius) that Adam was not created holy and upright but with an indifference or equilibrium of will, for the same objections Edwards raised earlier against indifference would apply here with equal force (414).

Dana merely asserts that how sin came to be permitted is more than one can comprehend. But if God knew (and all but contemporary open theists would affirm he did) that Adam would sin if left to himself, a condition Dana affirms came from the Creator and for which he, therefore, is ultimately responsible, and without that assistance which was absolutely necessary to the avoiding of sin (which assistance God surely could have provided had he so willed), then in the nature of the case God is as properly the reason why Adam sinned as if he (God) were the efficient

---

[36] Dana, *Examination Continued*, 68.

cause of it. Thus the mere existence of sin, and not just the question of its original cause, poses a problem that seems to defy explanation.

It would appear that Dana is unable and Edwards unwilling to explain how Adam fell. Dana is unable because spontaneity, self-determination, and indifference fail to account for the transition of Adam's will from obedience to rebellion. Edwards is unwilling in that his deterministic concept of human volition, if consistently applied, must trace every effect in the universe, and therefore every act of will, to the ultimate, all-sufficient, uncaused cause, the eternal Deity.

CONCLUSION

I began this essay with Edwards's insistent claim that if libertarian freedom is embraced, one must relinquish any hold on a Calvinistic soteriology and those doctrines essential to it. I trust that whether or not the reader agrees with Edwards's conclusions, he will acknowledge the truth of that assertion. As mysterious and unsettling as Edwards's treatise so often proves, I for one remain convinced that he is correct in his reasoning and reading of Scripture. Perhaps, then, I should close by leaning heavily on that text with which Edwards himself concluded his most famous work:

> For it is written, "I will destroy the wisdom of the wise, and the discernment of the discerning I will thwart." Where is the one who is wise? Where is the scribe? Where is the debater of this age? Has not God made foolish the wisdom of the world? . . . But God chose what is foolish in the world to shame the wise; God chose what is weak in the world to shame the strong; God chose what is low and despised in the world, even things that are not, to bring to nothing things that are, so that no human being might boast in the presence of God. (1 Cor. 1:19-20, 27-29)

ANNOTATED BIBLIOGRAPHY

Fiering, Norman. *Jonathan Edwards' Moral Thought and Its British Context*. Chapel Hill, N.C.: University of North Carolina Press, 1981.

A wide-ranging treatment of Edwards's ethical theory with extensive discussion of his treatise on the will.

Guelzo, Allen C. *Edwards on the Will: A Century of American Theological Debate.* Middletown, Conn.: Wesleyan University Press, 1989.

An encyclopedic treatment of the historical and theological context and aftermath of Edwards's treatise. One should also consult Guelzo's article, "The Return of the Will: Jonathan Edwards and the Possibilities of Free Will," in *Edwards in Our Time: Jonathan Edwards and the Shaping of American Religion* (Grand Rapids, Mich.: Eerdmans, 1999), 87-110, where he address the relationship of Edwards's theory to contemporary open theism.

Holmes, Stephen. "Strange Voices: Edwards on the Will." In *Listening to the Past: The Place of Tradition in Theology,* 86-107. Grand Rapids, Mich.: Baker, 2002.

A brief but insightful overview of Edwards on the will that goes beyond his comments in *God of Grace & God of Glory: An Account of the Theology of Jonathan Edwards* (Grand Rapids, Mich.: Eerdmans, 2000).

McCann, Hugh J. "Edwards on Free Will." In *Jonathan Edwards: Philosophical Theologian,* edited by Paul Ielm and Oliver D. Crisp, 27-43. Aldershot, Hants/Burlington, Vt.: Ashgate, 2003.

A critical response to Edwards's treatise in which he affirms the truth of libertarian freedom.

McClymond, Michael J. *Encounters with God: An Approach to the Theology of Jonathan Edwards.* New York: Oxford University Press, 1998.

Although somewhat brief (the text itself is only 112 pages), this is an excellent introduction to the theology of Edwards.

Storms, Sam. "Is Imputation Unjust? Jonathan Edwards on the Problem of Original Sin." *Reformation & Revival Journal* 12 (Summer 2003): 61-69.

In this article I argue that although ingenious, and perhaps correct, Edwards's view on personal identity and continuous creation does not solve the ethical problem posed by the imputation of Adam's sin.

— —. "Open Theism in the Hands of an Angry Puritan: Jonathan Edwards on Divine Foreknowledge." In *The Legacy of Jonathan Edwards: American Religion and the Evangelical Tradition,* edited by D. G. Hart, Sean Michael Lucas, and Stephen J. Nichols, 114-130. Grand Rapids, Mich.: Baker, 2003.

Here I unpack Edwards on foreknowledge and the way in which he would, no doubt, have responded to contemporary open theism.

— —. *Tragedy in Eden: Original Sin in the Theology of Jonathan Edwards*. Lanham, Md.: University Press of America, 1985.

This is an abbreviated version of my Ph.D. dissertation in which I analyze Edwards on both free will and original sin.

Talbot, Mark R. "True Freedom: The Liberty That Scripture Portrays as Worth Having." In *Beyond the Bounds: Open Theism and the Undermining of Biblical Christianity*, edited by John Piper, Justin Taylor, and Paul Kjoss Helseth, 77-109. Wheaton, Ill.: Crossway Books, 2003.

This is an excellent critique of libertarian free will and a biblical defense of the model found in Edwards's treatise.

Zakai, Avihu. *Jonathan Edwards' Philosophy of History: The Reenchantment of the World in the Age of Enlightenment*. Princeton, N.J.: Princeton University Press, 2003.

Although written in a somewhat repetitive style, this is an excellent analysis of Edwards's philosophy of history as found in his treatise, *A History of the Work of Redemption*.

10

GODLY EMOTIONS
(*RELIGIOUS AFFECTIONS*)

Mark R. Talbot

One of Scripture's most arresting incidents occurs in the book of Numbers. Numbers records Israel's wilderness wanderings. In chapter 25, Israel was encamped at Shittim getting ready to cross over the River Jordan into Canaan. But even there, right on the verge of the Promised Land, Israelite men began to indulge in sexual immorality and Baal worship with foreign women. God reacted fiercely to this and commanded Moses to execute the guilty Israelites. Yet even as Moses was carrying this out, Zimri, the son of one of the Simeonite leaders, brought a Midianite woman, Cozbi, into the Israelite camp in front of everyone. Here the text becomes a bit unclear, but it seems that Zimri and Cozbi went into his tent to have sex.[1] In any case, when Phinehas, one of Aaron's grandsons, saw what was happening, he grabbed a spear and killed Zimri and Cozbi with a single thrust. God then declared to Moses, "Phinehas . . . has turned back my wrath from the people of Israel in that he was jealous with my jealousy" (vv. 10-11). God praised Phinehas's act because it arose from godly jealousy; and because of

---

[1] It may have been much worse. In his commentary on Numbers in *The Expositor's Biblical Commentary*, 5 vols., ed. Frank E. Gaebelein (Grand Rapids, Mich.: Zondervan, 1990), 1:918ff., Ronald B. Allen speculates that this passage's obscurity may been prompted by the fact that "the scribes of Scripture found [the actions described here] to be quite repellant and that the precise nature of the offense was," consequently, "softened somewhat through time." He suggests that we understand verse 6 like this:

> Then a certain Israelite man brought *the* Midianite woman to *the* Tent [*of* God] right before the eyes of Moses and the eyes of all the congregation of Israel; *and they were sporting* at the entrance of the Tent of Meeting.

In other words, what this couple did was "to engage in a sexual embrace in the manner of Baal worship—right at the entrance of the holy Tent of God," right in front of Moses. If Allen is right (and it is worth reading the whole of his commentary on vv. 6-9 to assess his case), then the contempt shown by Zimri and Cozbi "for the holy things and the word of the Lord . . . is unimaginable" and Phinehas's emotional reaction becomes even more intelligible.

Phinehas's jealousy, God made a special covenant of peace and perpetual priesthood with him and his descendants forever (see vv. 12-13).

Jealousy is an emotion—a particularly intense emotion, as Scripture
sees it (see Prov. 27:4), and a negative one at that (see Deut. 29:20; Rom.
10:19). It is an emotion that arises from vigilance, when (rightly or
wrongly) we prize something so much that we guard it and then feel fear
when we think it is threatened, or resentment when we believe that it is
being dishonored or eclipsed.[2] For instance, in everyday situations we
often become jealous when we fear that our right to someone's exclusive
attachment or loyalty is being threatened or when we resent someone
else's advantages or success. Usually we think that jealousy is a bad thing
and something to be avoided, as it often is (see Acts 5:12-18; Rom. 13:13;
Jas. 3:13-16). Yet sometimes jealousy is a good thing (see 2 Cor. 11:2-3;
Ezek. 36:1-7; Zech. 8:1-8). If I am not jealous of my wife's affections, then
I don't love her as I should. And if God were not jealous for the exclusive affection of his people, then he would not be serious about his
covenant with them (see Exod. 20:1-6; Deut. 4:23-24; Ezek. 16:35-43).[3]

In other words, jealousy can be a godly emotion—an emotion that
Scripture either portrays God as having or as wanting his people to have
in particular circumstances. In these circumstances, being jealous is a sign
of true faith (see Ps. 106:28-31). It is, then, one of many emotions that
can indicate whether our hearts are right with God, as Jonathan Edwards
argues in his great book, *A Treatise Concerning the Religious Affections*.

THE HISTORICAL AND THEOLOGICAL BACKGROUND
TO *RELIGIOUS AFFECTIONS*

"Examine yourselves," the apostle Paul commanded the Corinthians,
"to see whether you are in the faith" (2 Cor. 13:5). Part of Jonathan
Edwards's reason for writing *Religious Affections* was to encourage professing Christians to obey this command.[4] Edwards published *Religious
Affections* in 1746 as part of a prolonged analysis and qualified defense

---

[2] This way of describing jealousy applies especially to human jealousy and not to divine jealousy, since God's jealousy for his people certainly involves no fear and probably should not be described as involving any resentment. For one attempt to understand divine jealousy, see John M. Frame, *The Doctrine of God* (Phillipsburg, N.J.: Presbyterian & Reformed, 2002), 458ff.

[3] Much of these first two paragraphs and a few sentences and paragraphs in what follows come from my article, "Godly Emotions," in *Modern Reformation* 10/6 (November/December 2001): 32-37, used with the permission of the Alliance of Confessing Evangelicals. This article is also available on the Alliance of Confessing Evangelicals website: www.alliancenet.org.

of the first "Great Awakening" in America, which began in his church in Northampton, Massachusetts, around 1734.[5] Some historical and theological background here will help us to appreciate Edwards's great book and understand why we should still study it today.

Contemporary observers described what was happening in New England after 1734 as a time of general "awakening"—that is, a time when significant numbers of people began to realize that they were under God's judgment and thus needed his mercy and saving grace. Describing what was happening in New England after 1734 in this way involves some careful theological thinking.[6] The Puritans who landed at Massachusetts Bay in 1620 intended New England to be a great experiment, the experiment of Calvinistic Christians sojourning to a new country to set up a whole way of life that would glorify God—a "city set on a hill" that could not be hid (Matt. 5:14),[7] a holy commonwealth that would manifest God's righteousness on earth and that might, by doing so, usher in the religious renewal of the whole world through God's millennial reign.[8] They recognized, as all Christians should, that a person must do more than merely profess Christian belief to be saved. Merely saying, "Lord, Lord" to Jesus is not enough to insure that we will enter Christ's kingdom (see Matt. 7:21). Conversion is necessary.[9] And they knew that true Christian conversion makes people active and

---

[4] See his *Religious Affections* in *The Works of Jonathan Edwards*, vol. 2, ed. John E. Smith (New Haven, Conn.: Yale University Press, 1959), 169, where Edwards cites this passage in the midst of arguing that Christian assurance is available to all Christians and should indeed be sought by each. See also the prefatory material to Part Three, 193-197. I will be citing this edition of *Religious Affections*, since it is part of the authoritative Yale edition of Edwards's works. Yet *Religious Affections* is available in many editions, including an inexpensive paperback edition from The Banner of Truth Trust.

[5] Usually the first Great Awakening is taken to start around 1740, with special reference to George Whitefield and the results of his preaching. But in reality the causes of what happened around that time include reports of and writings about—to say nothing of the continuing spiritual effects of—what had happened in Northampton around 1734. I think that proper hindsight should lead us, then, to see the Holy Spirit's great visitation on America beginning then and there.

[6] There is biblical warrant for this use of "awakening." See, e.g., Isaiah 26:19, 52:1; Joel 1:5; Ephesians 5:8-14; 1 Thessalonians 5:4-8; and Revelation 3:1-4.

[7] This image recurs repeatedly in the writings of the New England Puritans. Edwards himself uses it to describe Northampton. See, for instance, his sermon of that title in *The Works of Jonathan Edwards*, vol. 19, *Sermons and Discourses 1734-1738*, ed. M. X. Lesser (New Haven, Conn.: Yale University Press, 2001), 537-559, as well as his other references to the same idea as found in the index to that volume.

[8] For Edwards's own hopes that the awakening that started in Northampton and that then spread much more broadly under the influence of itinerant preachers like George Whitefield would eventually result in God's millennial reign, see C. C. Goen's introduction to *The Great Awakening*, WJE, vol. 4 (New Haven, Conn.: Yale University Press, 1972), especially 71f. George Marsden also examines this aspect of Edwards's thought in *Jonathan Edwards: A Life* (New Haven, Conn.: Yale University Press, 2003), especially 265-267, 315, 335-337.

[9] For a scriptural and theological exposition of the claims that I make here about conversion, saving faith, regeneration, and so on, please see my booklet, *The Signs of True Conversion* (Wheaton, Ill.: Crossway Books, 2000).

fervent for Christ because it involves their deliberately and consciously repenting of all sin and wickedness as well as their turning decisively to the Triune God in saving faith.

Most of the Pilgrims who crossed the Atlantic to come to America in the 1600s had showed signs of true conversion; indeed, it was their religious fervency that brought them here. Yet that fervency had cooled as the earliest generations of settlers spread out and gave way to later generations who shared the form of their parents' faith but not necessarily the power thereof. New England's churches, even in Jonathan Edwards's grandfather's time,[10] were clearly becoming "mixed companies" of some who showed evidence of true Christian conversion and some who did not.

Puritans on both sides of the Atlantic had been convinced by Scripture that salvation is entirely from God; they knew that true conversion depends on God having regenerated a person's heart. They also knew that Scripture represents God as ordinarily working in regular ways. They knew, for instance, that God has ordained preaching as the ordinary means by which sinners come to call upon the name of Christ in saving faith (see Rom. 10:8-17; Mark 16:14-16; Acts 10:34-48). Gathering together all that they thought they had found in Scripture regarding the usual steps or stages that sinners will pass through on the way to true conversion, they developed a "morphology of conversion"—that is, a step-by-step analysis of what sinners would normally experience up to and through the moment when God regenerated their hearts.[11]

This morphology remained somewhat flexible and could include more or fewer steps. For instance, in Jonathan Edwards's father's hands, it can be taken to involve just three essential steps: conviction, humiliation, and regeneration.[12]

As Timothy Edwards saw it, the first essential step in the process involves "conviction" or a person's "awakening sense of [his or her] sad

---

[10] Solomon Stoddard (1643-1729) was Edwards's grandfather and his immediate predecessor in the Northampton pulpit. He was a great churchman and sophisticated theological writer in his own right.

[11] For a careful description of the Puritan morphology of conversion with primary reference to Jonathan Edwards's own understanding of it, see again C. C. Goen's introduction in WJE, 4:25-32. I think the Puritan morphology, in the form in which I am about to give it, fails to acknowledge the full range of scriptural examples of true conversion. In particular, Timothy Edwards's second step of "humiliation"—which, Marsden informs us, he was particularly insistent about—seems to me to be a step or stage in Christian development that many Christians reach late or perhaps even never in their earthly lives and that is not clearly present in every case of conversion in the Scriptures.

[12] Timothy Edwards (1669-1758) was himself a pastor who oversaw several local "awakenings" in his church in East Windsor, Connecticut. In my next paragraph, I am quoting from his 1695 sermon on Acts 16:29-30 as portions of it are found in Marsden's biography, op. cit., 26-28, as are the points that I summarize from Marsden in that and the next paragraph.

estate with reference to eternity." Because this step involves someone beginning to realize that he or she is breaking God's law, it usually evokes some typical reactions, such as a sense of foreboding or fear at the prospect of angering God and then perhaps a resolution to change and do better. Of course, reactions like these are natural when anyone is starting to wake up to his or her wrongdoing or sinfulness[13]—for instance, children tend to react similarly to their parents when they realize that they have done what displeases them—and so they don't in and of themselves guarantee that God has begun the process that will eventuate in regeneration. Mere awakening, then, needs to be followed by something more, namely, these Puritans thought, by a sinner's clearer sense of his or her true state.

Timothy Edwards called this second step or stage "humiliation," when sinners recognize that, despite their best resolutions, they are bound to sin and fully deserve eternal damnation. At this stage, as George Marsden observes, the Puritan morphology required potential converts to "be 'truly humbled' by a total sense of their own unworthiness." So it involves a lot of emotional disturbance, even though, once again, a non-Christian could have similar emotions, and thus having them is not itself a sure sign of true conversion.[14] Yet, as Marsden notes, the Puritans believed that it was only by going through this emotionally harrowing stage that a person became "sufficiently prepared to reach the third step" of receiving, by God's grace, the radical change of heart that is known as regeneration. Ordinarily, regeneration then manifests itself in signs of true conversion—that is, with evidence of sincere, wholehearted repentance and saving faith.[15] So it was only at this third step or stage that the Puritans looked for what they considered to be "satisfying evidences" that God was savingly at work in someone's life.[16] Yet

---

[13] As James observes, even the demons can believe certain truths about God "and shudder" (James 2:19).

[14] The initial stage of this awakening in Northampton seemed to end with the suicide of Jonathan Edward's uncle, Joseph Hawley II, on June 1, 1735, who was mired in a terror-filled belief that he was bound for eternal damnation. Many of Hawley's contemporaries seem to have assumed that his suicide showed that he never was truly converted, even though he seemed to have been "truly humbled." So, for them at least, emotions that at least appeared very much like the emotions proper to Timothy Edwards's second stage in his morphology of conversion might apparently not result in regeneration. I myself am cautious about drawing any conclusions about a person's spiritual condition from the fact that he or she has committed suicide.

[15] "Ordinarily" because, for instance, God may mercifully regenerate an infant's heart and yet that act will not immediately manifest itself in signs of true conversion.

[16] See, e.g., Jonathan Edwards, *A Faithful Narrative of the Surprising Work of God in the Conversion of Many Hundred Souls in Northampton, and the Neighbouring Towns and Villages of the County of Hampshire in New-England*, in *WJE*, 4:148.

even then they often remained more cautious than many modern evangelists about identifying who is truly saved because they knew that, since salvation depends on God's secretly regenerating our hearts, it is not itself directly observable and thus can only be surmised from the signs of true conversion that follow in our lives.[17]

Because the Puritans took awakening to be an essential if still insufficient first step on the way to regeneration, Puritan home and church life was geared toward producing it. Children died frequently, and so parents and primers drove home the point that life is precarious and, unless God showed mercy, a flame-filled eternity awaited each and every human being. The same lesson was often preached. And so the seeds were planted in Puritan New England for sporadic awakenings.

Early in the 1730s, people in Northampton began to awake. The primary earthly catalyst was the "very sudden and awful death of a young man in the bloom of his youth" in April 1734, "who," Jonathan Edwards relates, "being violently seized with a [lungs' infection] and taken immediately very delirious, died in about two days."[18] Edwards then preached the young man's funeral sermon on Psalm 90:5-6—

> You sweep them away as with a flood; they are like a dream,
>   like grass that is renewed in the morning:
> in the morning it flourishes and is renewed;
>   in the evening it fades and withers

—with the design of convincing Northampton's young people of the utter unreasonableness of their not immediately and completely turning

---

[17] In line with the way that the Puritans thought about it, Wayne Grudem defines regeneration as "*a secret act of God in which he imparts new spiritual life to us*" (*Systematic Theology: An Introduction to Biblical Doctrine* [Grand Rapids, Mich.: Zondervan, 1994], 699). His chapters on effectual calling, regeneration, and conversion cast a lot of useful light on these topics. See also Robert L. Reymond's *A New Systematic Theology of the Christian Faith* (Nashville: Thomas Nelson Publishers, 1998), chapter 19, on "The Application of the Benefits of the Cross Work of Christ." Iain H. Murray, in *Evangelicalism Divided* (Edinburgh: Banner of Truth, 2001), 51-57, argues that recent imprecision about when salvation has actually taken place—such as counting everyone who comes forward in a evangelistic meeting as saved—has damaged the Christian cause. (See also his *Revival and Revivalism: The Making and Marring of American Evangelicalism, 1750-1858* [Edinburgh: Banner of Truth, 1994], 366-374.) In contrast, Edwards typically qualified what he thought was true because he knew that he could not be absolutely sure. So in his *Faithful Narrative* he writes, "there were, very suddenly, one after another, five or six persons who were *to all appearance* savingly converted" (149; my emphasis) and "it *appeared to me* that what she gave an account of was a glorious work of God's infinite power and sovereign grace" (ibid., my emphasis).

[18] Edwards, *A Faithful Narrative*, 147. Edwards notes that the young people in his congregation started to show "a very unusual flexibleness, and yielding to advice" at the end of 1733. Marsden gives a good account of all of this in *Jonathan Edwards*, 150-163.

from this world's fleeting pleasures to embrace by faith God's eternal pleasures as offered in Christ. This sermon seemed to precipitate a stream of conversions among Northampton's young people. "By March and April of 1735," Marsden observes, "the spiritual rains had turned the stream to a flood."[19]

This awakening, although it was somewhat similar to earlier ones in Puritan New England, was unique in its speed, depth, and extent. For instance, the news of the conversion of a frivolous young woman, Edwards reports,

> seemed to be almost like a flash of lightning, upon the hearts of young people all over the town, and upon many others. Those persons amongst us who used to be farthest from seriousness, and that I most feared would make an ill improvement of [her change], seemed greatly to be awakened with it. . . .

And soon,

> . . . a great and earnest concern about the great things of religion and the eternal world became universal in all parts of the town, and among persons of all degrees and all ages . . . . All other talk [except] about spiritual and eternal things was soon thrown by; all the conversation in all companies and upon all occasions, was upon these things only, unless so much as was necessary for people, carrying on their ordinary secular business.

Religion was, as Edwards continues,

> with all sorts the great concern. . . . The only thing in their view was to get the kingdom of heaven, and everyone appeared pressing into it. The engagedness of their hearts in this great concern could not be hid; it appeared in their very countenances. It then was a dreadful thing amongst us to lie out of Christ [that is, not to have put one's faith in Christ] . . . and what persons' minds were intent upon was to escape for their lives, and to fly from the wrath to come. All would eagerly lay hold of opportunities for their souls; and were [accustomed] very often to meet together in private houses for religious pur-

---

[19] Marsden, *Jonathan Edwards*, 159.

poses: and such meetings when appointed were [apt] greatly to be thronged.[20]

"There was scarcely a single person in the town, either young or old," Edwards writes, that "was left unconcerned about the great things of the eternal world."

> Those that were [inclined] to be the vainest and loosest, and those that had been most disposed to think and speak slightly of vital and experimental religion, were now generally subject to great awakenings. And the work of conversion was carried on in a most astonishing manner, and increased more and more; souls did as it were come by flocks to Jesus Christ.

In contrast with past patterns, about as many males as females seemed to have been saved, and God seemed to have extended his saving mercy not only to teens and early adults but also and much more unusually "both to elderly persons and also those that are very young." This led Edwards to "hope that by far the greater part of persons in this town, above sixteen years of age, are such as have the saving knowledge of Jesus Christ." Northampton, as well as some neighboring towns, certainly seemed to have become "a city on a hill." And even after the initial awakening ceased, Edwards saw so much spiritual good remain that he concluded, "we still remain a reformed people, and God has evidently made us a new people."

Yet within a few years of writing these words in 1737, Edwards retracted this blanket endorsement of what had happened in Northampton, acknowledging that he had been unduly confident about his own ability to

---

[20] Edwards, *A Faithful Narrative*, 149-150. The remaining quotations in this paragraph are from pp. 150, 158, and 209. It is worthwhile to read the whole of Edwards's account of the initial awakening, which is found on pp. 147-159. Edwards notes, at the end of this account, some other ways in which it appeared to be extraordinary, and which no doubt led him to hope that it was the beginning of God's great work that would usher in his millennial kingdom. He says, for instance, that

> God has also seemed to have gone out of his usual way in the quickness of his work, and the swift progress of his Spirit has made in his operations on the hearts of many. 'Tis wonderful that persons should be so suddenly, and yet so greatly, changed. . . . God's work has also appeared very extraordinary in the degrees of the influences of his Spirit, both in the degree of awakening and conviction, and also in the degree of saving light, and love, and joy, that many have experienced. (159)

Marsden casts some doubt on the accuracy of some of Edwards's report by claiming that "Edwards was scrupulously honest, but he was also prone to hyperbole in his zeal to inspire others" (159). But others made essentially the same claims. See, for instance, Benjamin Trumbull's assessment of later moments in the same revival as quoted in Iain H. Murray, *Jonathan Edwards: A New Biography* (Edinburgh: Banner of Truth, 1987), 167.

tell when someone had been truly converted. In times of great awakening, he came to understand, there are many fair blossoms that fail to produce mature fruit. We must be cautious, then, in declaring what God is doing with other human beings. As he writes at the end of his *The Distinguishing Marks of a Work of the Spirit of God*, published in 1741:

> I know by experience that there is a great aptness in men, that think they have had some experience of the power of religion, to think themselves sufficient to discern and determine the state of others' souls by a little conversation with them; and experience has taught me that 'tis an error. I once did not imagine that the heart of man had been so unsearchable as I find it is. I am less charitable, and less uncharitable than once I was.[21]

In other words, by now Edwards was fully convinced that God alone has the ability and the right to determine the spiritual state of another person's heart. Regeneration, as the basis of true conversion, really is a secret act of God that none of us can perceive directly in another human being.

Yet, in agreement with the Scriptures, Edwards remained convinced that the unregenerate and the regenerate are fundamentally different, and that this difference normally manifests itself in ways that allow us to assess our own and others' spiritual states.[22] Indeed, Edwards declares in the *Religious Affections*, Christ has given us rules that help us to assess others' spiritual states "so far as is necessary for [our] own safety, and to prevent [us from] being led into a snare by false teachers, and false pretenders to religion," even if "it was never God's design to give us any rules, by which we may certainly know, who of our fellow professors are his, and to make a full and clear separation between sheep and goats."[23] These rules, which specify the "marks" or

---

[21] Edwards, *The Distinguishing Marks of a Work of the Spirit of God*, WJE, 4:285. For a page or so before and after this passage, Edwards develops scriptural arguments to show that God alone has the ability and the right to determine the spiritual state of human hearts.

[22] In the New Testament, the Greek term for "regeneration"—*palingenesia*—is used only once to refer to the spiritual renewal of individuals (see Titus 3:5), but the idea of spiritual renewal or rebirth or regeneration is often found in passages like John 3:1-8; Ephesians 2:1-5; Colossians 2:13; 1 Peter 1:3, 23; and throughout 1 John. As Grudem stresses (see his *Systematic Theology*, 699ff.), "Exactly what happens in regeneration is mysterious to us," yet we know that it is entirely God's work and that it involves his making a radical, instantaneous change in us that rescues us from spiritual death by making us spiritually alive. This change then manifests itself over time in the regenerated person's daily life.

[23] Edwards, *Religious Affections*, 193. "Marks" and "signs" (mentioned next in the text) are taken from the same page. Edwards thought that the properly appointed officers of the visible church have a right and a duty to judge who are "*visibly*" saints—that is, who to all outward appearances "have a right to be received as [Christians or saints] in the eye of a public charity" (*Distinguishing Marks*, 286ff.; cf. 244f.). The final quotation in this paragraph is from page 84 of *Religious Affections*.

"signs" of true conversion, can guide ministers as they tend their flocks; and they can also assure individual Christians that they themselves are truly converted, provided they are not so far removed from a properly spiritual state of mind that it is impossible for them to tell, while they are in that poor state, whether they are regenerate. Knowing what these marks or signs of true conversion are may even help some non-Christians to stop fooling themselves about their standing with God. Everyone, then, should know them; and Edwards wrote *Religious Affections* to show that Scripture sheds "clear and abundant light" on them.

EDWARDS'S THESIS: "TRUE RELIGION, IN GREAT PART, CONSISTS IN HOLY AFFECTIONS"

To that end, Edwards bases *Religious Affections* on these words from the apostle Peter's first epistle: "Though you have not seen him, you love him. Though you do not now see him, you believe in him and rejoice with joy that is inexpressible and filled with glory" (1 Pet. 1:8). Peter's words, Edwards observes, reveal the spiritual state of the Christians to whom he was writing. They were under persecution— "grieved by various trials," as Peter puts it (1 Pet. 1:6)—and these trials tested the authenticity of their faith, which then manifested itself in the *love* and *joy* mentioned in verse 8. True faith, in other words, inevitably gives rise to godly desires and emotions.

Edwards's antique way of putting this is to say that "True religion, in great part, consists in holy affections."[24] He then dedicates Part One of his book to explaining and defending this statement.

Edwards knows that we will not understand what he means when he says that true religion consists very largely in holy affections if we don't understand what he means by *affections*. Modern dictionaries often take this term to refer merely to what we call the emotions—and

---

[24] Edwards, *Religious Affections*, 95. All other quotations from Edwards in this section of my chapter are from Part One of the *Religious Affections*, which is entitled, "Concerning the Nature of the Affections, and Their Importance in Religion." In general, this section's later quotations will be found later in that Part than earlier ones.

Reading Edwards can be discouraging because of his eighteenth-century vocabulary and grammar. We have to use dictionaries to look up the unfamiliar words and then learn how to construe his sentences by reading a lot of them. It often helps to read his more difficult sentences aloud. Yet what Edwards has to teach us is so valuable that it is clearly worth the effort. For further thought on reading Edwards, see Justin Taylor's appendix, "Reading Jonathan Edwards: Objections and Recommendations."

perhaps only to the more moderate emotions at that.[25] But for Edwards our *affections* involve a lot more than just our emotions. They have to do with the whole side of us that values and desires and chooses and wills as well as feels.

Edwards contrasts this side of our nature with another side that we can call our *cognitive* side. Our cognitive side includes our power to perceive and to speculate; it is what we use to discern and think about things. Conforming to the standard terminology of his day, Edwards sometimes calls the cognitive side of our nature our "faculty of understanding." He claims that God has endued human nature with understanding and one other faculty, namely, the faculty "by which the soul does not merely perceive and view things, but is some way inclined [or disinclined] with respect to the things it views or considers"—that is, either likes or dislikes them, is pleased or displeased by them, or approves or disapproves of whatever it is perceiving or thinking about.[26]

---

[25] For instance, the first definition for *affection* in *Webster's Seventh New Collegiate Dictionary* (Springfield, Mass.: G. & C. Merriam Company, 1971) is "a moderate feeling or emotion," and the fourth definition is "the feeling aspect of consciousness" (15). It is not until the fifth definition that we are told that *affection* can mean a propensity or disposition. *The Random House Dictionary of the English Language*, 2nd ed., unabridged (New York: Random House, 1987) starts with a definition that involves something more than mere emotion—"fond attachment, devotion, or love: *the affection of a parent for an only child*" (33)—but then defines the affections as emotions, which are themselves defined as affective states of consciousness "in which joy, sorrow, fear, hate, or the like, [are] experienced, as distinguished from cognitive and volitional states of consciousness" (637).

Evidently this tendency to reduce the affections to the emotions was also present in Edwards's day, which is what leads him to say that "The will, and the affections of the soul, are not two faculties; the affections . . . differ from the mere actings of the will and inclination of the soul . . . only in the liveliness and sensibleness of exercise." In other words, affections are those inclinations that are lively enough to be felt as emotions.

[26] As Conrad Cherry notes in his *The Theology of Jonathan Edwards: A Reappraisal* (Bloomington and Indianapolis: Indiana University Press, 1966), 15ff., Edwards is quite aware that traditional faculty psychology errs in considering the faculties of understanding and will to be "separate, self-activating entities" within the person rather than powers of the whole person. This, as Cherry goes on to show, affected how Edwards conceived of saving faith and led him to reject or at least deeply qualify the traditional Puritan analysis of it as consisting of three elements: *assent*, or believing what God claims is true; *consent*, or willfully accepting these truths; and *affiance*, or emotionally resting in these truths. Edwards, as Cherry stresses, understood that it is the whole person who is involved in each of these acts and consequently not some faculty of understanding that is involved in the first, some faculty of volition with the second, and some faculty of affection with the third. Edwards himself puts it this way:

The distinction of the several constituent parts or acts of faith, in assent, consent, and affiance, if strictly considered and examined, will appear not to be proper and just, or strictly according to the truth and nature of things; because the parts are not all entirely distinct one from another, and so are in some measure confounded one with another. ("Concerning Faith," in *The Works of Jonathan Edwards*, ed. Edward Hickman, 2 vols. [1884; reprint, Edinburgh: Banner of Truth, 1974], 2:587)

Elsewhere he says, "the Scriptures are ignorant of the philosophic distinction of the understanding and the will" ("The Mind," in *The Works of Jonathan Edwards*, vol. 6, *Scientific and Philosophical Writings*, ed. Wallace E. Anderson [New Haven, Conn.: Yale University Press, 1980], 389). Ultimately, Edwards's refusal to accept a full-blown faculty psychology has tremendous ramifications for how we understand human knowledge. It can also keep us from believing, with many Roman Catholics, that original sin affects primarily our wills and not so much our reason.

In other words, this second faculty involves our taking some sort of stance toward what we are considering. In Edwards's time, this "choosy" side of human nature was usually called the *will* or the *faculty of volition*, but Edwards recognized that calling it that tended to narrow our conception of it too much because we are then really referring to only "the actions that are determined and governed by" this part of us. This leaves out the affective side's more fundamental motions of merely being inclined—or mentally (but not necessarily physically) "carried out towards"—various objects and being disinclined—or mentally repulsed by—others. These motions start in the secret recesses of our souls; and we may resolve—or *will*—never to act on them. This is one of the reasons why Scripture refers to this side of our natures as our *hearts* (see Ps. 36:1ff.; Prov. 4:20-23; Matt. 15:17-19) and declares that only God can know them (see 2 Chron. 6:30; Jer. 17:9ff.).

Of course, our inclinations can be weaker or stronger. Sometimes, Edwards observes, the soul, in considering something, "is carried out [just] a little beyond a state of perfect indifference." In such cases, our preferences are so weak that it would not be right even to call them desires. At other times, "the approbation or dislike, pleasedness or aversion, are stronger." And sometimes our heart's motions are so strong that "the soul comes to act vigorously and sensibly, and the actings of the soul are with that strength that (through the laws of the union which the Creator has fixed between soul and body) the motion of the blood and animal spirits begins to be sensibly altered," and then we feel our inclinations as emotions. Our affections, Edwards tells us, are these "more vigorous and sensible exercises of the inclination and will of the soul."[27]

In claiming, then, that true religion consists very largely in holy affections, Edwards means that those who have been truly converted will manifest the fact that God has regenerated their hearts by their having godly desires and emotions, such as the sort of Christian love and joy that Peter sees in his persecuted readers.

Edwards then argues, both from Scripture and by reason, that this

---

[27] Edwards admits that "language is here somewhat imperfect" and that in a sense "the affection of the soul differs nothing at all from the will and inclination" because insofar as we are moved at all in considering something, even if that movement is too weak to be sensed physiologically, it still involves our being "affected." But he wants, in accordance with more ordinary eighteenth-century English usage, to reserve the term "affection" for the stronger and more sensible movements that we experience as, e.g., love and hatred, joy and grief, delight and sorrow.

claim must be true. For instance, he asks, "who will deny that true religion consists, in great measure, in vigorous and lively actings of the inclination and will of the soul, or the fervent exercises of the heart?" He answers this question by quoting biblical passages where God commands us to be "fervent in spirit" (Rom. 12:11) and to fear and love and serve him with our whole hearts and our whole souls (see Deut. 10:12; cf. 6:4-5 and Matt. 22:34-40). Such "a fervent, vigorous engagedness of the heart in religion . . . is the fruit of a real circumcision of the heart, or true regeneration," he observes; and it is this that "has the promises of life" (see Deut. 30:6). He also reasons that for us not to be "in good earnest in religion," with "our wills and inclinations . . . strongly exercised" when we consider the great Christian truths, indicates that we are not truly converted, because the "things of religion are so great, that there can be no suitableness in the exercises of our hearts, to their nature and importance, unless they be lively and powerful."

This follows from a principle that we all generally acknowledge; namely, that our desires and emotions ought to be proportioned to the real value of their objects. For example, virtually everyone recognizes that there is something really wrong with spouses who don't love their husbands or wives much more than they love their dogs or with parents who aren't much more emotionally involved with their children than with their cars. According to this principle, human beings should love God more than anything else: "In nothing, is vigor in the actings of our inclinations so requisite, as in religion; and in nothing is lukewarmness so odious." This is what Edwards had preached to his young people in 1734 as he tried to convince them, after the sudden death of one of their own, of the utter unreasonableness of their not immediately and completely turning from this world's fleeting pleasures to embrace in faith God's eternal pleasures as offered in Christ.

As I have noted, New England's Puritans were well aware that true Christian conversion makes people active and fervent for Christ, and they also saw New England's fervency cooling as its earliest generation of pilgrims gave way to later generations. These later generations almost invariably shared the "form" of their parents' faith—that is, they subscribed to the same truths—but they often lacked the power thereof. Edwards now tackles this problem head-on, arguing that

True religion is evermore a powerful thing; and the power of it appears, in the first place, in the inward exercises of it in the heart, where is the principal and original seat of it. Hence true religion is called the power of godliness, in distinction from the external appearances of it, that are the form of it, "Having a form of godliness, but denying the power of it" (II Tim. 3:5).

Those who are reborn of the Spirit are also indwelt by him (see John 3:1-8 with 14:15-17; Rom. 8:9); and, Edwards observes, "The Spirit of God in those that have sound and solid religion, is a spirit of powerful holy affection; and therefore, God is said to have given them the spirit of power, and of love, and of a sound mind (II Tim. 1:7)." Consequently, regeneration always manifests itself in godly desires and emotions. Edwards grants that "true grace has various degrees, and there are some that are but babes in Christ, in whom the exercise of the inclination and will towards divine and heavenly things is comparatively weak"; but even in such babes in the faith, the Spirit who indwells them will ultimately prevail over "all carnal or natural affections." So one sign of true conversion is the persistence of godly desires and emotions throughout a Christian's life.[28]

This summarizes just the first of ten arguments Edwards gives in support of the claim that true conversion will manifest itself in godly desires and emotions. His second and third arguments appeal to general features of human nature and thus are primarily philosophical, but all the rest of his arguments are primarily scriptural and theological. They stress that the Scriptures "do everywhere place religion very much in . . . affections . . . such as fear, hope, love, hatred, desire, joy, sorrow, gratitude, compassion and zeal"; that Scripture's greatest saints—such as David and the apostles Paul and John and our Lord Jesus Christ him-

---

[28] Edwards stresses this point especially in the last of the twelve signs of true conversion that make up *Religious Affections'* third part:

> True saints may be guilty of some kinds and degrees of backsliding, and may be soiled by particular temptations, and may fall into sin, yea great sins: but they can never fall away so, as to grow weary of religion, and the service of God, and habitually to dislike it and neglect it; either on its own account, or on account of the difficulties that attend it. . . . Nor can they ever fall away so, as habitually to be more engaged in other things, than in the business of religion; or so that it should become their way and manner to serve something else more than God; or so as statedly to cease to serve God, with such earnestness and diligence, as still to be habitually devoted and given up to the business of religion. (390ff.)

True saints, Edwards insists, will always be manifestly different after conversion than before, because the truly converted "are new men, new creatures; new, not only within, but without; . . . [with] new hearts, and new eyes, new ears, new tongues, new hands, new feet; i.e. a new conversation and practice; and they walk in newness of life, and continue to do so to the end of life" (391). Lack of perseverance is, then, "a sign that [those who don't persevere] never were risen with Christ" (391).

self—were full of godly desires and emotions;[29] that the Scriptures very much condemn hardness of heart; and that they "represent true religion, as being summarily comprehended in *love*, [which is] the chief of the affections, and [the] fountain of all other affections."

The truth of Edwards's claim about the centrality of godly desire and emotion in true conversion can be driven home like this. Our emotions can be considered to arise from our beliefs and concerns. Our *beliefs* are what we take to be real or true—I believe right now, for instance, that I am composing this chapter on my Dell laptop computer, that I am looking at the Yale edition of Edwards's *Religious Affections*, that God exists and that he speaks to me through the Christian Scriptures, and so on. Our *concerns* are our more persistent or insistent inclinations and desires. They are what we care about. For example, I am concerned for my own and my wife's welfare, for the salvation of my daughter's children, for my ability to work and pay the bills, and (near dinnertime) for eating enough to get rid of my hunger pangs.

Now our emotions arise from our beliefs and concerns like this. Suppose I care deeply about something, let's say my wife's welfare. And then suppose that I hear that she has just been in a car accident. If I believe what I've heard, then the combination of that belief and that concern will prompt an emotion, something like *fear* or *anxiety* about her physical state. Suppose that I then hear that it was a very minor car accident and that she wasn't hurt. As my belief changes while my care for Cindy remains constant, my emotion will also change from fear or anxiety to something like *relief* and then perhaps to *gratitude to God* for keeping her safe.

Picture the linkage among our beliefs and concerns and emotions like this:

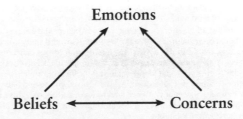

---

[29] Indeed, God commends David as a man after his own heart (see 1 Sam. 13:14 with Acts 13:22). David's Psalms, then, being "nothing else but the expressions and breathings of devout and holy affections" that are "penned for the use of the church of God in its public worship" in every age, model the kind of affectionate religion that is to be the norm for godly persons at all times and in all places.

The line between beliefs and concerns with its double arrows signifies the way that our beliefs and concerns interact in producing our emotions. The lines with single arrows pointing from beliefs and concerns to emotions represent how our emotions arise out of the interaction of our beliefs and concerns.[30]

This picture helps us to understand what our emotions can reveal about our beliefs and concerns. Suppose a teenage girl has just been seriously hurt in an automobile accident and then observes that her father is more distraught about the damage to his new Mercedes than about her injuries. If she loves her father and has always assumed that he loves her, then observing this will probably shatter her heart. For the fact that he is more emotionally distressed about his car than about her injuries manifests what he cares for most.[31] Or suppose that a staunchly orthodox pastor preaches regularly about the danger of everlasting punishment and yet doesn't seem to be at all disturbed by the fact that none of his children is seeking salvation. His apparent lack of emotion about his children's apparent spiritual destiny may tell us something about either his concerns or his beliefs: It may tell us either that he does not care enough about his children or that he doesn't really believe what he

---

[30] Careful thought about the linkage among our beliefs and concerns and emotions will convince us that all three of the lines should probably have double arrows because our emotions affect our beliefs and concerns as well as being affected by them. Think, for instance, of how much more likely you are to believe a negative report about someone (e.g., "I hear that he cheats on his taxes") if you are already angry with him. (For a biblical example linking the condition of someone's heart to her beliefs, see Acts 16:14, where Luke says that God opened Lydia's heart to pay attention to what Paul was saying.) This confirms Edwards's rejection of faculty psychology as I reported it in footnote 26; human nature is much more a unity of somewhat but not fully distinguishable powers than an amalgamation of separate faculties or parts. Such was in fact Edwards's own experience, as his description of his own contemplation of God's absolute sovereignty in salvation as involving "a *delightful* conviction" shows. See his "Personal Narrative" of his own spiritual life in *WJE*, vol. 16, *Letters and Personal Writings*, ed. George S. Claghorn (New Haven, Conn.: Yale University Press, 1998), 792 (Edwards's emphasis). (Portions of Edwards's "Personal Narrative" can also be found at the beginning of Volume One of the two-volume Banner of Truth edition of Edwards's works in Sereno E. Dwight's "Memoirs of Jonathan Edwards, A. M." This passage is found on xiii.)

I owe my understanding of emotions as products of our beliefs and concerns to the thinking that Robert C. Roberts's book, *Spirituality and Human Emotion* (Grand Rapids, Mich.: Eerdmans, 1982), prompted me to do many years ago. He first taught me to think of our concerns as emotion-dispositions that produce specific emotions when we have or acquire specific beliefs. Roberts should not, however, be held responsible for my particular way of picturing the linkages among our beliefs and concerns and emotions or for the conclusions I subsequently draw. Those who would like to pursue the topic of emotion much more thoroughly cannot do better than to look at Roberts's more recent *Emotions: An Essay in Aid of Moral Psychology* (Cambridge: Cambridge University Press, 2003), which is a full-blown philosophical treatment of emotions.

[31] This example is not merely hypothetical. I had a female student some years ago who was suffering from serious depression, and after much counseling it came out that something very like this had happened to her during her senior year in high school and had triggered her depression. She had heard her father, outside the curtain of the emergency-room bay she was in, inquiring first about the damage to his car and only afterwards about how badly she was hurt.

preaches. For otherwise that concern and that belief would be likely to produce fear and anxiety about his children's spiritual states.[32]

Now transfer these general insights to Edwards's claim about the centrality of godly desire and emotion in true conversion. These insights show how our desires and emotions can be signs or marks of our spiritual states. My spiritual state depends on whether or not God has regenerated my heart. Regeneration involves God giving me a radically different set of inclinations and desires (see Ezek. 36:22-32; Jer. 32:37-41). I go from being a child of the devil who does what he desires (see John 8:44; Eph. 2:1-3) to being a child of God who is now capable of doing what the Spirit, who is living within me, desires (see Gal. 5:16-25; Col. 3:1-17). It is the Spirit living within me who gives me this whole new set of desires and concerns (see Rom. 8:5, 9; Gal. 4:6). And these godly desires and concerns, combined with my beliefs, dispose me to have specific godly emotions. My having these emotions, then, indicates that my heart is regenerate. And my not having these emotions would indicate that my heart is not. My emotions, as feelings that indicate what I am genuinely concerned about, betray my spiritual state.[33]

PRACTICAL INFERENCES

In typical Puritan fashion, Edwards draws some practical inferences from his claim that "True religion, in great part, consists in holy affections" before closing Part One of his book.

The first practical inference is that it is a very great error to denigrate all religious affections "as having nothing solid or substantial in them." This, as Edwards observes, was the position of many in his day, especially after the first Great Awakening had ceased. One main criticism of the first Great Awakening even while it was occurring was that it was marked by a lot of odd behavior. Even while fostering it, Edwards himself readily admitted that it was accompanied by many "impru-

---

[32] I have tried to state this example carefully because (1) the pastor may actually be feeling a lot of emotion about his children's apparent spiritual state and yet attempt not to show it because he thinks that manifesting it would make it even harder for his children to deal with their spiritual states or (2) his concern and his belief may prompt him just to place the salvation of his children even more into God's hands. He may then know a peace that passes all understanding about what God is doing with his children.

[33] For Edwards's own sense of these things and the way that he understood his own affections as indicating his own spiritual state, see his "Personal Narrative," in *Letters and Personal Writings*, 790-804. The first couple of paragraphs deal with his early and carnal religious affections and then there is a transition to the sort of spiritual affections that arise from a regenerated heart.

dences and irregularities."[34] For instance, George Marsden reports that in some meetings in 1741 in New Haven, Connecticut, it seemed that "all order had disappeared, [with] 'some praying, some exhorting and terrifying, some singing, some screaming, some crying, some laughing and some scolding,'" so that a contemporary observer claimed it was "the most amazing confusion that ever was heard." How, some asked, could spectacles like this come from God?

After it ended, the criticism sharpened. And thus, writing in about 1745, Edwards remarks that because

> many who, in the late extraordinary season, appeared to have great religious affections, did not manifest a right temper of mind, and [ran] into many errors, in the time of their affection, and the heat of their zeal; and because the high affections of many seem to be so soon come to nothing, and some who seemed to be mightily raised and swallowed with joy and zeal, for a while, seem to have returned like the dog to his vomit: hence religious affections in general are grown out of credit, with great numbers, as though true religion did not at all consist in them.

This, Edwards says, seems to have been in reaction to the earlier, uncritical attitude that many took to the whole range of affections that displayed themselves during the Great Awakening. For despite the fact that some doubted such displays even during "those extraordinary circumstances and events," there was overall, at that time,

> a prevalent disposition to look upon all high religious affections, as eminent exercises of true grace, without much inquiring into the nature and source of those affections, and the manner in which they arose: if

---

[34] I take the phrase "imprudences and irregularities" from Edwards's August 31, 1741, letter to Deacon Lyman, who had formerly lived in Northampton. See Edwards, *Letters and Personal Writings*, 97. The context of that phrase is instructive:

> Concerning the great stir that is in the land, and those extraordinary circumstances and events that it is attended with, such as persons crying out, and being set into great agonies, with a sense of sin and wrath, and having their strength taken away, and their minds extraordinarily transported with light, love and comfort, I have been abundantly amongst such things, and have had great opportunity to observe them, here and elsewhere, in their beginning, progress, issue and consequences, and however there may be some mixtures of natural affection, and sometimes of temptation, and some imprudences and irregularities, as there always was, and always will be in this imperfect state; yet as to the work in general, and the main of what is to be observed in these extraordinary things, they have all the clear and incontestable evidences of a true divine work. If this ben't the work of God, I have all my religion to learn over again, and know not what use to make of the Bible.

The next quotation is from Marsden, *Jonathan Edwards*, 232.

persons did but appear to be indeed very much moved and raised, so as to be full of religious talk, and express themselves with great warmth and earnestness, and to be filled, or to be very full, as the phrases were; it was too much the manner, without further examination, to conclude such persons were full of the Spirit of God, and had eminent experience of his gracious influences.

Similar polarizations to the display of religious affection are as prevalent in our day as they were then and as they were even in biblical times (see 2 Sam. 6:16-23; Acts 2:1-13).

Edwards always maintained that the awakening that began in Northampton around 1734 and then was renewed and spread through the preaching of George Whitefield and others in the early 1740s could only be explained as involving a great movement of God's Spirit that had indeed resulted in many true conversions—and, that, consequently, could be ignored or denigrated only at great spiritual peril.[35] He published his *Distinguishing Marks of a Work of the Spirit of God* in 1741 to defend the thesis that the Great Awakening was a bona fide work of God's Spirit, even if many of those who were then being influenced by God's Spirit were not in fact regenerated by him. Edwards opened that book with these words from 1 John 4:1: "Beloved, believe not every

---

[35] Writing in 1742 about the first Great Awakening overall, Edwards said:

> And now let us consider—Is it not strange that in a Christian, orthodox country, and such a land of light as this is, there should be many at a loss whose work this is, whether the work of God or the work of the Devil? Is it not a shame to New England that such a work should be much doubted of here? . . . We need not say, "Who shall ascend into heaven" [Rom. 10:6], to bring us down something whereby to judge of this work. Nor does God send us beyond the seas, nor into past ages, to obtain a rule that shall determine and satisfy us. But we have a rule near at hand, a sacred book that God himself has put into our hands, with clear and infallible marks, sufficient to resolve us in things of this nature; which book I think we must reject, not only in some particular passages, but in the substance of it, if we reject such a work as has now been described, as not being the work of God. The whole tenor of the Gospel proves it; all the notion of religion that the Scriptures gives us confirms it. (*Some Thoughts Concerning the Revival of Religion in New-England*, in WJE, 4:330-331)

Later in the same book we find him claiming:

> This work that has lately been carried on in the land is the work of God, and not the work of man. Its beginning has not been of man's power or device, and its being carried on depends not on our strength or wisdom; but yet God expects of all that they should use their utmost endeavors to promote it, and that the hearts of all should be greatly engaged in this affair. (384)

Elsewhere in the same book we find him speculating that this awakening may eventuate in God's millennial reign: "'Tis not unlikely that this work of God's Spirit, that is so extraordinary and wonderful, is the dawning, or at least a prelude, of that glorious work of God, so often foretold in Scripture, which in the progress and issue of it, shall renew the world of mankind" (353). And a few pages later, he warns of the dangers of resisting the Holy Spirit's work in this awakening:

> It is very dangerous for God's professing people to lie still, and not to come to the help of the Lord, whenever he remarkably pours out his Spirit, to carry on the work of redemption in the application of it; but above all, when he comes forth in that last and greatest outpouring of his Spirit, to introduce that happy day of God's power and salvation. (358)

spirit, but *try the spirits* whether they are of God; because many false prophets are gone out into the world" (KJV, my emphasis). That is then what he attempted to do, articulating nine kinds of considerations that don't indicate, one way or another, whether some extraordinary awakening is a work of God's Spirit,[36] then developing from 1 John 4 five "sure, distinguishing, Scripture evidences and marks of a work of the Spirit of God, by which we may proceed in judging of any operation we find in ourselves, or see among a people, without danger of being misled."[37]

Edwards reprises and expands his analysis of "some things, which are no signs that affections are gracious, or that they are not" in Part Two of *Religious Affections*. This part of his book can be very valuable to us, for there is little doubt, to use Edwards's own words, that in much of the emotion that we see displayed in various quarters of the contemporary church there are "some mixtures of natural affection, and sometimes of temptation, and some imprudences and irregularities, as there always was, and always will be in this imperfect state."[38] Observing these mixed displays can tempt us to dismiss these odd and sometimes aberrant ways of fellowshiping and worshiping as being entirely beyond the realm in which God works. But Edwards's arguments can help us to remember that such dismissals are unwarranted. We can and should deplore unscriptural and sinful excesses of affection among those who call on the name of Christ while recognizing that even in their midst God may be gathering some of his children to himself.

Yet Edwards's main point in the first of his three applications in Part One of his text is that as much as we may be uneasy about excessive or aberrant displays of affection during times of awakening (or in specific quarters of the Christian church), condemning all religious affection is much more deadly. "If the great things of religion are rightly understood," he declares, "they will affect the heart." Granted, there are false and true religious affections and, consequently, someone's "having much affection [doesn't] prove that he has any true religion." Yet "if he has no

---

[36] And especially, he adds, "what are no evidences that a work that is wrought amongst a people, is not the work of the Spirit of God" (*Distinguishing Marks*, 228). In other words, Edwards is particularly concerned in this portion of his book to discredit those who said that specific observable phenomena—e.g., great physiological effects, strong impressions on the imagination, utilization of some standard means to produce an effect, imprudent or unbiblical conduct, errors of judgment and delusions of Satan, apostasy, etc.—were clear indicators that God was *not* at work.

[37] Edwards, *Distinguishing Marks*, 248ff.

[38] For these words, see footnote 34, above.

affection, it proves that he has no religion," because those with no religious affections are "in a state of spiritual death." The right way forward, then, "is not to reject all affections, nor to approve all; but to distinguish between affections, approving some, and rejecting others; separating between the wheat and the chaff, the gold and the dross, the precious and the vile." Edwards's fullest account of Scripture's approved affections is found in Part Three of *Religious Affections*; and his fullest account of those to be rejected is found in several chapters of *Charity and Its Fruits*.[39]

The next practical implication that Edwards draws from the fact that "true religion lies much in the affections" is that Christians will then want to convey their faith in ways that are most likely to move the affections. "Such books," Edwards explains,

> and such a way of preaching the Word, and administration of ordinances, and such a way of worshiping God in prayer, and singing praises, is much to be desired, as has a tendency to affect the hearts of those who attend these means.[40]

Edwards recognizes that "there may be such means, as may have a great tendency to stir up the passions of weak and ignorant persons, and yet have no great tendency to benefit their souls" because these means act on natural human capacities that work independently of any saving grace. But, he insists,

> undoubtedly, if the things of religion, in the means used, are treated according to their nature, and exhibited truly, so as tends to convey just apprehensions, and a right judgment of them; the more they have a tendency to move the affections, the better.

He felt so strongly about this that, for example, with regard to music, he urged all Christian parents to give their children singing lessons and

---

[39] *Charity and Its Fruits* is found in *The Works of Jonathan Edwards*, vol. 8, *Ethical Writings*, ed. Paul Ramsey (New Haven, Conn.: Yale University Press, 1989). It is not in the two-volume Banner of Truth edition of Edwards's works, although Banner of Truth puts it out individually in an inexpensive paperback.

[40] One secular book that corroborates this point is Antonio R. Damasio, *Descartes' Error: Emotion, Reason, and the Human Brain* (New York: G. P. Putnam's Sons, 1994), which shows from a clinical and medical point of view how central emotion is to human life. Books such as Damasio's show that our emotions hold our thoughts in place and that, when people lose their capacity to feel emotionally (through an accident or a brain tumor or whatever), they also lose their ability to function well in the normal everyday world. Of course, Scripture has always recognized the truth of this and this is why it takes, e.g., the fear of the Lord to be fundamental to a godly life.

proudly notes that his own congregation, especially during its times of awakening, sang loudly and heartily and in three parts.[41] As he says a bit earlier in Part One of *Religious Affections*:

> The duty of singing praises to God, seems to be appointed wholly to excite and express religious affections. No other reason can be assigned, why we should express ourselves to God in verse, rather than in prose, and do it with music, but only, that such is our nature and frame, that these things have a tendency to move our affections.

In typical English translations of the Scriptures, words such as "sing," "singers," "singing," and "songs" appear around 300 times.[42]

Finally, he declares, as his third practical implication, that if true religion lies so much in godly affections, then we may learn "what great cause we have to be ashamed and confounded before God, that we are no more affected with the great things of religion." If God has given to us the capacity to desire and to feel

> for the same purpose which he has given all the faculties and principles of human life for, [namely] that they might be subservient to man's chief end, and the great business for which God has created him, that is the business of religion,

then the fact that our desires and emotions are usually much more engaged and aroused regarding worldly things is a very bad sign about the sanctity of our hearts. We should be most moved by the great things that God has done for us through his Son, Jesus Christ. And the fact that we are not moved by this work means that we should "be humbled to

---

[41] For Edwards's remarks about singing, see his *Faithful Narrative*, 151 and *Religious Affections*, 115. His more general emphasis on a proper use of means is reiterated by many other Puritans. Here, for instance, is a passage from Richard Baxter's *A Christian Directory* (1673; reprint, Morgan, Penn: Soli Deo Gloria, 1990), 59:

> We are no sooner warmed with the celestial flames, but natural corruption is inclining us to grow cold; like hot water, which loseth its heat by degrees, unless the fire be continually kept under it. Who feeleth not that as soon as in a sermon, or prayer, or holy meditation, his heart hath got a little heat, as soon as it is gone, it is prone to its former earthly temper, and by a little remissness in our duty, or thoughts, or business about the world, we presently grow cold and dull again. Be watchful, therefore, lest it decline too far. Be frequent in the means that must preserve you from declining: when faintness telleth you that your stomach is emptied of the former meat, supply it with another, lest strength abate. You are rowing against the stream of fleshly interest and inclinations; and therefore intermit not too long, lest you go faster down by your ease, then you get up by labour.

[42] For more about the importance of singing to the Christian life, see my "Why We Sing," *Modern Reformation* 11/6 (November/December 2002): 22-25.

the dust." We should turn our hearts and minds to hearken to the things of God, even while confessing that we know we are incapable of being moved properly by these things, and then pray that God's indwelling Holy Spirit will move us to love and to take joy in what is godly above all else. Then, if God graciously grants our prayer, we will possess one of the chief marks of true conversion, as Paul's words to the Thessalonians makes clear: "For we know, brothers loved by God, that he has chosen you, because our gospel came to you not only in word, but also in power and in the Holy Spirit and with full conviction. . . . And you became imitators of us and of the Lord, for you received the word in much affliction, with the joy of the Holy Spirit" (1 Thess. 1:4-6).

THE ROLE OF NEGATIVE DESIRES AND EMOTIONS IN THE CHRISTIAN LIFE

Christians sometimes seem to assume that godliness ought to be proof against having any negative desires or emotions. Numbers 25 contradicts that assumption. Phinehas had an intensely negative emotion, and God blessed him for it.

Negative desires and emotions involve our reacting against something. Our perceiving or considering something is then tinged with dislike, displeasure, disapproval, aversion, or something like that. It would be nice if it were possible to experience only positive desires and emotions[43]—desires and emotions involving only mental states like pleasure, approval, and attraction. But the linkage that holds among our beliefs, concerns, and emotions is such that, in a world where we can know or believe or worry that something we care about is or may be threatened, the same concerns that give rise to positive emotions when we have certain beliefs will inevitably give rise to negative emotions when we have other beliefs. For the very same care or concern that disposes me to feel a particular positive emotion under certain conditions will dispose me to feel a particular negative emotion under others. If I am able to feel joy at my wedding, then I am also capable of feeling sorrow if something bad happens to my wife.

Indeed, when we think carefully about it, we see that many desires

---

[43] I say this even though negative desires and emotions aren't always unpleasant. For example, getting angry can sometimes feel pretty good. And someone can "nurse" a negative emotion like envy in a way that involves its being a familiar and somehow even a welcome presence in the person's life. So to classify something as a "negative" desire or emotion is not to say that we necessarily feel badly while having it.

and emotions come in complementary pairs: love and hatred, joy and sorrow, fear and hope, gratitude and resentment, and so on. A desire or emotion is not "right," then, just because it is a positive desire or emotion; it is right when it is the desire or emotion that is appropriate to the situation at hand, whether it is positive or negative.[44] If, upon hearing that my wife has just been in a very serious automobile accident, I don't experience any negative emotion, there is probably something wrong with me.

Edwards, utilizing both reason and Scripture, recognizes all of this and more.[45] He says,

> As all the exercises of the inclination and will, are either in approving and liking, or disapproving and rejecting; so the affections are of two sorts; they are those by which the soul is carried out to what is in view,

---

[44] C. S. Lewis makes a very similar point, in the second chapter of *Mere Christianity* (San Francisco: Harper Collins, 2001), 10-12, when he warns us against elevating any affection—which he calls "instincts" or "impulses"—to the place where we consider it always to be good:

> It is a mistake to think that some of our impulses—say mother love or patriotism—are good, and others, like sex or the fighting instinct, are bad. All we mean is that the occasions on which the fighting instinct or the sexual desire need to be restrained are rather more frequent than those for restraining mother love or patriotism. But there are situations in which it is the duty of a married man to encourage his sexual impulse and of a soldier to encourage the fighting instinct. There are also occasions on which a mother's love for her own children or a man's love for his own country have to be suppressed or they will lead to unfairness towards other people's children or countries. Strictly speaking, there are no such things as good and bad impulses. . . .
>
> The most dangerous thing you can do is to take any one impulse of your own nature and set it up as the thing you ought to follow at all costs. There is not one of them which will not make us into devils if we set it up as an absolute guide. You might think love of humanity in general was safe, but it is not. If you leave out justice you will find yourself breaking agreements and faking evidence in trials 'for the sake of humanity', and become in the end a cruel and treacherous man.

Lewis's claims here may need some qualification if we include among possible impulses or instincts ones such as love of God the Father of Jesus Christ or a desire that the Trinity will receive their proper glory. (Of course, these impulses are only had by the regenerate, so Lewis may be right concerning "natural"—meaning "unregenerate"—instincts and impulses.) In addition, no matter whether there are any desires or emotions that are always right, there are probably some that are always wrong—the desire to be maliciously cruel, for example, or the emotion of spite. Edwards does a good job in isolating some of these sorts of desires or emotions in *Charity and Its Fruits*.

[45] While Edwards clearly acknowledges that our ultimate guide is *sola Scriptura*, he also (and properly, I think) recognizes that human reasoning can start us on the way towards right views on some theological issues. And so he often investigates important theological questions both from the standpoint of reason and of Scripture. For instance, in his *Dissertation Concerning the End for which God Created the World*, in *WJE*, vol. 8, the first chapter is entitled, "Wherein Is Considered What Reason Teaches Concerning This Affair," and the second chapter, "Wherein It Is Inquired, What Is to Be Learned from Holy Scriptures Concerning God's Last End in the Creation of the World." (The most readable version of Edwards's *Dissertation* is found in John Piper, *God's Passion for His Glory: Living the Vision of Jonathan Edwards* [Wheaton, Ill.: Crossway Books, 1998].)

It is always important to remember that, while Edwards was one of the most biblically literate Christians of all time and so we should take anything that he says seriously, he occasionally reasons in ways that outrun or contradict Scripture. So, with him as with anyone else, we must always check his claims and conclusions against Scripture.

cleaving to it, or seeking it; or those by which it is averse from it, and opposes it.

Of the former sort are love, desire, hope, joy, gratitude, complacence. Of the latter kind, are hatred, fear, anger, grief, and such like. . . .

And there are some affections wherein there is a composition of each of the aforementioned kinds of actings of the will; as in the affection of pity, there is something of the former kind, towards the person suffering, and something of the latter, towards what he suffers. And so in zeal [which is another term for what Phinehas was feeling in Numbers 25], there is in it high approbation of some person or thing, together with vigorous opposition to what is conceived to be contrary to it.[46]

He then lists some of the positive and negative desires and emotions that, in appropriate circumstances, are among the signs of true conversion: "fear, hope, love, hatred, desire, joy, sorrow, gratitude, compassion and zeal." He also argues that the Scriptures "represent true religion, as being summarily comprehended in *love*, the chief of the affections," citing our Lord's declaration that love to God and neighbor make up the two great commandments (see Matt. 22:37-40) as well as the apostle Paul's commendation of love "as the greatest thing in religion, and as the vitals, essence and soul of it," as found especially in 1 Corinthians 13. He then claims that love is the "fountain of all other affections." From love, he argues,

arises hatred of those things which are contrary to what we love, or which oppose and thwart us in those things that we delight in: and from the various exercises of love and hatred, according to the circumstances of the objects of these affections, as present or absent, certain or uncertain, probable or improbable, arise all those other affections of desire, hope, fear, joy, grief, gratitude, anger, etc.

This general claim, applied to Christianity, yields claims like these:

---

[46] *Religious Affections*, 98ff. The next quotation is from 102 and the remaining ones in this paragraph from pp. 106-108. I am unsure whether Edwards's claim that love is the "fountain of all other affections" is true. It is certainly the source of many other affections, as my observations from Scripture will show. But it isn't clear to me, either rationally or biblically, that it is the source of *all* of our other desires and emotions.

From a vigorous, affectionate, and fervent love to God, will necessarily arise . . . an intense hatred and abhorrence of sin, fear of sin, and a dread of God's displeasure, gratitude to God for his goodness, complacence and joy in God when God is graciously and sensibly present, and grief when he is absent,

as well as "a joyful hope when a future enjoyment of God is expected and fervent zeal for the glory of God."

Edwards buttresses these claims with various Scriptures, but some additional biblical reflection is in order. I will concentrate on the emotional aspects of love and hatred, highlighting especially what Scripture claims about hate, since we tend to think that having strong negative emotions like it couldn't possibly be godly.

Ecclesiastes confirms that "For everything there is a season, and a time for every matter under heaven: . . . a time to weep, and a time to laugh; a time to mourn, and a time to dance; . . . *a time to love, and a time to hate*" (Eccl. 3:1, 4, 8). Moreover, Scripture takes love and hatred as complementary, presenting some juxtapositions of them as inevitable: Those who fear God and love his law inevitably hate and abhor falsehood and evil (see Ps. 119:163; Prov. 8:13); fools love being simple and hate knowledge (see Prov. 1:22); and it is impossible to love both God and money (see Matt. 6:24). And sometimes Scripture commands us to juxtapose them: "O you who love the LORD, hate evil!" (Ps. 97:10; cf. Amos 5:15); "Let love be genuine. Abhor what is evil; hold fast to what is good" (Rom. 12:9).

In addition, Scripture informs us that wrong loves and hates provoke God's wrath. For example, Jehu the prophet at one point confronts King Jehoshaphat by saying, "Should you help the wicked and love those who hate the LORD? Because of this, wrath has gone out against you from the LORD" (2 Chron. 19:2; cf. Exod. 20:5). Earlier, Moses warns the Israelites,

Know . . . *that the LORD your God is God, the faithful God who keeps covenant and steadfast love with those who love him and keep his commandments, to a thousand generations, and repays to their face those who hate him, by destroying them. He will not be slack with one who hates him. He will repay him to his face. You shall therefore be careful to do the commandment and the statutes and the rules that I command you today. (Deut. 7:9-11; cf. 32:41)*

Since the whole affective side of our natures involves our hearts, this means that God's wrath rests on those who have wrong—that is, unregenerate—hearts.

This allows us to understand why David and some of the other psalmists cite their hatreds as proof of their pure hearts. Sometimes they say they hate the ways and works of those who sin (see Ps. 101:3; 119:128; cf. Rev. 2:6) or the gatherings of liars, hypocrites, evildoers, and sinners:

> *Prove me, O LORD, and try me;*
> *   test my heart and my mind.*
> *For your steadfast love is before my eyes,*
> *   and I walk in your faithfulness.*
> *I do not sit with men of falsehood,*
> *   nor do I consort with hypocrites.*
> *I hate the assembly of evildoers,*
> *   and I will not sit with the wicked. (Ps. 26:2-5; cf. 119:161-163)*

Sometimes, however, they declare that they hate not just ungodliness but ungodly people: "I hate those who pay regard to worthless idols" (Ps. 31:6); "I hate the double-minded" (Ps. 119:113); and, most shockingly,

> *How precious to me are your thoughts, O God! . . .*
> *Oh that you would slay the wicked, O God! . . .*
> *Do I not hate those who hate you, O LORD?*
> *   And do I not loathe those who rise up against you?*
> *I hate them with complete hatred;*
> *   I count them my enemies.*
> *Search me, O God, and know my heart!*
> *   Try me and know my thoughts!*
> *And see if there be any grievous way in me,*
> *   and lead me in the way everlasting! (Ps. 139:17, 19, 21-24)*[47]

This is shocking to us because we have uncritically accepted the saying, "Love the sinner; hate the sin." But David's claims in Psalm 139 parallel Scripture's claims about what God himself hates: God hates evil (see,

---

[47] Traditionally, this psalm is ascribed to David. But if, as I noted in footnote 29, the Scriptures themselves describe David as a person after God's own heart, we may then expect that David's emotions will generally be godly. And so it is especially significant that we find Scripture recording David's declaration that he hates ungodly people.

e.g., Deut. 12:31; 16:22; Prov. 6:16-18; Isa. 1:14; 61:8) and also evil-doers (see Ps. 5:5; 11:5; Prov. 6:19; Hos. 9:15).

Furthermore, hating specific things qualifies human beings for specific divinely sanctioned tasks, offices, and blessings. Thus Jethro, Moses's father-in-law, advises him on how to manage his workload by urging him to appoint others to help with specific tasks and says: "look for able men from all the people, men who fear God, who are trustworthy and hate a bribe, and place such men over the people . . . [to] judge the people" (Exod. 18:21ff.; cf. Prov. 15:27). In Psalms, this sort of qualification gets picked up and applied to the kind of kings God blesses (see Ps. 45:6ff.), and ultimately it is applied in Hebrews to God the Son:

> Your throne, O God, is forever and ever,
>   the scepter of uprightness is the scepter of your kingdom.
> You have loved righteousness and hated wickedness;
>   therefore God, your God, has anointed you with the oil of gladness
>   beyond your companions. (Heb. 1:8-9)

Finally, Jesus makes the right hates key to Christian discipleship and obtaining eternal life by declaring that "If anyone comes to me and does not hate his own father and mother and wife and children and brothers and sisters, yes, and even his own life, he cannot be my disciple" (Luke 14:26), and "Truly, truly, I say to you, unless a grain of wheat falls into the earth and dies, it remains alone; but if it dies, it bears much fruit. Whoever loves his life loses it, and whoever hates his life in this world will keep it for eternal life" (John 12:24ff.).

Hatred, dictionaries inform us, involves feeling extreme enmity or a strong aversion toward something or someone. When we hate something, we usually can't stand the sight of it, and we want it damaged or destroyed. And so these declarations by Jesus seem a bit puzzling, especially in the light of 1 Timothy 5, where Paul declares that Christians who do not provide for their relatives are worse than unbelievers—and how likely are we to do that if we bear them such ill will? In these cases we need to remember that sometimes Scripture uses the word *hate* comparatively, as a way of contrasting how much we must value being Christ's disciples over everything else, including our families or ourselves. In those cases, if we must choose, then we only avoid idolatry by choosing Christ and eternal life as if we hate everything else.

Scripture ascribes not only hatred but many other strong negative desires and emotions both to God and to God's people. For instance, it often characterizes God as *jealous* (see Exod. 34:14; Deut. 6:13-15; Nah. 1:2), and its references to God's *anger* and *wrath* are too frequent to be easily counted (see, e.g., Exod. 4:14; Josh. 7:1; Ezra 8:22; Ps. 78:49; John 3:36; Rom. 1:18; Rev. 14:9-11). Moreover, any adequate treatment of anger in Scripture must deal with what B. B. Warfield established in his article on "The Emotional Life of our Lord," namely, that Jesus himself, as the sinless God/man, was often angry or upset (see Mark 3:5; 10:14; John 2:14-16).[48]

Why does Scripture do this? It is not merely because we need to remember that strong negative desires and emotions are inevitable in a fallen world so that we will not be too discouraged or shocked when (in appropriate circumstances) we have them. It is also because we need the reassurance of knowing that *God* has them.[49] God is majestic in his holiness (see Exod. 15:11; 1 Chron. 16:29), which is manifested in his perfect righteousness, absolute justness, and moral purity (see Isa. 5:16; Zeph. 3:5), and which necessitates his inveterate hatred of all sin,

---

[48] See "The Emotional Life of our Lord," in Benjamin Breckenridge Warfield, *The Person and Work of Christ* (Philadelphia: Presbyterian & Reformed, 1950), 93-145. Warfield opens that article's second section like this:

> The moral sense is not a mere faculty of discrimination between the qualities which we call right and wrong, which exhausts itself in their perception as different. The judgments it passes are not merely intellectual, but what we call moral judgments; that is to say, they involve approval and disapproval according to the qualities perceived. It would be impossible, therefore, for a moral being to stand in the presence of perceived wrong indifferent and unmoved. Precisely what we mean by a moral being is a being perceptive of the difference between right and wrong and reacting appropriately to right and wrong perceived as such. The emotions of indignation and anger belong therefore to the very self-expression of a moral being as such and cannot be lacking to him in the presence of wrong. We should know, accordingly, without instruction that Jesus, living in the conditions of this earthly life under the curse of sin, could not fail to be the subject of the whole series of angry emotions, and we are not surprised that even in the brief and broken narratives of his life-experiences which have been given to us, there have been preserved records of the manifestation in word and act of not a few of them. (107)

Warfield then shows that these emotions are particularly on display in the Gospel of Mark, when various Greek phrases within it are properly translated.

Moses, who is a type of Christ (see Deut. 18:18-19 with Acts 3:18-23), was often angry (see Exod. 11:8; 16:20; 32:19-20). Occasionally, his anger was sinful (see Num. 20:2-13 with Ps. 106:32-33), but it usually arose out of a proper concern for God's honor or for the welfare of God's people. On at least one occasion, it anticipated God's own anger (see Num. 16).

Sometimes it is claimed that Scripture's attitude to strong negative emotions like hatred, jealousy, and anger changes radically in the New Testament. For a refutation of this claim, see my piece "Godly Emotions" in *Modern Reformation* magazine as cited in footnote 3.

[49] There are deep philosophical and theological questions about the sense in which God has desires and especially emotions. When Scripture represents God as having emotions, it may be speaking only analogically. In other words, it may be saying no more than that, e.g., God is righteous and consequently must have whatever is the appropriate divine analogical equivalent of a righteous human being's emotional reaction to sin.

wickedness, and evil (see Isa. 61:8). We need to know that he hates these things because our fallen world contains so much that is wrong and evil. For instance, each of us gives and gets small but real affronts and injuries every day. Then there are less frequent but more horrifying evils and crimes against humanity. Encountering these things reminds us that the world is not the way it is supposed to be and that these wrongs need righting. Yet often we cannot right them, and no one else rights them. So we need the reassurance of knowing that it is part of God's nature and glory to get angry about sin (see Rom. 2:6-11) and to be continuously indignant at the world's many evils (Ps. 7:11; Nah. 1:2-13). God now disciplines us less than we deserve so that we are not consumed (see Ezra 9:13; Ps. 78:37-39; 103:8-14). Yet his anger and hatred against all wrongdoing and sin will endure until all wrongdoing is finally confronted and fully requited (see Deut. 7:10; Ps. 1:5-6; 21:8-13; Prov. 11:19-21; Zeph. 3:8-10; Rom. 2:1-5; Rev. 18:4-8).[50]

Scripture ascribes hatred and other strong negative desires and emotions not only to God but also to God's people because we must be encouraged to have them in the right circumstances. As counterintuitive as this may at first seem, to have such desires and emotions in the right circumstances is part of our glory, as creatures made in God's image.[51] They show that our hearts are attuned to God's own heart and thus that we are indwelt by God's Holy Spirit. Thus if God's standards are flouted, then we should feel sorrow or indignation (see Jer. 13:15-17; Ps. 119:53). Consequently, one sign of true conversion is that we feel strong negative emotions when we should. As Edwards puts it, Christians "are

---

[50] For a much fuller examination of why it is part of God's glory to requite every wrong, see my "The Morality of Everlasting Punishment," *Reformation & Revival Journal* 5 (Fall 1996), 117-134. This is also available on the Alliance of Confessing Evangelicals website: www.alliancenet.org.

One reason why we need to be reassured that God will ultimately requite every wrong is that we then can often leave the dispensing of justice up to God. Indeed, Scripture sometimes commands us to do this: "Do not say, 'I will repay evil'; wait for the LORD, and he will deliver you" (Prov. 20:22; cf. Rom. 12:19). Christ, of course, is our exemplar in this: "When he was reviled, he did not revile in return; when he suffered, he did not threaten, but continued entrusting himself to him who judges justly" (1 Pet. 2:23).

[51] For instance, it is part of a mother's glory that she does not approve of any one of her children mistreating or endangering any other. Suppose, as can happen with very young children, that a young boy were to endanger his younger sister by (in a fit of pique) pushing her down some steps. In that situation, their mother should react very negatively to what her boy has done, which (among other things) shows him how unacceptable she takes his behavior to be. In these circumstances, we should think *less* and not *more* of this mother if she didn't react negatively. As Calvin makes clear in his commentary on Genesis 9:5-7, God commands us to be vigilant in protecting and nurturing the well-being of each other precisely because we are each made in his image, and thus to dishonor each other is the same as dishonoring him. For more on this, see my "Morality of Everlasting Punishment."

called upon to give evidence of their sincerity by this, 'Ye that love the Lord, hate evil.'"[52]

But in addition to being reliable signs of true conversion, strong negative emotions in the right circumstances help us to be more godly in particular ways. One of the chief characteristics of a strong negative emotion like anger is that it motivates us. My being righteously angry can help me to think clearly and then act decisively.[53] Of course, anger can be sinful or turn sinful; and so we must be very careful not to indulge it inappropriately and thus, as Paul says, "give . . . opportunity to the devil" (Eph. 4:27). But this does not mean all anger is wrong, as Paul's counsel, "Be angry and do not sin" (Eph. 4:26), makes clear.

Again, hatred's tendency to persist can keep us focused on confronting and countering truly horrific evils in exactly the way that God's people should; and detesting wickedness—that is, loathing and abhorring it—is good. Scripture calls various sexual acts and practices *detestable* (see Lev. 18:22; Deut. 22:5; Jer. 13:24-27), which means that God detests them (see 1 Kings 14:22-24 with Deut. 23:18), and so should we (see Deut. 7:26). In Moses and the prophets, these acts and practices are detestable partly because they were associated with pagan religious rituals (see Deut. 23:17-18; Jer. 5:7-9). Engaging in them thus meant breaking covenant with Yahweh and making covenant with pagan deities deliberately and explicitly (see Num. 25:1-3 and 31:15-16 with Rev. 2:14). Yet even then, the detestation that such acts and practices should produce was never completely separate from the fact that they fly in the face of the created order as God intended it (see, for instance, Deut. 24:1-4 with Gen. 2:24). This aspect of their immorality or perversity becomes more central in the Wisdom literature and in the New Testament (see Prov. 11:20; Rom. 1:24-27; 1 Cor. 6:18; 2 Pet. 2:4-16). And it remains the primary reason why we, as God's New Covenant people, should detest them.[54]

As Michael Grisanti says, in his *New International Dictionary of Old Testament Theology and Exegesis* articles on the Hebrew terms

---

[52] Edwards, *Religious Affections*, 104.

[53] Think here of a father who discovers that a good friend of his has been abusing his daughter sexually. His anger can prompt him to think carefully about what has happened as well as what he should do and then goad him to do it in spite of his previous love for his friend.

[54] As I understand it, if an act or practice—such as homosexual sexual practice and homosexual marriage—perverts the natural moral order as God intended it (see Rom. 1:26-27), then it is supposed to be recognized as wrong by everyone and not merely by Christians; and so it is appropriate for a government to legislate against it.

that the *New International Version* translates as "detestable," "Yahweh's demand for Israel's heartfelt obedience . . . provided Israel with a tangible means to fulfill her divine commission to be a 'treasured possession . . . a kingdom of priests and a holy nation' (Exod. 19:5-6)."[55] Yahweh demanded that his people reject and loathe certain sexual acts and practices because they were incompatible with his holiness. He desired "to preserve the purity of his chosen people so as to enable them to clearly mirror his character to the surrounding pagan nations." Whether or not they loathed these acts and practices "demonstrated their spiritual condition and served as an indicator of their coming fate."

We, in God's New Covenant times, are God's new royal priesthood and holy nation (see 1 Pet. 2:9). And we also are called to be holy because he is holy (see Lev. 20:7-26; 1 Pet. 1:15-16). This means that "there must not be *even a hint* of sexual immorality, or of any kind of impurity [among us], . . . because these are improper for God's holy people" (Eph. 5:3, NIV; see 5:3-20; 1 Thess. 4:3-8). In the Beatitudes, Jesus stresses that the threshold for sexual immorality is much lower than the Jewish people had taken it to be (see Matt. 5:27-32). Paul is so averse to any sexual impurity that he rules even "foolish talk" and "crude joking" "out of place" (Eph. 5:4).

But in our time the floodgates of sexual immorality and moral perversity have been thrown wide open. Many in our culture are constantly attempting to make us more tolerant and thus less inclined to react strongly against such things. One of their primary strategies involves their redescribing various forms of sexual immorality and moral perversity in ways that make those acts and practices less likely to arouse emotional aversion. For instance, some segments of the homosexual community are working hard to destigmatize the sexual molestation of pre- and post-pubescent boys by homosexual adults. In 1998, an article appeared in the American Psychological Association's prestigious *Psychological Bulletin* claiming that scientific evidence does not support the common belief that such sexual encounters invariably harm the boys involved. Consequently, it concluded, it is inappropriate to label all such encounters "sexual abuse." Willing encounters "with positive reac-

---

[55] Michael Grisanti, in *New International Dictionary of Old Testament Theology & Exegesis*, 5 vols., ed. Willem A. VanGemeren (Grand Rapids, Mich.: Zondervan, 1997), 4:315. The other two quotations from Grisanti in this paragraph are found, respectively, at 4:315 and 4:244.

tions" should just be labeled "*adult-child* sex."[56] Similarly, in 2001 Peter Singer of Princeton University's Center for Human Values published an essay on the webzine Nerve.com that tried to normalize bestiality by highlighting some of the "science" in Midas Dekkers's pro-bestiality book, *Dearest Pet*.

In both cases, this strategy involved comparing these still generally abhorred practices with sexual practices that our culture no longer decries. The *Psychological Bulletin* article compared pedophilia with behaviors like masturbation, homosexuality, oral sex, and sexual promiscuity, all of which were once but are no longer classified as pathologies in the American Psychological Association's *Diagnostic and Statistical Manual of Mental Disorders*. Singer associates bestiality with the once-widespread beliefs that contraception and masturbation were wrong as well as with practices such as heterosexual sodomy and homosexuality that our society now tolerates and sometimes celebrates.

It is clear that, with the likely exception of contraception, God detests practices like these (see Lev. 18:22-30; 20:13, 15-16; Deut. 27:21). Yet is it clear that *we* do? Do we feel emotional aversion in the face of sexual immorality and moral perversion? Are we willing to serve as mirrors of God's character to our culture by expressing it? On any given evening, any number of us watch television programs that break the bounds of propriety that the Scriptures set. We may think that our assent to Scripture's sexual standards is enough and that it does not really matter that we do not emotionally detest what we see, but Scripture tells us otherwise: "O you who love the Lord, *hate* evil."

Have we allowed the culture around us to "squeeze [us] into its own mould" rather than allowing "God [to] re-make [us] so that [our] whole attitude of mind is changed" (Rom. 12:2, *Phillips*)? In Jeremiah, God condemns those who do not know how to blush (see 8:12). Paul declares that "it is shameful even to mention what the disobedient do in secret" (Eph. 5:12, NIV). Strong negative emotions are important indicators of who—and *whose*—we are. To claim to be Christians and yet not to feel emotional aversion when Christian moral standards are violated is, at

[56] See Mary Eberstadt's "'Pedophilia Chic' Re-considered," *Weekly Standard* (January 1/January 8, 2001).

best, to exhibit a kind of mental schizophrenia between our heads and our hearts.

The Psalmist declares that God's wrath against human beings brings him praise and that its survivors are restrained by that very wrath (see 76:10, NIV). It is part of our task, as God's holy people, to manifest his holiness through our emotions. Moral perversion makes headway in our culture when we are not moved to decry the less-shocking forms of sexual immorality. How much better might the moral situation of our time be if many of us could say, "I never sat in the company of revelers, never made merry with them; I sat alone because your hand was on me and you had filled me with indignation" (Jer. 15:17, NIV)?

"TAKE AND READ!"

Negative desires and emotions like jealousy, hatred, anger, indignation, and fear can be godly, then, if we have them in the appropriate circumstances. But then how can we tell that a desire or emotion is or is not godly, since we can't just assume that all positive desires and emotions are godly and all negative ones are not?

The only sure indicator is that our desires and emotions conform to those that God approves of in his Scriptures. Holy affections are desires and emotions that God has or that he wants his people to have. The way that we know what he wants us to desire and feel is by reading the Scriptures and noting what his saints are represented as properly desiring and feeling as well as what God commands and counsels his saints to desire and feel. This is what Edwards sets out to do in Part Three of his *Religious Affections*. Its whole purpose is to show us what in Scripture distinguishes "truly gracious and holy affections" from all others.

Thus Part Three is the treasure trove in Edwards's great work. Everything that I have written just gets you ready to appreciate it. And, somewhat in the manner of Philip's reply to Nathanael early in John's Gospel, to any Christian who doubts what is to be found there, I would say, "Come and see" (see John 1:43-46). Pore through those pages of Edwards's great book, and you will find much to enlighten your mind and warm your heart. Indeed, you will find truths that will bring you joy from now throughout eternity.

ANNOTATED BIBLIOGRAPHY

Cherry, Conrad. *The Theology of Jonathan Edwards: A Reappraisal.*
   Bloomington and Indianapolis, Ind.: Indiana University Press, 1966.
   Perhaps the most reliable survey of Edwards's theological thinking.

McDermott, Gerald. *Seeing God: Jonathan Edwards and Spiritual Discernment.* Vancouver: Regent College Publishing, 2000.
   McDermott, an accomplished Edwards scholar, uses the outline and arguments of *Religious Affections* to provide a contemporary rendition of this classic work. McDermott's more recent work on Edwards needs to be read more critically.

Plantinga, Alvin. *Warranted Christian Belief.* Oxford: Oxford University Press, 2000.
   This is the third volume in Plantinga's justly famous trilogy on epistemology. In chapter 8 he explores the cognitive aspects of faith. Then in chapter 9 he examines the affective side of faith, using Edwards's *Religious Affections* as the basis for his discussion.

Roberts, Robert C. *Emotions: An Essay in Aid of Moral Psychology.* Cambridge: Cambridge University Press, 2003.
   A helpful, full-blown philosophical treatment of emotions by a noted philosopher.

Robinson, Jeff. "*Religious Affections*: Sorting the Wheat from the Chaff." *Founders Journal* (Summer 2003): 25-30.
   A shorter article that uses *Religious Affections* to help us sort the good from the bad in intense religious experience.

Spring, Gardiner. *The Distinguishing Traits of Christian Character.* Phillipsburg, N.J.: Presbyterian & Reformed, 1966.
   This is a nice attempt to restate much of Edwards's *Religious Affections* in simpler language.

Talbot, Mark R. *The Signs of True Conversion.* Today's Issues Booklets. Wheaton, Ill.: Crossway Books, 2000.
   A booklet exploring the scriptural steps for and signs of true conversion.

Wainwright, William. *Reason and the Heart: A Prolegomenon to a Critique of Passional Reason.* Ithaca, N.Y.: Cornell University Press, 1995.

Chapter 1 of this work—previously published in part as "Jonathan Edwards and the Sense of the Heart," *Faith and Philosophy* 7 (1990): 43-62—utilizes Edwards's *Religious Affections* to examine the relationship between reason and our "passional nature" (or the reasons of our hearts).

Walton, Brad. *Jonathan Edwards, Religious Affections, and the Puritan Analysis of True Piety, Spiritual Sensation and Heart Religion.* Lewiston, N.Y.: Edwin Mellen, 2002.

A scholarly work that explores the connection between Edwards's view of the religious affections and his sixteenth- and seventeenth-century Puritan forerunners, arguing that the former extends the latter.

Warfield, B. B. "The Emotional Life of our Lord." In Benjamin Breckenridge Warfield, *The Person and Work of Christ*, 93-145. Philadelphia: Presbyterian & Reformed, 1950.

In this brilliant essay, Warfield argues that since Christ has "all sinless emotions," it behooves us to note the full range of our Lord's emotions.

Appendix 1

A DIVINE AND SUPERNATURAL LIGHT IMMEDIATELY IMPARTED TO THE SOUL BY THE SPIRIT OF GOD: AN EDWARDSEAN SERMON (2 CORINTHIANS 3:18—4:7)

John Piper

The following sermon was delivered at the close of the Jonathan Edwards Conference. We present it here as an example of an Edwardsean sermon for today, and also to answer Objection #6 in chapter 1 of this volume.

> [18] *And we all, with unveiled face, beholding the glory of the Lord, are being transformed into the same image from one degree of glory to another. For this comes from the Lord who is the Spirit.* [4:1] *Therefore, having this ministry by the mercy of God, we do not lose heart.* [2] *But we have renounced disgraceful, underhanded ways. We refuse to practice cunning or to tamper with God's word, but by the open statement of the truth we would commend ourselves to everyone's conscience in the sight of God.* [3] *And even if our gospel is veiled, it is veiled only to those who are perishing.* [4] *In their case the god of this world has blinded the minds of the unbelievers, to keep them from seeing the light of the gospel of the glory of Christ, who is the image of God.* [5] *For what we proclaim is not ourselves, but Jesus Christ as Lord, with ourselves as your servants for Jesus' sake.* [6] *For God, who said, "Let light shine out of darkness," has shone in our hearts to give the light of the knowledge of the glory of God in the face of Jesus Christ.* [7] *But we have this treasure in jars of clay, to show that the surpassing power belongs to God and not to us.*

Focus with me for a few moments on the root of Jonathan Edwards's God-entranced vision of all things. The root is sunk into three levels of salvation. And what makes Edwards's vision of all things so God-entranced and God-centered and God-exalting is that in each of these three levels of salvation God himself is sovereign and decisive and beautiful. You can see these three levels of salvation in 2 Corinthians 4:4 and 4:6.

I'll point them out and then come back and look at them more closely with you. Focus first on the last part of verse 4.

In their case [those who are perishing] the god of this world has blinded the minds of the unbelievers, to keep them from seeing the light of the gospel of the glory of Christ, who is the image of God.

Then notice the close parallel to the last words of verse 4 in the last part of verse 6:

For God, who said, "Let light shine out of darkness," has shone in our hearts to give the light of the knowledge of the glory of God in the face of Jesus Christ.

Notice the similar words in verses 4 and 6:

Verse 4: "the light *of the* gospel *of the* glory of Christ, *who is the image of God."*

Verse 6: "the light *of the* knowledge *of the* glory of God *in the face of Jesus Christ."*

In both verses the word "light" is parallel. Then the words "gospel" and "knowledge" are parallel: "light of the gospel" and "the light of the knowledge." Then the term "glory of Christ" is parallel to "glory of God": "the light of the gospel *of the glory of Christ*" and "the light of the knowledge of *the glory of God*." And in both verses Paul adds words to show how the "glory of God" is in fact "the glory of Christ." He does it in verse 4 by saying Christ is "the image of God"; so Christ's glory is the glory of God. And he does it in verse 6 by saying that God's glory is seen "in the face of Jesus Christ"; so God's glory is the glory of Christ.

Now notice the three levels of salvation in these two parallel verses. The deepest level of salvation is in the term, "the glory of Christ, who is the image of God," or "the glory of God in the face of Jesus Christ." This is the deepest level of Edwards's vision—*the glory of God in Christ, or the glory of Christ who is God*. You cannot go beneath this. There is no deeper reality and no greater value than the glory of God in Christ. There is no prize and no satisfaction beyond this. When you have this, you are at the end. You are home. The glory of God is not a means to anything greater. This is ultimate, absolute reality. All true salvation ends here, not before and not beyond. There is no beyond. The glory of God in Christ is what makes the gospel *gospel*.

The second level of salvation, moving up from the deepest level of the glory of Christ, is *the gospel of Christ*. This is the good news (verse 4, or, as verse 6 says, the "knowledge") of what Christ has done in history to make access to the deepest level of salvation possible for guilty sinners. What makes the good news ultimately good is that it opens the way for sinners to approach the glory of God with all-satisfying joy instead of being incinerated. We will come back in a moment to see what Christ did.

The third level of salvation, moving up from the glory of Christ and the gospel of Christ, is *the shining of divine light in the human heart that enables it to see and savor the gospel of the glory of Christ*. You see this in the word "light" in verse 4 ("light of the gospel") and verse 6 ("light of the knowledge"). But you see most clearly how this light comes in verse 6: "For God, who said, 'Let light shine out of darkness,' has shone in our hearts to give the light . . ." It is not enough to hear "the gospel" mentioned in verse 4 or to have "the knowledge" mentioned in verse 6. There must be a divine work of illumination or awakening. God himself, by his Spirit, must do an act of creation as he did at the beginning of the universe when he said, "Let there be light." Edwards will call this act of God "regeneration"—being born again.

These are the three levels of salvation in which Edwards's God-entranced vision of all things is rooted. Most deeply and ultimately salvation is seeing and savoring the glory of Christ forever. But sinners cannot approach the glory of God without being destroyed. Therefore Christ came into the world to save sinners through the gospel of his death and resurrection. But sinners, left to themselves, will never see the beauty of the gospel. Christ crucified for sinners will always be foolishness to the natural man. There is only one hope—a divine and supernatural light immediately imparted to the soul by the Spirit of God.

So I want to let Edwards speak to us about these three levels of salvation where his God-entranced vision is rooted.

FIRST, THE DEEPEST LEVEL OF SALVATION: THE GLORY OF CHRIST

Edwards believed that the glory of Christ is revealed most clearly in the gospel, and that this glory carries its own evidence of truth. It is self-authenticating. If you see it, you know for sure that you are looking at divine reality.

> Thus the soul may have a kind of intuitive knowledge of the divinity of the things exhibited in the gospel; not that he judges the doctrines of the gospel to be from God, without any argument or deduction at all; but it is without any long chain of arguments; the argument is but one, and the evidence direct; the mind ascends to the truth of the gospel but by one step, and that is its divine glory.[1]

So Edwards labored in his preaching to put the glory of Christ on display in the gospel. One of his most beautiful examples of this is his sermon, "The Excellency of Christ," based on Revelation 5:5-6 where Christ is described as the conquering "Lion of the tribe of Judah" (v. 5) and the "Lamb, standing as though it had been slain" (v. 6). Edwards states his theme: "There is an admirable conjunction of diverse excellencies in Jesus Christ."

Then he puts his lens to the gospel and describes Christ in one of the most compelling, Christ-exalting sermons you will ever read. In the person of Christ, he says, meet together

> infinite highness and infinite condescension . . . infinite justice and infinite grace . . . infinite glory and lowest humility . . . infinite majesty and transcendent meekness . . . deepest reverence towards God and equality with God . . . infinite worthiness of good, and the greatest patience under sufferings of evil . . . an exceeding spirit of obedience, with supreme dominion over heaven and earth . . . absolute sovereignty and perfect resignation . . . self-sufficiency, and an entire trust and reliance on God.[2]

---

[1] Jonathan Edwards, *Religious Affections*, in *The Works of Jonathan Edwards*, ed. Edward Hickman, 2 vols. (1884; reprint, Edinburgh: Banner of Truth, 1974), 1:290.

[2] Jonathan Edwards, "The Excellencies of Christ," in *Works*, ed. Hickman, 1:681-682.

This is the glory of Christ. To see him and be with him and to enjoy him will be our final, all-satisfying salvation. This is the end for which we were made—to spend eternity knowing evermore and enjoying evermore the infinite riches of the glory of Christ.

But the problem is that we are sinful and deserving of hell. We dare not even approach the glory of God, lest we be consumed by his holiness and wrath. Therefore, we need the gospel. That is level two of the salvation in this text. We cannot get to the bottom level of the glory of Christ except through the second level of the gospel of Christ.

THE SECOND LEVEL OF SALVATION: THE GOSPEL

Second Corinthians 4:4 refers to "the light of *the gospel* of the glory of Christ." Because he was a sinner, Edwards loved the double truth of the gospel that Christ satisfied the righteous wrath of God by dying in our place, and that he performed for us a perfect righteousness that God reckons to be ours by faith alone. This double truth is the heart of the gospel, and both are crucial. Edwards was jealous that Christ get glory not only as the one who pardons our sins, and not only as the one who imparts to us a sanctifying righteousness, but also as the one who performed the perfect righteousness that God imputes to us and on the basis of which alone we are justified and declared to be righteous.

The gospel of Christ's blood and righteousness cannot be cherished as it ought without realizing the horrific situation we are in before God because of our sin. Edwards helps us treasure the gospel by describing this situation:

> If it be allowed that it is requisite that great crimes should be punished with punishment in some measure answerable to the heinousness of the crime . . . because of their great demerit and the great abhorrence and indignation they justly excite:—it will follow that it is requisite that God should punish all sin with infinite punishment, because all sin, as it is against God, is infinitely hateful to him, and so stirs up infinite abhorrence and indignation in him.[3]

This infinite punishment that is justly owing to our sin can be meted out in two ways: either through the infinitely precious sacrifice of the Son

---

[3] Jonathan Edwards, "Satisfaction for Sin," in *Works*, ed. Hickman, 2:565.

of God for those who believe, or everlasting punishment in hell for those who don't. Every Christian exults with Edwards in the words of Galatians 3:13, "Christ redeemed us from the curse of the law by becoming a curse for us—for it is written, 'Cursed is everyone who is hanged on a tree.'" The infinite punishment owing to us was laid on Christ, and by faith alone, we enjoy the forgiveness for our sins.

But Edwards was jealous to show that this is not the limit of the gospel or the glory of Christ in our salvation. We are not only *pardoned* in the courtroom of heaven, we are *justified*—that is, we are declared righteous. A punishment is not merely taken away, but perfection is provided—the perfection of Christ. Not only is the title to hell canceled, but the title to heaven is created.

And what is that title? The righteousness of Christ. "We are accepted, and approved of God as the heirs of salvation," Edwards says, "not out of regard to the excellency of our own virtue or goodness, or any moral fitness therein . . . but only on account of the dignity and moral fitness of Christ's righteousness."[4] "[That I] be found in him, not having a righteousness of my own that comes from the law, but that which comes through faith in Christ, the righteousness from God that depends on faith" (Phil. 3:9). "For Christ is the end of the law for righteousness to everyone who believes" (Rom. 10:4). "For as by the one man's disobedience the many were made sinners, so by the one man's obedience the many will be made righteous" (Rom. 5:19). "For our sake he made him to be sin who knew no sin, so that in him we might become the righteousness of God" (2 Cor. 5:21).

It is a glorious thing to have pardon for all our sins because of Christ. And it is doubly glorious to have the perfect righteousness of Christ credited to us by faith alone. "For we hold that one is justified by faith apart from works of the law" (Rom. 3:28). This is the double truth of the gospel that Edwards saw and loved. Because of this gospel alone does any sinner have access to the all-satisfying glory of Christ. The gospel is the blood and righteousness of Christ providing pardon and perfection. And with that we will inherit the glory of Christ as our everlasting treasure.

But there is another problem. The natural mind—the fallen, worldly mind—does not want the glory of Christ as its treasure. And we all have

---

[4] Jonathan Edwards, "Justification by Faith Alone," in *Works*, ed. Hickman, 1:643.

this fallen mind by nature. We wouldn't mind escape from hell. And we wouldn't mind the healing of our bodies and removal of guilt feelings and reunion with our relatives and loved ones in heaven. All that is natural. But treasuring Christ above all, enjoying the glory of Christ above all joys—for that we have no taste. And that brings us finally to the third level of salvation.

THE THIRD LEVEL OF SALVATION:
THE SHINING OF DIVINE LIGHT INTO THE HUMAN HEART
THAT ENABLES IT TO SEE AND SAVOR THE GOSPEL OF
THE GLORY OF CHRIST ABOVE ALL OTHER JOYS

Just as God was sovereign and decisive in levels one and two, so he is sovereign and decisive here at level three. He is the glory we inherit in the deepest level. He is the one who sent Christ to do the work of the gospel for us in level two. And now it is God who breaks into our natural, rebellious, darkened minds and changes our nature so that we see Christ crucified no longer as foolishness but as the wisdom of God and the power of God.

Edwards saw this in 2 Corinthians 4:6: "For God, who said, 'Let light shine out of darkness,' has shone in our hearts to give the light of the knowledge of the glory of God in the face of Jesus Christ." The way anybody gets converted—the way anybody comes to see and savor the glory of Christ as the greatest treasure and sweetest joy—is that God sovereignly causes the darkened soul to see the beauty of Christ in the gospel. Just as he once said, "Let there be light" and there was light, so now he says, "Let the glory of Christ shine as an irresistible beauty," and it does.

Edwards calls this "a divine and supernatural light immediately imparted to the soul by the Spirit of God"—the name of one of his most famous sermons.[5] Being converted to Christ—being saved—is a supernatural work of God. It is being born again by the Spirit of God—being given a new nature, a new spiritual taste, and a new way of seeing, and by that, an awakening of joy in Christ that you never knew before.

In Edwards's understanding, this is what regeneration is. This is what God does in shining into the heart of a darkened sinner: "The first

---

[5] Jonathan Edwards, "A Divine and Supernatural Light Immediately Imparted to the Soul by the Spirit of God," in *Works*, ed. Hickman, 2:12-16.

effect of the power of God in the heart in regeneration, is to give the heart a Divine taste or sense; to cause it to have a relish [for] the loveliness and sweetness of the supreme excellency of the Divine nature."[6] This is how any of us comes to rejoice in the glory of Christ. Before regeneration—before God creates a new taste for Christ—money and comfort and ease and security and sexual stimulation and food and success and family and productivity and the praise of men tasted better to us than Christ.

But now something has happened. "God . . . has shone in our hearts to give the light of the knowledge of the glory of God in the face of Jesus Christ." We have been born again. We have a new taste for reality. The created things that we thought were the fountain of pleasure turned out to be empty, and the one we thought was a boring, bloody fool turns out to be a beautiful treasure chest of holy joy.

Therefore Edwards says, "The change that takes place in a man, when he is converted . . . is not that his love [or desire] for happiness is diminished, but only that it is regulated."[7] Now we have a new spiritual, supernatural taste for what will truly satisfy. Our longing for happiness now looks to God and says, "You make known to me the path of life; in your presence there is fullness of joy; at your right hand are pleasures forevermore" (Ps. 16:11).

CONCLUSION

I argued in chapter 1 that Jonathan Edwards's God-entranced vision of all things has near its heart this sentence: "*God is glorified not only by His glory's being seen . . . but by its being rejoiced in.*"[8] This implies that our passion for satisfaction is the barometer of our passion to glorify God. It also implies that not to pursue your joy in God is to insult his glory.

Objection #6, you recall, to this elevation of joy to such a central place in God's purposes to be glorified in the world was that it seems to have little to do with the cross, justification by faith, and regeneration by the Holy Spirit.

---

[6] Jonathan Edwards, *Treatise on Grace and Other Posthumous Writings*, ed. Paul Helm (Cambridge: James Clarke and Co., 1971), 48-49.

[7] Jonathan Edwards, *Charity and Its Fruits* (Edinburgh: Banner of Truth, 1969), 161-162.

[8] "Miscellanies," no. 448, in *The Works of Jonathan Edwards*, vol. 13, *The "Miscellanies,"* ed. Thomas Schafer (New Haven, Conn.: Yale University Press, 1994), 495.

To this objection I now answer by summing up this sermon.

By the cross—that is, by the blood-shedding and the completed righteousness of Christ—the wrath of God was removed as the great obstacle to my hope of everlasting joy at God's right hand. His suffering became my punishment. His obedience became my righteousness. The curse of the law and the command of the law were fulfilled for me by the death of Christ and the righteousness of Christ.

As a hell-deserving sinner I never could have dreamed of spending eternity with God in ever-increasing joy in the ever-increasing revelation of God himself. All I could expect was destruction and misery. But wonder of wonders, "Christ also suffered once for sins, the righteous for the unrighteous, that he might bring [me] to God" (1 Pet. 3:18).

That was my rescue from the guilt and punishment of sin. But what about sin's power? What about my corruption and my spiritual blindness and my rebellion and my addiction to the poison of sin and my slavery to the fleeting pleasures of the world? What about my preference for all that is not God? How shall I ever lay claim to the purchase of Christ, when I prefer anything and everything to God?

The answer is not that I have free will, but that my will must be set free. The answer is that something supernatural must happen in my heart that causes me to see Christ as the image of God, and to see God in the face of Christ, and to see the cross as the wisdom and power of God, and to see Jesus as a treasure so valuable that I count everything else as rubbish in comparison with him. A divine and supernatural light must shine in my heart, so that Christ appears compellingly glorious. That is, I must be born again. I must be regenerated by the Holy Spirit.

I conclude therefore that the sin-bearing cross of Christ and the imputation of his righteousness through faith alone and the supernatural work of regeneration are the indispensable divine works of salvation that usher us into the ultimate goal of God in creation: namely, the display of the infinite worth of his glory in the never-ending increase of our joy in him.

Appendix 2

READING JONATHAN EDWARDS:
OBJECTIONS AND RECOMMENDATIONS

Justin Taylor

W hat would happen if you ate fast food and nothing else? Some questions are apparently too difficult for some to resist. New York filmmaker Morgan Spurlock decided to answer the question by eating McDonalds food three times a day for a month. The result? He gained twenty-four pounds and increased his cholesterol level from 165 to 230, as recorded in his appropriately titled documentary, *Supersize Me*.[1]

Evangelicalism suffers from an analogous condition with respect to the mind.[2] We often stuff ourselves with intellectual junk food while failing to feast upon the rich banquets that are available to us. We have become unwitting co-conspirators to the ancient heresy that "the newer is the truer, only what is recent is decent, every shift of ground is a step forward, and every latest word must be hailed as the last word on its subject."[3] My purpose here, however, is not to bemoan the contemporary situation but rather to offer encouragement toward a solution.

Having read *about* Edwards, it is our hope that you would now turn to read Edwards for yourself. There are, however, some perceived obstacles that have been thought to block this endeavor. Both objections have to do with a reluctance to read difficult things. The first is the general hesitancy about reading older works due to their archaic style and vocabulary. The second is that Edwards in particular is difficult to understand due to complicated sentences and complex thoughts. Before

---

[1] See www.supersizeme.com (accessed 1-26-04).
[2] Note the title and content of Os Guinness's *Fit Bodies, Fat Minds: Why Evangelicals Don't Think and What to Do About It* (Grand Rapids, Mich.: Baker, 1994).
[3] J. I. Packer, "Is Systematic Theology a Mirage? An Introductory Discussion," in *Doing Theology in Today's World: Essays in Honor of Kenneth S. Kantzer*, ed. John D. Woodbridge and Thomas Edward McComiskey (Grand Rapids, Mich.: Zondervan, 1991), 21.

offering a list of recommended books, I would like to address both of these seemingly plausible concerns.

Related to the issue of reading old books versus new ones is the issue of reading good books versus bad ones. For most of us, the choice is not between reading and not reading. As C. S. Lewis wrote: "You are not, in fact, going to read nothing . . . if you don't read good books you will read bad ones."[4] And according to Lewis, the good books are by and large the old books. But why shouldn't we simply content ourselves with modern restatements of the old truths—like the book you hold in your hands!—rather than also returning to the original sources? I will let Lewis answer:

> There is a strange idea abroad that in every subject the ancient books should be read only by the professionals, and that the amateur should content himself with the modern books. . . . The error is rather an amiable one, for it springs from humility. The student is half afraid to meet one of the great philosophers face to face. He feels himself inadequate and thinks he will not understand him. But if he only knew, the great man, just because of his greatness, is much more intelligible than his modern commentator. . . . It has always therefore been one of my main endeavours as a teacher to persuade the young that first-hand knowledge is not only more worth acquiring than second-hand knowledge, but is usually much easier and more delightful to acquire. . . . Naturally, since I myself am a writer, I do not wish the ordinary reader to read no modern books. But if he must read only the new or only the old, I would advise him to read the old.[5]

Even if one is persuaded that it is wise to read older works, the myth is perpetuated that Edwards is a particularly difficult writer to read. This complaint is not new; it dates back at least to evangelical theologians of the nineteenth century. But J. I. Packer offers a counter-perspective:

> One has only to make the experiment to find that this is not so at all. The levelling of this charge was in fact a case of the mote and the beam. It is true that Edwards does not go in for the flowery padding which the nineteenth century regarded as essential to good style, but this is to his

---

[4] C. S. Lewis, "Learning in War-Time," in *The Weight of Glory and Other Addresses*, rev. and exp. ed. (New York: Macmillan, 1980), 23.
[5] C. S. Lewis, "On the Reading of Old Books," in *C. S. Lewis: Essay Collections and Other Short Pieces*, ed. Lesley Walmsley (London: HarperCollins, 2000), 438-439.

credit rather than otherwise. He is today far more palatable as a writer than are many of his older critics. The most one can say against him is that on occasion his desire for clinical precision of language leads him to write sentences that are too long and complex for easy assimilation on first reading. But this is his only stylistic fault, and that not a common one; most of the time he is admirably clear, exact, and pointed.[6]

All of this is prolegomena to our overarching exhortation: *Take up and read!* Martyn Lloyd-Jones has said it best:

> My advice to you is: Read Jonathan Edwards. Stop going to so many meetings; stop craving for the various forms of entertainment which are so popular in evangelical circles at the present time. Learn to stay at home. Learn to read again, and do not merely read the exciting stories of certain modern people. Go back to something solid and deep and real. Are we losing the art of reading? Revivals have often started as the result of people reading volumes such as these two volumes of Edwards' works [see below]. So read this man. Decide to do so. Read his sermons; read his practical treatises, and then go on to the great discourses on theological subjects.[7]

Here are some recommended resources to aid you in this task.

The Works of Jonathan Edwards

In 1834 Edward Hickman published a two-volume edition of *The Works of Jonathan Edwards*. This edition has been reproduced in facsimile by publishers Banner of Truth (1974) and Hendrickson (1998).[8] At 1,660 pages it would take at least twenty volumes in conventional format to equal what is in this small-print, two-column edition. Lloyd-Jones wrote:

> In my early days in the ministry there were no books which helped me more, both personally and in respect of my preaching, than the two-volume edition of the *Works of Jonathan Edwards*. . . . I devoured these volumes and literally just read and reread them. It is certainly true

[6] J. I. Packer, *A Quest for Godliness: The Puritan Vision of the Christian Life* (Wheaton, Ill.: Crossway Books, 1990), 315.

[7] D. Martyn Lloyd-Jones, "Jonathan Edwards and the Crucial Importance of Revival," *Puritans: Their Origins and Successors* (Edinburgh: Banner of Truth, 1987).

[8] The jacket copy of the second volume of the Banner of Truth edition of the *Works*.

that they helped me more than anything else. . . . . If I had the power I
would make these two volumes compulsory reading for all ministers![9]

For those serious about understanding Edwards, it is certainly the most
economical way to acquire a large number of his writings.

The most thorough, critical, and expensive version of Edwards's
works is being published by Yale University Press. Twenty-three volumes
have been published thus far, with four more forthcoming.[10] Yale has
also produced a one-volume selection of his writings: *A Jonathan
Edwards Reader.*[11]

Sermons

For those being introduced to Edwards for the first time, the most helpful place to begin may be the sermons he preached to ordinary people
week in and week out. We recommend:

GROWING IN GOD'S SPIRIT[12]

The first volume in a new series entitled Jonathan Edwards for Today's Reader.
It contains Edwards's classic sermons "A Divine and Supernatural Light,"
"Christian Knowledge," and "The Christian Pilgrim." The editor has supplied
helpful headings and thoughtful study questions.

PRAYING TOGETHER FOR TRUE REVIVAL[13]

The second volume in the Jonathan Edwards for Today's Reader series, con-
taining "A Humble Attempt to Promote Explicit Agreement and Visible Union
of God's People in Extraordinary Prayer, for the Revival of the Church and the
Advancement of Christ's Kingdom on Earth."

THE SERMONS OF JONATHAN EDWARDS: A READER[14]

An anthology from the critical Yale edition.

---

[9] The latter edition is available for purchase at Desiring God Ministries for 50 percent off the retail price. See www.desiringGod.org.

[10] For a complete listing, see www.yale.edu/wje/.

[11] Ed. John E. Smith, Harry S. Stout, and Kenneth P. Minkema (New Haven, Conn.: Yale University Press, 1995).

[12] Ed. T. M. Moore (Phillipsburg, N.J.: P & R, 2003).

[13] Ed. T. M. Moore (Phillipsburg, N.J.: P & R, 2004).

[14] Ed. Wilson H. Kimnach, Kenneth P. Minkema, and Douglas A. Sweeney (New Haven, Conn.: Yale University Press, 1999).

THE SALVATION OF SOULS:
NINE PREVIOUSLY UNPUBLISHED SERMONS ON THE CALL OF
MINISTRY AND THE GOSPEL BY JONATHAN EDWARDS[15]

THE BLESSING OF GOD:
PREVIOUSLY UNPUBLISHED SERMONS OF JONATHAN EDWARDS[16]
Most of Edwards's 1,400 sermons will not be published in the critical Yale edition. These two works contain previously unpublished sermons, freshly transcribed as labors of love by these scholars.

Theological Writings with Helps

When beginning to study Edwards's longer theological works, many will welcome the help of explanatory footnotes and introductions. For example, see:

GOD'S PASSION FOR HIS GLORY:
LIVING THE VISION OF JONATHAN EDWARDS[17]
Includes an introduction to Edwards by John Piper, the complete text of *The End for Which God Created the World*, and explanatory notes by Piper.

THE SPIRIT OF REVIVAL:
DISCOVERING THE WISDOM OF JONATHAN EDWARDS[18]
A modernized version of *The Distinguishing Marks of a Work of the Spirit of God* by Archie Parrish, with an introduction by R. C. Sproul.

SEEING GOD: JONATHAN EDWARDS AND SPIRITUAL DISCERNMENT[19]
Does not contain the actual text of *Religious Affections* but is rather an excellent analysis by Gerald McDermott using the skeleton of Edwards's work. Packer writes: "I wish [McDermott's book] would be made compulsory reading in every evangelical congregation."

[15] Ed. Richard A. Bailey and Gregory A. Wills (Wheaton, Ill.: Crossway Books, 2002).
[16] Ed. Michael D. McMullen (Nashville: Broadman & Holman, 2003).
[17] (Wheaton, Ill.: Crossway Books, 1998).
[18] (Wheaton, Ill.: Crossway Books, 2000).
[19] Reprint, Vancouver: Regent College Publishing, 2000). Originally published by InterVarsity Press under the title, *Seeing God: Twelve Reliable Signs of True Spirituality* (1995).

Biographical Materials

For those interested in biographical materials, we would recommend (in ascending order of comprehensiveness and length):

STEPHEN J. NICHOLS—
JONATHAN EDWARDS: A GUIDED TOUR OF HIS LIFE AND THOUGHT[20]

IAIN H. MURRAY—
JONATHAN EDWARDS: A NEW BIOGRAPHY[21]

GEORGE M. MARSDEN—
JONATHAN EDWARDS: A LIFE[22]

As you can see, publishers have produced a plethora of accessible resources on Edwards in recent years. Any reasons for not reading him have significantly dwindled! May God bless you as you read and study to the glory of God.

---

[20] (Phillipsburg, N.J.: P&R, 2001).
[21] (Edinburgh: Banner of Truth, 1987).
[22] (New Haven, Conn.: Yale University Press, 2003).

✳ desiringGod

Desiring God exists to spread a passion for the supremacy of God in all things for the joy of all peoples through Jesus Christ. We love to spread the truth that God is most glorified in us when we are most satisfied in him. John Piper receives no royalties personally from the books he writes—they are all reinvested back into the ministry of Desiring God. It's all designed as part of our vision to spread this passion to others.

With that in mind, we invite you to visit the Desiring God website at desiringGod.org. You'll find twenty years' worth of free sermons by John Piper—in manuscript and downloadable audio formats—hundreds of free articles, and information about our upcoming conferences. An online store allows you to purchase audio albums, God-centered children's curriculum, books and resources by Noël Piper, and over 25 books by John Piper. You can also find information about our growing radio ministry at desiringGodradio.org.

DG also has a whatever-you-can-afford policy, designed for individuals without discretionary funds. If you'd like more information about this policy, please contact us at the address or phone number below.

We exist to help you make God your treasure. If we can serve you in any way, please let us know!

Desiring God
2601 East Franklin Avenue
Minneapolis, MN 55406-1103

Telephone: 1.888.346.4700
Fax: 612.338.4372
Email: mail@desiringGod.org
Web: www.desiringGod.org

Desiring God Europe
Unit 9-10 Spencer House
14-22 Spencer Road
Londonderry
Northern Ireland
BT47 6AA

Telephone/Fax: 011.44.28.713.429.07
Email: info@christisall.com
Web: www.christisall.com/dgm

SCRIPTURE INDEX

PERSON INDEX

Subject Index